Multilingualism in Mathematics Education in Africa

Multilingualisms and Diversities in Education Series

Editors: Kathleen Heugh, Christopher Stroud and Piet Van Avermaet

Multilingualism and diversity are fast becoming defining characteristics of global education. This is because human mobility has increased exponentially over the past two decades, bringing about an increase in socioeconomic, cultural and faith-based diversity with consequences for citizenship, identity, education, and practices of language and literacy (among others).

The **Multilingualisms and Diversities in Education** series takes a global perspective on the 21st century societal diversities. It looks at the languages through which these diversities are conveyed, and how they are changing the theoretical foundations and practice of formal and non-formal education. Multilingualisms and diversities in this series are understood as dynamic and variable phenomena, processes and realities. They are viewed alongside: classroom practices (including curriculum, assessment, methodologies); teacher development (pre- and in-service; and in non-formal education); theory-building; research and evaluation; and policy considerations.

Volumes in the series articulate the opportunities and challenges afforded by contemporary diversities and multilingualisms across global settings at local, national and international levels. A distinctive aim of the series is to provide a platform for reciprocal exchanges of expertise among stakeholders located in different southern and northern contexts.

Also Available in the Series:

Engaging with Linguistic Diversity: A Study of Educational Inclusion in an Irish Primary School, David Little and Déirdre Kirwan

Language and Decoloniality in Higher Education: Reclaiming Voices from the South, edited by Zannie Bock and Christopher Stroud

Language Narratives and Shifting Multilingual Pedagogies: English Teaching from the South, Belinda Mendelowitz, Ana Ferreira and Kerryn Dixon

Forthcoming in the Series:

Multilingual Pedagogies in Practice: Life and Learning in a Diverse Australian Secondary School, Mei French

Multilingualism in Mathematics Education in Africa

Edited by Anthony A. Essien

BLOOMSBURY ACADEMIC
LONDON • NEW YORK • OXFORD • NEW DELHI • SYDNEY

BLOOMSBURY ACADEMIC
Bloomsbury Publishing Plc, 50 Bedford Square, London, WC1B 3DP, UK
Bloomsbury Publishing Inc, 1359 Broadway, New York, NY 10018, USA
Bloomsbury Publishing Ireland, 29 Earlsfort Terrace, Dublin 2, D02 AY28, Ireland

BLOOMSBURY, BLOOMSBURY ACADEMIC and the Diana logo are trademarks of
Bloomsbury Publishing Plc

First published in Great Britain 2024
This paperback edition published in 2025

Copyright © Anthony A. Essien, 2024

Anthony A. Essien and Contributors have asserted their right under the Copyright,
Designs and Patents Act, 1988, to be identified as Authors of this work.

For legal purposes the Acknowledgements on pp. xxi, 15, 142, 213 constitute an
extension of this copyright page.

Cover design: Grace Ridge
Cover image © Anthony A. Essien

All rights reserved. No part of this publication may be: i) reproduced or transmitted
in any form, electronic or mechanical, including photocopying, recording or by means
of any information storage or retrieval system without prior permission in writing from the
publishers; or ii) used or reproduced in any way for the training, development or operation
of artificial intelligence (AI) technologies, including generative AI technologies. The rights
holders expressly reserve this publication from the text and data mining exception as
per Article 4(3) of the Digital Single Market Directive (EU) 2019/790.

Bloomsbury Publishing Plc does not have any control over, or responsibility for,
any third-party websites referred to or in this book. All internet addresses given
in this book were correct at the time of going to press. The author and publisher
regret any inconvenience caused if addresses have changed or sites have ceased
to exist, but can accept no responsibility for any such changes.

A catalogue record for this book is available from the British Library.

A catalog record for this book is available from the Library of Congress.

ISBN: HB: 978-1-3503-6920-7
PB: 978-1-3503-6924-5
ePDF: 978-1-3503-6921-4
eBook: 978-1-3503-6922-1

Series: Multilingualisms and Diversities in Education

Typeset by RefineCatch Limited, Bungay, Suffolk

For product safety related questions contact productsafety@bloomsbury.com.

To find out more about our authors and books visit
www.bloomsbury.com and sign up for our newsletters.

Contents

List of Figures	vii
List of Tables	viii
List of Contributors	ix
Series Editors' Foreword	xiii
Preface	xix
Acknowledgements	xxi

1. The Concept of Language-as-Resource/Sources of Meaning from an African Perspective: Challenges and Opportunities in Mathematics Education *Anthony A. Essien, Ingrid Sapire and Matshidiso M. Moleko* — 1

Part One Critical Engagement of Language Policies and Their Implementation or Reforms in Mathematics Education

2. Exploring the Implications of the Multilingual Turn in Mathematics Education Research for South African Policy-Makers, Researchers and Educators *Sally-Ann Robertson and Mellony Graven* — 23

3. Teaching and Learning Mathematics in Algeria as a Multilingual Country: Difficulties, Challenges and Hints for Future Research Studies *Nadia Azrou* — 47

4. Novice Teachers' Use of the Mother Tongue in Mathematics Junior Primary Multilingual Classrooms in Northern Namibia *Tulonga T. Shuukwanyama, Caroline Long and Jeremiah S. Maseko* — 73

Part Two Curriculum and Pedagogy Issues in Multilingual Education within Mathematics in Africa

5. Multilingualism Challenges in Mathematics Education in Morocco *Moulay Driss Aqil* — 95

Part Three Support and Development of Mathematical Practices in the Teaching and Learning of Mathematics in a Specific Linguistic Setting in Africa

6   Supporting the Development of Content-Specific Language-Responsive Mathematical Teaching Practices in Multilingual Classrooms in Africa *Jill Adler and Anthony A. Essien*   115

7   African Language/English Bilingual Curriculum Materials: What Educative Supports Does the Bala Wande Package Offer Teachers? *Hamsa Venkat and Samantha Morrison*   147

8   A Case of English Medium Instruction in Rwanda: Issues for Mathematics Teaching and Learning Research *Rachel Bowden, Innocente Uwineza, Jean Claude Dushimimana and Alphonse Uworwabayeho*   171

Part Four Language Issues in Teaching with Mathematics Register in an Indigenous (African) Language and Directions for Future Research

9   Preparing Teachers to Teach Mathematics in Home Languages in Malawi: What We Know, What We Need to Know and Directions for Future Research *Justina Longwe, Fraser Gobede and Mercy Kazima*   195

Epilogue

10   Whose Languages? Whose Mathematics? An Epilogue *Richard Barwell*   219

Index   227

Figures

1.1	The rainfall task	1
2.1	Some key models for bilingual education	30
2.2	Representation of Cummins' linguistic interdependence hypothesis	32
2.3	Ms P's numeric flow diagram	35
2.4	Synthesis of Cummins' BICS/CALP distinction	38
3.1	Street names and signs written in both Arabic and French	51
5.1a	Jayid (2012 edition)	100
5.1b	Mathematics analysis, problems and solutions, first year of baccalaureate	101
5.2a	What's interesting in mathematics, third year secondary preparatory	103
5.2b	Mathematics analysis, problems and solutions, first year of baccalaureate	104
6.1	Geometric task	115
6.2	Task adapted from Wits Maths Connect Project course materials	127
6.3	The transport company task	132
7.1	Bala Wande register poster	153
7.2	Teacher Guide notes	161
9.1	A place value box being used by a pre-service teacher	204
9.2	Writing numbers under place value headings	208
9.3	Adding numbers on a place value box and on the chalkboard	209
9.4	Individual work	209

Tables

1.1	Some linguistic dynamics of the African contexts	2
1.2	Operationalization of criteria for language use	11
1.3	Excerpt from a Grade 3 lesson on number patterns	13
5.1	Different forms of sums of cubic roots	105
5.2	Arabic mathematical limits, functions, derivatives and integrals notations	106
5.3	Arabic inverse trigonometric functions	106
5.4	Three sets of numbers	106
6.1	The transport company task	134
7.1	Bala Wande Teacher Guide	160
9.1	An example of coding	203

Contributors

Jill Adler is Professor of Mathematics Education at the University of the Witwatersrand (Wits), Johannesburg, South Africa. Jill was President of the International Commission on Mathematical Instruction (ICMI), 2017–2020, and held the SARChI Mathematics Education Chair at Wits during 2010–2019. She was awarded the ICMI Hans Freudenthal Medal in 2015 in recognition of a major cumulative programme of research.

Moulay Driss Aqil holds a PhD in Mathematics Education from Columbia University, New York, USA. He currently teaches Mathematics at Pace University and New York City College of Technology, City University of New York, USA. His research interests include multilingualism, cultural identity and mathematics education.

Nadia Azrou holds a PhD in Mathematics Education. Her research interests include proof and proving at university level and multilingualism/multiculturalism in the teaching and learning of mathematics. She also teaches Mathematics at the University of Medea, Algeria.

Richard Barwell is Dean and Professor of Mathematics Education at the Faculty of Education, University of Ottawa, Canada. His research interests include language, language diversity and discourse in mathematics classrooms. He also studies how mathematics education can contribute towards a sustainable future for planet Earth.

Rachel Bowden is Research Associate at the University of Bristol Centre for Comparative and International Research in Education (CIRE), UK, and at the Technical University Dresden, Centre for Teacher Education and Education Research (ZLSB), Germany. Her research interests are multilingual education, education for sustainability and teacher professional development.

Jean Claude Dushimimana is Assistant Lecturer and PhD student at the University of Rwanda-College of Education, Kigali, Rwanda. He is Associate

Member of the African Centre of Excellence for Innovative Teaching and Learning Mathematics and Science (ACEITLMS), University of Rwanda-College of Education, Kayonza District, Eastern Province, Rwanda. Jean Claude has participated in international conferences and published a number of articles. His research interest is statistics education, especially the impact of technology integration.

Anthony A. Essien is Associate Professor in Mathematics Education and the Interim South African Numeracy Chair at the Wits School of Education, Johannesburg, South Africa. He was the Deputy Head of School for Research at the Wits School of Education from June 2020 to September 2022. He is series editor of Studies on Mathematics Education and Society, and an Editorial Board member of Educational Studies in Mathematics (ESM). Anthony was an associate editor of *Pythagoras* for eleven years.

Fraser Gobede is Postdoctoral Fellow at the University of Malawi, Zomba, Malawi. He has an overall experience of twenty years, which includes twelve years of teaching secondary school and college mathematics; and over eight years in both mathematics teacher education and research in the teaching of early grade mathematics.

Mellony Graven holds the South African Numeracy Chair at Rhodes University, Grahamstown, Makhanda, South Africa. She has edited several books and special issues of journals, and serves on the editorial board of several leading journals. Her work focuses on the creation of a hub of mathematical activity and innovation-seeking solutions to mathematics education challenges.

Mercy Kazima is Professor of Mathematics Education at the University of Malawi, Zomba, Malawi. Her work includes leading research and development projects. Mercy has substantial experience in mathematics education research in the areas of teaching mathematics in multilingual contexts, mathematical knowledge for teaching, and mathematics teacher education and professional development.

Caroline Long is Senior Research Associate at the University of Johannesburg, South Africa. Her fields of specialization are mathematics teacher education and assessment. She holds a PhD (UCT) and has completed courses in measurement theory through the University of Western Australia, Crawley, Australia. Her publications include works on mathematics education, teacher education, teacher agency and assessment and measurement.

Justina Longwe is Postdoctoral Fellow at the University of Malawi, Zomba, Malawi. Her research interest is in mathematics teacher education with a special focus on the teaching of mathematics in the early years of primary school. She recently completed her PhD, which explored the area of pre-service mathematics teacher education.

Jeremiah S. Maseko is Lecturer in the Department of Childhood Education at the University of Johannesburg, South Africa. With a PhD in Mathematics Education and a Masters in Information and Communication Technology (ICT) Education, his research focuses on mathematics teacher education, the application of ICTs in education and the development of professional graduate attributes in student teachers.

Matshidiso M. Moleko is Mathematics Education Lecturer and the Discipline Coordinator for Mathematics in the School of Mathematics, Natural Sciences and Technology Education in the Faculty of Education at the University of the Free State, South Africa, where she also obtained her PhD.

Samantha Morrison obtained her PhD at the University of the Witwatersrand (Wits), Johannesburg, South Africa, and is currently Project Manager for the SARChI Mathematics Education Numeracy Chair at the same university. She is involved in a number of research projects within the SARChI Chair where she does research and development work.

Sally-Ann Robertson worked initially as a primary school teacher, later moving into teacher education at Rhodes University's Education Faculty, Grahamstown, Makhanda, South Africa. Her doctorate, obtained under the supervision of Professor Mellony Graven, explored the place of language in supporting children's mathematical development, work she now continues as part of Mellony's Numeracy Chair Project.

Ingrid Sapire is a primary mathematics education expert. Her work centres on the teaching of mathematics for understanding, with a particular emphasis on language use in the multilingual South African context. She is currently Head of

Maths Content for the Bala Wande programme, based at the University of the Witwatersrand (Wits), Johannesburg, South Africa.

Tulonga T. Shuukwanyama is Lecturer in the Department of Early Childhood Education and Care, lecturing on Mathematics and Numeracy Education at the University of Namibia (Hifikepunye Pohamba Campus), Ongwediva, Namibia. She completed her PhD at the University of Johannesburg, South Africa. Her research interests are on teaching experiences of novice teachers and pre-service teacher education.

Innocente Uwineza is Assistant Lecturer in Mathematics Education and PhD student at the University of Rwanda-College of Education. She develops teaching modules and facilitates face-to-face and online CPD training for secondary school teachers. Her research focuses on gender and ICT in mathematics education.

Alphonse Uworwabayeho is Professor of Mathematics Education at the University of Rwanda-College of Education, Kigali, Rwanda. He is Commissioner on Mathematics Education for the African Mathematics Union (AMU) and member of Rwanda Mathematics Union. His research interest lies in mathematics teacher professional development on enhancing active learning.

Hamsa Venkat holds the Naughton Chair in Early Years/Primary STEM Education at Dublin City University, and holds visiting professorships at University of the Witwatersrand (Wits), Johannesburg, South Africa and Jönköping University, Sweden. She has extensive experience of research and development work in primary mathematics, and of publication in mathematics education.

Series Editors' Foreword

Multilingualism in Mathematics Education in Africa is a significant contribution to Bloomsbury's series, *Multilingualisms and Diversities in Education*. Richard Barwell, author of the Epilogue to the volume, locates this volume within internationally leading African research, particularly from Southern Africa, on linguistic diversity (multilingualism) and mathematics. Barwell points out that it is surprising that so little research effort has been directed at the relationship between linguistic diversity and mathematics teaching and learning beyond Africa. Anthony A. Essien brings together the first book collection of African research in mathematics education in multilingual societies. With many of the authors building on earlier path-breaking African research, the volume is a unique contribution of careful thinking through how linguistic diversity and multilingualism manifest in ways that differ from one geopolitical context to another. Complex histories and layers of human mobility, conquest, coloniality, epistemologies, practices of faith, languages, scripts and scholarship come together differently, with varying implications for the teaching and learning of mathematics in each setting. The implications present critical challenges and opportunities for students and teachers, followed in turn by a sequence of socioeconomic consequences for the societies in which they live, and those to which they migrate and into which they are received. Yet, to be more fully understood are the necessary responses for mathematics and science education that need to be taken by ethical and responsible policymakers, planners and providers of professional learning of teachers.

To illustrate the complexity of multilingual societies as these intersect with mathematics and education, Essien has brought together authors of studies from six of the fifty-four countries of Africa. In each case, authors grapple with the multilingual ecology of their context and how to deploy multilingual approaches that best navigate conceptual differences in mathematical thinking that accompany historically different epistemologies, languages and scripts. There is no simple template, or model that can be designed to address all the complexities here. Northern perspectives of what bilingual and multilingual education look like, especially those curated in contemporary texts and critiques of multilingualism based on a relatively few programme designs from North

America, lack relevance in African contexts. These programmes and accompanying critiques are similarly inappropriate for contexts across the Asia-Pacific and Euro-North countries experiencing increasing in-migration and societal diversification. For these reasons, this volume is an important contribution to growing recognition of multilingualism as the global 'linguistic dispensation' (Aronin & Singleton, 2008) especially for implications in mathematics and science education.

Two of the country studies in this volume, Algeria and Morocco, in North Africa, are countries that have witnessed millennia of mobility, conquest, linguistic, faith-based and epistemological influences from across Africa to the South, the Mediterranean and Middle East. Historical layers of linguistic complexity and multiple writing scripts in these countries include Tifinagh scripts with origins in ancient Libyco-Berber that can be traced to 600 BCE and that spread across North Africa to the Canary Islands. Latin was to follow the Roman Empire from about 150 BCE, and Maghrebi (or Maghribi) script – an African version of Arabic script – from about 650 CE was to spread across North Africa and the Sahara, together with Classical Arabic script used for religious observance. Azrou (Algeria) and Aqil (Morocco) point out that the different directionality of scripts implicate comprehension. Whereas Arabic script runs from right to left, the Latin script runs from left to right. Attempts to use bilingual Arabic–French texts in the teaching of mathematics, can be conceptually tricky to navigate with scripts running in different directions, for example when working with algebraic formulations. At the same time, bi/multilingual pedagogies necessary for speaking and explaining concepts and making meaning are essential.

In each country-setting, both earlier conquest and later colonial history have left hierarchical or stratified (Barwell, this volume) linguistic ecologies. Most significant of these is that whereas in Europe and North America, the school language is usually a language of widest communication, this is not the case in most African countries, especially when a language of a former European or colonial administration has become the medium of instruction. In most African countries, the range of 'international' language dispersal and functional use is between 0 per cent in remote areas and a possible maximum of 40 per cent in some urban contexts. This leaves most students in Africa at risk when one of the former colonial languages remains the dominant and single language of instruction. The situation is little different across South-East and South Asia, and the outcomes are dire for minoritized communities everywhere. The studies in this volume then, speak to contexts way beyond Africa.

Rwanda, located in Central Africa, is a country that has experienced a century of ongoing genocide and the aftermath of trauma, with recent implications for language education policy. The genocide perpetrated during 1885–1908 under King Leopold II of Belgium, followed by inept Belgian administration after the First World War fomented interethnic violence that was to continue to the mid-1990s. Colonial use of the French language over a majority Kinyarwanda-speaking population with significant multilingual capability in regional languages of trade, including Kiswahili and Lingala, was suddenly replaced in 2008 with English (Bowden et al., this volume). Strong lobbying of Rwandese political refugees in Uganda led to French being replaced as the sole medium of instruction in schools in a country where English has little societal diffusion or functional use. Despite considerable external support from the British Council, this move poses significant risk for educational catastrophe and intergenerational poverty in Rwanda since most teachers are unlikely to be able to use English effectively, especially for mathematics teaching, for decades to come. Despite inventive interventions by teachers, the prioritization of English undermines teachers' and community multilingual capabilities and repertoires (including Kinyarwanda–Kiswahili–French). This case is an example, for language policy and planning stakeholders everywhere, of *what not to do*, the ethical questions that arise when multilingual ecologies are disrupted or encouraged, and high-risk consequences of educational failure and systemic exclusion.

Six chapters address Southern Africa countries. Two of these, Malawi, sometimes also included as an eastern or central African country (Kazima et al.) and Namibia, located in south-western Africa (Shuukwanyama et al.), are highly multilingual countries administered through English. They have different highly contested colonial and post-colonial histories, characterized by inequality. Upon independence, both Malawi and Namibia adopted English as the official language and primary language of education. This was predictable for Malawi, with a prior history of British colonial administration. However, there was no prior history of English in Namibia, colonized by Germany and then largely administrated through Afrikaans from after the First World War to 1990. It was only after more than fifteen years of lobbying for a multilingual education policy that curriculum changes began to occur, and teachers, as evident in this volume, have been left confused and underprepared. What have become monolingual English Medium Instruction (EMI) curriculum and state-led implementation practices, have been resisted by teachers and educators as illustrated in the four chapters that address research and practice in South Africa over the last three decades (post-apartheid period). South Africa has had a vexed bifurcated bilingual and multilingual and unequal education system for more than a century – despite variations of this over the last seven decades. This is also the country in which the greatest body of research in bilingual and multilingual education has occurred internationally. Authors and collaborators in this volume have been at the forefront of this research. Teachers, educators of mathematics and non-for-profit bodies, recognizing that state-led initiatives have led to few, if any, positive outcomes for students exiting schooling systems, have contributed significantly to this research, as evidenced by authors Adler, Essien, Graven, Moleko, Morrison, Robertson, Sapire and Venkat in this volume, and Setati and others elsewhere. Regrettably, as Barwell points out in the Epilogue, much of this research has been overlooked in what we, as Series Editors, suggest is a 'slimmed'-down literature of bilingual education programmes designed in or replicated elsewhere from North America.

Essien's volume and the four chapters on the intersection of multilingual education and mathematics drawn from South African research, and wider discussions of the complexity of mathematics teaching from Algeria, Morocco, Namibia, Malawi and Rwanda, are thus most welcome. They draw attention to the need for 'talk' and 'conversation' about mathematics and mathematical thinking. They offer compelling rationale for why and how everyday talk, about what students know when they enter classrooms, is important. It is important for both students and teachers to understand and grapple with in order to navigate the epistemological frames of reference, and sources of knowledge and belief upon which these frames rest. The authors offer compelling reasons why mathematical thinking and discourse in contemporary curricula require the acquisition of a corpus of mathematical vocabulary and conceptual building blocks in the languages most often used in their linguistic repertoires for successful journeys of mathematical learning. This is not straightforward, as the authors demonstrate. Some languages and scripts in students' repertoires are more suitable and useful for certain mathematical concepts, formulations and functions, whereas different languages (and scripts) may be more suitable for others.

The way students and teachers exercise purposeful choice (selecting elements of their multilingual repertoires) was identified as part of multilingual capability and societal 'functional multilingualism' in earlier South African research three decades back. The linguistic agency linked to this capability, reflected in the concept of 'linguistic citizenship' in educational contexts (discussed in Heugh & Stroud, 2020), and in the pedagogical use of 'functional multilingual learning' (Van Avermaet et al., 2018) evidenced in multilingual school populations in

Europe are evident throughout this volume. This volume offers a powerful move for students and teachers, heightening awareness of the potential of teachers and students' linguistic choices (agency and citizenship), and functional use of these in productive pedagogies (functional multilingual learning) to facilitate comfortable conversations that enhance mathematical thinking.

Finally, Essien and colleagues draw attention to both multilingualism as a resource in and for mathematics in education, and as sources of and for mathematical education. Mathematics is not a discipline that began in English or any other European or so-called international language. Thus far, the earliest archaeological and palaeontological evidence of geometric patterns, including triangles, dating back 74,000 years, have been found in Blombos Cave on the southernmost coast of Africa (Henshilwood et al., 2001). These, as far as we can surmise, indicate spatial concepts that are central to mathematical thinking (Heugh, 2022), predating the pyramids of the Kingdom of Kush in present-day Sudan and Egypt by thousands of years. As series editors, we are proud of this volume. The time has come to straighten historical records and to acknowledge the longue durée sources of conceptual knowledge fundamental to global knowledge systems. This is much more than a contribution to teacher education and the teaching of mathematics to students around the world. It is an invitation to rethink the origin and sources of mathematics and how we might pay more attention to the multilingual agency and capabilities of both students and teachers to ensure greater access and equality in the teaching of mathematics everywhere.

Kathleen Heugh, Christopher Stroud and Piet Van Avermaet

References

Aronin, L., & Singleton, D. (2008). Multilingualism as a new linguistic dispensation. *International Journal of Multilingualism, 5*(1), 1–16.

Henshilwood, C. S., Sealy, J. C., Yates, R., Cruz-Uribe, K., Goldberg, P., Grine, F. E., Klein, R. G., Poggenpoel, C., van Niekerk, K., & Watts, I. (2001). Blombos Cave, Southern Cape, South Africa: Preliminary report on the 1992–1999 excavations of the Middle Stone Age levels. *Journal of Archaeological Science, 28*(4), 421–448.

Heugh, K. (2022). Linguistic and epistemic erasure in Africa: Coloniality, linguistic human rights and decoloniality. In T. Skutnabb-Kangas & R. Phillipson (eds), *The handbook of linguistic human rights* (pp. 55–70). Hoboken, NJ: John Wiley & Sons.

Heugh, K., & Stroud, C. (2019). Multilingualism in South African education: A southern perspective. In R. Hickey (ed.), *English in multilingual South Africa: The linguistics of contact and change*. Studies in English Language, 216–238. Cambridge: Cambridge University Press.

Van Avermaet, P., Slembrouck, S., Van Gorp, K., Sierens, S., & Maryns, K. (eds) (2018). *The multilingual edge of education*. London: Palgrave Macmillan.

Preface

It was Gorgias' (483–375 BCE) book entitled *On Not-Being or On Nature* that sparked off much debates about language and communication that would last centuries amongst philosophers, psychologists and linguists. In his book, Gorgias sets out to prove that 'first, nothing exists; second, that even if it does, it is incomprehensible by men; and third, that even if it is comprehensible, it is certainly *not expressible and cannot be communicated to another*' (Borgmann, 1974, p. 17, my emphasis). Although this philosophical position was regarded as sophism and thus rejected by many philosophers after him (e.g. Socrates, Plato, Aristotle, etc.), Gorgias' work nonetheless opened up avenues for the recognition and investigation of language as a philosophical problem. The attention to the intertwinement of language and mathematics, that is, how language is a tool for the advancement of mathematics and also how language issues are embedded in mathematics, has seen exponential growth in the last couple of decades. Teaching and learning mathematics, although perhaps stereotypically associated with manipulating numbers, is now fundamentally seen as inextricably interwoven with language. This is key in mathematics education given that language is core in meaning-making and communicating mathematics meaning. It is impossible to talk about conceptual understanding without language, given that mathematics is imbedded in language.

But while language issues in the teaching and learning of mathematics have received considerable research interest lately, there is a need for a concerted effort in continuing to investigate how to harness the epistemic potential of multiple languages in contexts of language diversity, like the African context. The challenges posed by language diversity – by multilingualism in education (and more specifically in mathematics education) – are a majority issue rather than a minority issue (Probyn, 2019). This is so because the African continent is one of the most linguistically diverse continents in the world, and as Heugh (2019) argues, multilingualism in Africa is not only multifaceted and but also multiscaled within changing linguistic hierarchies.

The book *Multilingualism in Mathematics Education in Africa* chronicles current research in different linguistic contexts across the African continent on issues of language diversity (or multilingualism) in the teaching and learning of mathematics, but more importantly, it foregrounds pertinent issues for mathematics education research in the next decades through: the language as resource/sources of meaning orientation (Chapter 1); through studies that critically engage with language policies/planning and their implementation or reforms in mathematics education (Chapters 2, 3 and 4); curriculum and pedagogy issues in multilingual education within mathematics in Africa (Chapter 5); support and development of mathematical practices in the teaching and learning of mathematics in a specific linguistic setting in Africa (Chapters 6, 7 and 8); and language issues in teaching with mathematics register in an indigenous (African) language and directions for future research (Chapter 9). The Epilogue, Chapter 10, by Richard Barwell, brings the international dimension to the African language diversity tensions and urges African education to pave the way (for the world) on how to teach mathematics in ways that honour, preserve and enrich language diversity.

The book brings together leading scholars in Africa, in the field of multilingualism and mathematics teaching and learning across a range of different country experiences. It is hoped that the pertinent issues raised in each chapter of this book will further induce research into the teaching and learning of mathematics in an African context (and beyond) that is deeply multilingual.

Unlike Gorgias, and like the philosophers mentioned above, the authors of the different chapters of this book firmly believe that mathematics can be 'comprehensible', 'expressible', and communicable if the epistemic potential of the presence of multiple languages in a context like that of Africa is harnessed.

This book has particular relevance in those countries and contexts in which English Medium Instruction (EMI) is increasingly introduced in the schooling system and in which there is an indisputable need for students learning to be built upon the foundations of strong home/local and national languages, without which EMI will fail. The book is also relevant to teacher education in all multilingual contexts of the world.

Anthony A. Essien

References

Borgmann, A. (1974). *The philosophy of language: Historical foundations and contemporary issues.* The Hague: Martinus Nijhoff.
Heugh, K. (2019) Multilingualism and education in Africa. In E. Wolff (ed.), *The Cambridge handbook of African linguistics* (pp. 577–600). Cambridge: Cambridge University Press.
Probyn, M. (2019). Pedagogical translanguaging and the construction of science knowledge in a multilingual South African classroom: Challenging monoglossic/post-colonial orthodoxies. *Classroom Discourse, 10*(3–4), 216–236. Available online: https://doi.org/10.1080/19463014.2019.1628792 (accessed 20 May 2023).

Acknowledgements

My appreciation goes to the National Research Foundation (NRF) under the South African Numeracy Chair: University of the Witwatersrand (Wits) (Grant Number: 74703), for providing the funding that enabled the initial reviewing work of the chapters in this book. My sincere gratitude also goes to Thulelah Takane and Avuzwa Essien for ensuring that the technical requirements for the manuscript were effected.

The Concept of Language-as-Resource/Sources of Meaning from an African Perspective: Challenges and Opportunities in Mathematics Education

Anthony A. Essien, Ingrid Sapire and Matshidiso M. Moleko

Introduction

Consider the task in Figure 1.1 which was given to postgraduate multilingual students who were also in-service teachers teaching mathematics at different grade levels in primary and secondary schools.

In the months below, the circles represent the number of days it rained per month. Which month has the least rainfall?			
January	February	March	April

Figure 1.1 The rainfall task.

Year after year, this task is given to postgraduate students who are in-service teachers, and it is interesting how the answers provided by these students are usually divided along two lines. While some (mainly the monolingual English first language students) say it is April, most of the multilingual students argue that the correct answer must be March. For the students who argue that the correct answer is April, this is not debatable. For them, the answer is somewhat clear-cut and they marvel at the students who think it is March. But the students who argue for March have their own argument, which is premised on the fact that the word 'least' means that a quantity is involved and that this quantity must be the smallest. They use a dictionary definition of the word 'least' to support their argument. The situation got so heated one year that one of the multilingual students, in making his point clear, said: '*this maths will make us fight. How can the answer be April? If four friends each have 5 dollars, 3 dollars, 1 dollar and the last no money respectively, who has the least money? Isn't it the one with 1 dollar?'* Langa and Setati (2006), who had used a similar task (but in their case, with English and home-language versions given to students) in an early grade mathematics class also reported a similar experience. A similar situation is further reported in a study by Kazima et al. (2023) in Malawi where teachers found the movement of zero as absence to zero as a number difficult to teach (also see Pitchford et al., 2021).

What linguistic issues are at stake in this task and in the way the students experience this task? What do we mean when we say that teaching and learning of mathematics is complex in situations of linguistic diversity? What does it take to teach/learn mathematics meaningfully in Africa? How does language diversity play a role? What are the critical issues? More often than not, discussions on the multilingual context in Africa dwell mainly on what is transparent across different African linguistic settings and what lurks behind the visible is often ignored. Yet, these less visible subtleties also contribute in no small measure to the complexity of teaching and learning in multilingual contexts. Table 1.1 depicts some of these subtle linguistic dynamics.

Table 1.1 Some linguistic dynamics of the African contexts

What stands out	What is less visible
High language diversity	Distinct nature of multilingualisms
Colonial history regarding language – colonial language versus indigenous language	Cross-linguistic issues (interaction between languages)
Transition from African languages to world languages	Translation issues • Teaching/Learning • Textbooks • Dialects/standardization
(Limited/varying) proficiency in LoLT (English/French)	• Varying proficiencies in home languages • Issues of dialects • Tonal variations • Structural linguistic differences

In terms of the distinct nature of multilingualism, while there are similarities between many linguistic contexts across the African continent (notably the multiplicity of languages and the dominance of colonial languages), the reality is that these contexts have their own particularities. For example, in South Africa where there are nine indigenous official languages in addition to English and Afrikaans, seven of these indigenous African languages are generally grouped into two groups based on their linguistic distance: the Sotho languages and the Nguni languages. Languages within the same group are mutually intelligible. The remaining two indigenous languages are autonomous languages with little or no common lexicon (Essien, 2020). Contrast this with the multilingual context in Nigeria, which boasts more than 400 indigenous languages, most of which are autonomous. In both contexts, the concept of language-as-resource as it pertains to certain practices like code switching takes on different meanings. In Algeria, there is cohabitation of four different languages, with the added complexity of reading both right-to-left and left-to-right, depending on which language one is using, including the structural differences between these languages (Azrou in this volume). This situation is also similar in Morocco (see Aqil in this volume), to mention but a few. Each of these contexts evokes the need for discursive practices that are attuned to their particularities.

Going back to the rainfall task in Figure 1.1, and to respond to the linguistic issues at stake in the task, two interrelated issues stand out. The first is the everyday understanding of the term 'least' versus the mathematical understanding. It must be noted that the 'everyday' understanding is always constrained by one's environment and what Zevenbergen (2000) has referred to as linguistic capital. Herein lies a key cross-linguistic issue: for many African indigenous languages, the word 'least' cannot be construed without 'something'. In other words, for there to be a 'least', there has to be something for which the 'least' is the smallest amount. It is completely nonsensical to think otherwise in these languages. The second issue is that of the concept of 'zero'. To demonstrate this with the class, the teacher educator, when using the Rainfall task, puts five pens on the desk and asks one of the students to translate the sentence, 'I have five pens on the table,' into the home language. The teacher educator then gradually takes away some pens until there are none left and asks for the translation: 'I have zero pens on the table.' The translation that is usually given is: 'I have no pens on the table.' When pressed to rather use the term 'zero', they are unable to.

In mathematics, zero is recognized as a quantity, while this is not so in many indigenous African languages. This cross-linguistic issue leads to many of the students proposing March as the month with the least rainfall. This is one of many cases where meaning-making in mathematics class is constrained by the interaction between languages. Halai (2009) also presents a case where the ways of showing degrees of comparison in Urdu are different compared to how this is done in English. Similar findings are noted in Mostert and Roberts (2020) in their work on the similarities and differences between isiXhosa (a South African indigenous language) and English regarding the language of comparison in early grade mathematics texts. What is clearly at stake here are intrinsic language issues concerning the teaching and learning of mathematics – a stark reminder of Durkin's (1991) words that mathematics starts in language, progresses through language, but also stumbles in language. No natural language is exempt from language-related issues in the teaching and learning of mathematic, hence African languages are no exception. This is so because mathematics subsumes a natural language to be communicated. Hence, in the above narrative regarding the concept of zero and the degree of comparison, what is at stake is not necessarily proficiency in either the home language or English (or both) but rather that of the linguistic capital (Zevenbergen, 2000) that students come to class with and how this capital shapes the way mathematics concepts are understood. As Barwell (2009) argues, those who have English as first language are already familiar with the linguist structures of the LoLT (English). This is not necessarily the case with those for whom English is an additional language.

Translation is another topical area that is prominent in discourse on the teaching and learning of mathematics in African indigenous languages, which raises many issues. These include the question as to whether or not particular African languages have sufficient mathematical/academic register to be used as languages of scholarship; how translations into indigenous languages are often long and sometimes windy because they are in fact descriptive appellation of the terms; what needs to be done when a particular mathematics vocabulary does not exist in the indigenous language; and how African indigenous language textbooks (especially early grade mathematics textbooks) are written in such a way that they are placeholders for English as they use English conventions that sometimes clash with the structure of the indigenous language (Kajoro, 2016). Related to this, Aqil (in this volume) noted a similar clash in linguistic structures in textbooks used in Morocco which are written in both Arabic (which is read from right to left), and French (which is read from left to right). In multilingual contexts, particularly where certain languages may be dominated by others, there could be a debate about the 'correct' mathematical register. This impacts more on written texts where fixed translations are required and where multiple meanings of words need to be monitored with care. Some mathematical terminology used in English might not carry over to other languages in the same way, where different words or phrases may have been established to convey specialized mathematical meanings. In spoken language, there is greater flexibility, where speakers can use language fluidly, using the words from one language while speaking another (translanguaging). Some authors have argued that the multi-bilingual presentation of print materials enables connections across different languages between meanings of terms which make up the mathematical register (Botes & Mji, 2010; Owen-Smith, 2012).

Another language-related issue that is visible across the continent is that students come to class with limited and/or varying levels of proficiency in the so-called world language that is used as LoLT. What is less visible is that there are also varying proficiencies in the indigenous languages students bring to class. This adds another layer of complexity to the teaching and learning of mathematics. And even more complex are issues of differences in dialect and issues of variations within the same language or dialect, where some terms in one dialect have a completely different meaning in another dialect.

Despite the complexities of the linguistic contexts discussed above, recent research in mathematics education in Africa has come to see language as a resource. This is attuned to global research whereby many educationists and researchers disagree with the view of linguistic pluralism as a deficit in the teaching and learning of mathematics. In fact, current research acknowledges multilingualism as a resource and language as sources of meaning in the teaching and learning of mathematics. The concepts of language as resource or language as sources of meaning have, thus, been a key underlying thrust in much research on the role of language in the teaching and learning of mathematics in multilingual settings. To this we now turn.

The Concept of Language-as-Resource/Sources of Meaning

A 'resource' is something that is valuable or experienced as helpful in a particular situation. Something is considered resourceful when it can create useful and unique solutions in challenging conditions. Research has long acknowledged the perspective of language-as-resource (Adler, 2001; Setati, 2005; Planas & Setati-Phakeng, 2014, Moschkovich, 2007; McLachlan & Essien, 2022). Research has also shown the role of language in education, especially in challenging contexts such as multilingual mathematics classrooms (Adler, 1999; Barwell, 2009; Mostert & Roberts, 2020). This research points to the fact that in these contexts, language can be used as a resource to aid learners' understanding of mathematics and to enable teachers to convey the mathematics content meaningfully.

The concept of language-as-resource, coined by Ruiz (1984), embraces the role languages play in teaching and learning. Moreso, it embraces the co-existence and usage of these languages. The concept, 'language-as-resource' requires that people acknowledge the use of multiple languages and see this as beneficial (Planas, 2011). This view means that the value of the use of more than one language should be acknowledged to help alleviate language-induced challenges often presented by the language of learning and teaching (English/ French), which is often not the home language of most learners. This is important, especially in the African context with such high linguistic diversities.

In the African context, the concept of language-as-resource has been used and is understood to encourage practices that support learners whose home language is not the language of learning and teaching (Setati, 2005, 2008). This concept is used to encourage efforts to enable learners to acquire meaningful learning. Language-as-resource is used to inspire the use of practices that would aid learners' comprehension and help clarify the concepts. Tensions that still exist between the use of home languages and English (in the African context) make it difficult for language to be used as a resource. In many African contexts where a world language is considered the medium of instruction, the use of 'subordinate languages' is not always fully integrated into the teaching and learning of mathematics. As we will explain later in this chapter, one way of optimizing language-as-resource is the use of translanguaging (rather than code-switching), bearing in mind the consideration that although the use of African languages seems helpful, at times the limited vocabulary of home languages for some mathematical concepts means that fluid use of more than one language will be needed.

The officialization of the colonial language as a medium of instruction in the past has resulted in its status being elevated above that of the other languages and has led to the perception that the colonial language is best for the teaching and learning of mathematics. This perception shows no consideration of the challenges that prevail in multilingual classrooms and underpins the view that multilingualism is a problem that must be fixed (Planas & Setati-Phakeng, 2014), aligning with the language-as-problem orientation, which puts emphasis on the regular use of only one language which is considered more powerful (Ruiz, 1984). In most African contexts where historic colonial politics still influence teaching and learning in schools, this orientation advocates for the use of the 'higher status' colonial language as the only preferred language (Setati, 2003), above the indigenous languages. In such instances, proficiency in the colonial language has come to be seen as the emblem of educatedness. In this vein, similar to Setati's (2008) findings, Posel and Casale (2011) also found in their study that most parents liked their children to learn through English because they believed that people proficient in English stand a good chance of being employed, unlike those who are not. Despite the arguments that continue to exist on which language (English or the indigenous home languages) should be used for teaching and learning mathematics, many researchers in the African context still argue for the use of home languages as resources for teaching and learning mathematics (Adler, 2001; Khisty, 1995; Moschkovich, 1999). These scholars acknowledge that English may be a more suitable language for teaching mathematics, considering that the assessments are also administered in it. However, they argue that the home languages as resources for learning can play a supportive role that is needed while the learners continue to develop English proficiency (Setati, 2008).

Code-switching enabling language-as-resource is prominently used in African countries such as South Africa, Kenya and Malawi (Maluleke, 2019; Halai & Karuku, 2013) to support the transfer of necessary/important knowledge to students to convey clarity. Botes and Mji (2010) assert that this practice may not be effective since teachers' explanations given in English may disadvantage learners who speak different languages. Robertson and Graven (2019) on the other hand, suggest the use of exploratory talk in another language as a tool for trying out different ways of thinking and understanding. They regard this strategy as useful in instances where learners must learn mathematics in English in which they are not yet proficient. However, a disadvantage of this language-as-resource strategy is that it requires more time, attention, practice and repetition for learners whose home language is not English.

It is worth noting that the work of Barwell (2018), drawing from the Bakhtinian perspective on language, critiques and reframes/expands the notion of language as a resource by providing limitations to this notion and proposing the concept of language as sources of meaning. According to Barwell (2018), four notions undergird the concept of language as sources of meaning: meaning-making is relational, language is agentive, language is diverse, and language is stratified and stratifying. He goes on to argue that to understand the role of language in the learning and teaching of mathematics in multilingual classrooms, there is a need to carefully look at the learners' repertoires of multiple sources of meaning, which can then be organized into three dimensions namely; languages, discourses and voices.

Our understanding of Barwell's notion of language as sources of meaning, is that language cannot only be viewed as a tool to support learning in line with the intended goal. Instead, language should be viewed beyond this goal. It should be seen as a tool for meaning-making, enabling learners to participate in class and construct new knowledge based on current constructions of reality and the repertoire of language practices they need to draw on. Meaning-making in a mathematics classroom requires the use of multiple languages, multiple discourses and multiple voices.

Drawing on the concepts of language-as-resource (Ruiz, 1984) and language as sources of meaning (Barwell, 2018), and given the complex nature of multilingualism across different linguistic contexts in Africa, we argue for the potential of translanguaging as a discursive practice for enabling the attainment of broader language roles.

Translanguaging and Its Potential in Africa

As seen above, the African education context is multilingual, with different numbers and combinations of languages in use to a greater or lesser extent across the various sites of educational activity. Although in the African context, mixed language use is the norm (Sapire, 2021) there is a tension that exists due to power relations that impact on language use (Setati, 2008) as discussed earlier in this chapter. At times, due to these power relations, pure language use, and of a dominant language, such as English rather than the mother tongue, is seen as the aspirational goal (Msila, 2019; Setati, 2008). The concepts of code-switching and translanguaging are used by researchers to differentiate between types of language mixing (Creese & Blackledge, 2010; García & Wei, 2014). Although code-switching is a form of language mixing, it can be seen as one caught in the monolingual mode (Essien & Sapire, 2022; Sapire & Essien, 2021). In contrast, translanguaging best allows multilinguals to draw on their multilingual language repertoire when using language to make meaning in educational settings. Our use of the term language or linguistic repertoire draws from our previous work (Essien and Sapire, 2022, p. 85) to mean 'an individual's linguistic "baggage", that is, the totality of the set of knowledge and skills an individual possesses of one or more languages that can be drawn upon in any instance of speaking, writing, reading and sense-making'.

Vogel and García (2017, p.1) summarize the concept and potential of translanguaging in the following excerpt:

> Translanguaging is a theoretical lens that offers a different view of bilingualism and multilingualism. The theory posits that rather than possessing two or more autonomous language systems, as has been traditionally thought, bilinguals, multilinguals, and indeed, all users of language, select and deploy particular features from a unitary linguistic repertoire to make meaning and to negotiate

particular communicative contexts. Translanguaging also represents an approach to language pedagogy that affirms and leverages students' diverse and dynamic language practices in teaching and learning.

Put differently, as García and Otheguy (2020, p. 25) note, 'translanguaging sees multilinguals as possessing a unitary linguistic system that they build through social interactions of different types, and that is not compartmentalized into boundaries corresponding to those of the named languages'. Research reporting on the practice of code-switching in multilingual African and international contexts, emerged in the 1990s and is still ongoing (e.g. Adler, 1999, 2001; Aineamani, 2018; Bunyi, 1997; Essien, 2010, 2013, 2018; Kaphesi, 2002; Langa, 2006; Moschkovich, 2007; Poo & Venkat, 2021; Setati, 2003). Code-switching (an alternation between two or more languages of expression) is seen as useful for both teachers and learners when mathematics is taught in multilingual contexts. More recently, a growing body of research into translanguaging and the role of language in mathematics teaching and learning has emerged, also in Africa and internationally (e.g. Creese & Blackledge, 2010; Prediger et al., 2019; Sorto et al., 2014; Poo & Venkat, 2021; Essien & Sapire, 2022). Translanguaging can be defined as the 'integration of language practices in the person of the learner' (García & Wei, 2014, p. 80) involving a 'shift within bilingual instruction from teaching two separate autonomous linguistic systems to a more flexible set of arrangements' (Cummins, 2015, slide 15). Flexibility is a core requirement for translanguaging in a mathematics class, but for this to be possible, transferability between languages is a necessity (Canagarajah, 2011). This means that, for both teachers and learners, knowledge of the mathematical register in more than one language is an advantage; but it is not a necessity and the freedom to draw on those different language resources flexibly is essential.

Researchers claim that translanguaging is a useful practice in the context of multilingual teaching, especially (but not exclusively) in the context of language learning (García & Wei, 2014, Lewis et al., 2012; Essien & Sapire, 2022). This has implications for the teaching of mathematics in the early grades. Recently in the South African context, Mostert (2019) and Poo and Venkat (2021) have written about the value of using the linguistic structure of number names in indigenous languages in the teaching of number concepts. Makalela (2014) argues that 'research on classroom and programme and practices has revealed a myriad of benefits that show the need for translanguaging policy in multilingual contexts' (p. 92). These benefits include language and cognitive development, since some researchers have shown that brain function is strengthened in learners who draw on two languages simultaneously. Many authors speak to the cognitive benefits of translanguaging for learners of all ages (e.g. Bialystok, 2006; Chin & Wigglesworth, 2007; Kovács & Mehler, 2009). For example, Castro (2015) suggests that 'translanguaging is one way in which [learners can] support their working memory' (p. 64). In addition to this, Castro's study that explored language use in mathematics lessons in multilingual spaces in a rural community in the Midwest USA found that the school worked at systemizing translanguaging as part of their bilingual programme, impacting learner engagement as it was experienced as a 'pedagogy of care' (2015). The benefits of translanguaging in multilingual contexts rest on the ability of teachers in these contexts to mediate learning in more than one language.

Harnessing the Power of a Multiplicity of Languages

Learning draws on language at every level and in the multilingual African context, this plays out in a multiplicity of manners, some of which have begun being researched but some of which remain an untapped source of potential learning about the concept of language-as-resource/sources of meaning. Core to all research on language and learning is knowledge of different types of language use and the development of criteria for the recognition of variation in language use. Drawing on literature, Sapire (2021) developed a set of six criteria for this purpose that make explicit the variations in language use, linking them to language ideology (mono/heteroglossic) which, at least to an extent, accounts for the power relations at play when language use choices are made. Monoglossic ideologies were seen as driving pure language use and heteroglossic ideologies drive mixed language use (Sapire, 2021; Sapire & Essien, 2021). The criteria also made a distinction between embedded and articulated language use.[1] Sapire (2021) referred to embedded language when a speaker uses language in a particular way without giving an explanation for the choice of language use. This is normal in all instances of language use apart from when speakers intentionally reflect on their language use choices. The examples given in the table are taken from survey and observation data collected as part of the project *Researching Multilingualism in Foundation Phase Mathematics*. The survey included some mathematics questions (where explanations of solutions were required) from which written language use data was obtained while the observation transcripts provided a record of spoken language use data. The way in which three of the criteria (for embedded language use) are operationalized shows the potential of translanguaging as demonstrated in Table 1.2.

Table 1.2 Operationalization of criteria for language use (Sapire, 2021, p. 91)

Criterion: language use	Indicator	Example
Pure language (embedded)	One language used when writing mathematical answers or giving mathematical explanations.	**Survey (maths questionnaire)** [I wrote two numbers and then I found the answer] **Observation** *Sometharo ke e (writes 13 on the board), a ke lekgolo? Ka na wa re ke lekgolo akere?* [Here is thirteen (writes 13 on the board) is it a hundred? You guys are saying it's hundred, right?]
Mixed language – code switching (embedded)	More than one language used, where the speaker made a choice to use these languages (showing awareness) when writing mathematical answers or giving mathematical explanations.	**Survey (maths questionnaire)** **Observation** So here, you must also know, *kufanele wazi ukuthi*, which rule that you must use. [So here, you must also know, you must know, which rule that you must use.]
Mixed language – translanguaging (embedded)	More than one language used, where the speaker used language fluidly and flexibly when writing mathematical answers or giving mathematical explanations.	**Survey (maths questionnaire)** [I counted in threes] **Observation** *Njengamanje ngikunikeze bani? U three angithi? Okay emva ka three ngifuna u jampe kangaki?* [Right now, what number have I given you? Three, right? Okay, after three I want you to jump how many times?]

The table shows a rich range of possibilities (written and spoken) for variation in language use, in the operationalization of the three criteria for embedded language use. In the first row of Table 1.2, there are examples of the criterion *pure (monolingual)* language use. In these examples, only one language is used in the utterance. In the second row, there are examples of the criterion *mixed codeswitching* language use. This criterion was developed to give recognition to mixed language utterances, where awareness of language use was evident, as seen in the repetition/translation of the same word, phrase or sentence in two languages. In the third row, we see examples of the criterion *mixed translanguaging* language use. Here we see fluid mixing of more than one language drawn from the language repertoire of the speaker. The mixing may simply involve using words/phrases from more than one language – evidence of a multilingual speaker drawing on their language repertoire. The potential for translanguaging lies in its fluidity and as can be seen in Table 1.2 where both students and teachers translanguage when speaking mathematics.

There is scope for many different forms of expression in multilingual contexts where speakers draw on a language repertoire of more than one language. Transcripts of observed lessons in South African classrooms as part of the Researching Multilingualism in Foundation Phase Mathematics project (Sapire, 2021) provide an example of a teacher using language-as-resource/sources of meaning. This can be done in various ways as discussed above and exemplified by the criteria for language use in Table 1.2. In Table 1.3 below, a brief excerpt of the interaction between a teacher and her Grade 4 class is given.

The language use in Table 1.3 is evidence of translanguaging using isiZulu, English and some words that are invented by the teacher using a mixture of isiZulu and English, referred to as 'trans' words (Sapire, 2021). Language use here is mixed fluidly. Teacher utterances in the dominant language (isiZulu) are *italicized* where language mixing occurs. Trans words are given in ***bolded italics*** in the original as well as in the English translation. Where the teacher used the English number word with an isiZulu prefix, this is also italicized. When the teacher uses an English word/phrase, this is **bolded** and student utterances (which are all in English) are also bolded to distinguish them. The fluidity of the language use shown in Table 1.3 is clear – there is a certain pattern in the way this teacher mixes languages as she draws on from her language repertoire. For example, she says most number names in English with or without an isiZulu prefix. The way in which she uses the prefixes (for example, ngo four, ka four) shows her using English while maintaining the structure of the isiZulu language. The trans words that she invents (for example, inamba, lenamba, jumpa) also show how she is combining elements of her language repertoire. The teacher's

Table 1.3 Excerpt from a Grade 3 lesson (isiZulu LoLT school) on number patterns

Speaker	Utterance	Translation
Teacher	Amaphethini ezinombolo esizowenza namhlanje amaphethini okubala ngobani?	Number patterns we will do today, which ones will we do?
Students (Chorus)	**Four**	**Four**
Teacher	***Ngo four.*** Lalelani ke … akuzukuphelela ekutheni sibala ***ngo four*** ngeba kade senza **but** okubalulekile ukuthi wazi ukuthi kune ***inamba*** ozoyinikezwa. Makuthiwa yeqa ***ka four then*** usuzokwazi ukubona ***inamba*** elandelayo. **It's not that** … iphethini lokubala ***ngo four, eight, twelve, sixteen*** kuphela … kuyezwakala yini?	***Fours.*** Listen then … it's not going to end with you counting in ***fours*** the way we have been doing **but** what is important is to know if there is a ***number*** you will be given. When they say count ***in fours then*** you will be able to see the next ***number***. **It's not that** … simply a pattern of counting ***four, eight, twelve, sixteen*** only … Do you understand?
Students (Chorus)	**Yes, mam.**	**Yes, mam.**
Teacher	**But** ukuthi wazi ukuthi mawunikezwe ***lenamba*** bese kuthiwa ***jampa ka four*** bese ubona ***inamba*** enjani elandelayo. Kuyezwakala yini nah?	**But** so you should know that if you are given a ***number*** … then they say ***jump four*** times … then you can see which ***number*** comes next. Are you getting it?
Students (Chorus)	**Yes, mam.**	**Yes, mam.**

language use shows that she is focusing on providing sources of meaning in her explanations and questions to the class. This is evidence of language-as-resource/sources of meaning in the multilingual context where translanguaging is being harnessed to support learning and teaching.

Concluding Reflections

In the literature, benefits of mixed language are often the focus. However, challenges and issues may also arise in multilingual contexts when mixed language is used (Canagarajah, 2011; Ticheloven et al., 2019). Vaish (2019) argues that the main challenges are created by the superdiversity of the language context and the hegemony of English, resulting in a preference for English even when it is not the home language.

The power and value of multilingualism are gaining recognition internationally (Wolff, 2018) and searching for ways to fully utilize language-as-resource/sources of meaning is an ongoing task – translanguaging is seen as key to this endeavour. Given the linguistic subtleties presented in the introductory section of this chapter, how can translanguaging space be opened up in such a way that accounts for and attends to the use of learners' full linguistic/semiotic repertoires freely and flexibly in the teaching and learning of mathematics?

The transcripts presented in Tables 1.2 and 1.3 have shown that some teachers (or learners) draw on a rich language repertoire when translanguaging. We argue that the necessity of understanding the two languages cannot be discounted for these speakers. But other forms of translanguaging can be done even if the teacher does not understand the home language. This can be done by drawing on any of the languages present in the class through a carefully planned lesson where the teacher can call on a learner to express a mathematical idea in her or his home language and allow the class to engage with what this idea translates to in English/French or any other language in use as the LoLT. For example, in isiZulu – one of the South African languages, the term for multiplication is *phinda Phinda*, which in English translates literally to 'repeat repeatedly'. Students in the early grade could be asked to express multiplication in their home language. Once this is done, they could then, as a class have a robust discussion as to what this term means in mathematics. In so doing, the teacher can work with the class on the difference (if any) and similarity between the terms expressed in the home language, and the mathematical meaning of that term. Enabling indigenous forms of expression / local languages to be visible in lessons and therefore used as a valuable learning resource to explore the meaning of particular mathematical terms is one way of creating opportunities for meaning-making in multilingual classrooms.

Challenges arise when there is a mismatch between the choices made by speakers and the ability of listeners not just to comprehend what may be a unique choice on the part of a speaker, but also to respect that choice. If these challenges are used to create opportunities for teachers to engage with learners, drawing on language-as-resource/sources of meaning, then they create opportunities for the deepening of mathematics learning and teaching in multilingual contexts.

In terms of the issue of translation raised in the introductory section, translanguaging presents itself as a response given its take on being able to move fluidly between languages. As argued in Essien and Sapire (2022), why confine oneself to one language when there are others that can be drawn on in the class?

The concept of translanguaging has become topical in situations of English/French/Welsh immersion. Given the linguistic subtleties discussed in the introductory section of this chapter, the knowledge/understanding of what it means to fully benefit from translanguaging practice is yet to be fully understood in the context of Africa. These include, but are not limited to, the varying proficiencies in home languages that students bring to class and the issue of dialects and tonal variations. Translanguaging using the epistemic potential of multiple languages that characterizes the African context therefore presents a potentially rich field for future research in the teaching and learning of mathematics in Africa. But this does not in any way mean that translanguaging practices should look the same in all African contexts. Translanguaging should enable differentiated and locally relevant language practices – transgressing modernist/colonial views of standard languages and respectfully engaging local language practices in learning processes. By this, we mean that translanguaging will look different in different contexts, on the spectrum from translation between fixed standard written forms to fluid and flexible language practices, rather than a single universal solution or method for diverse contexts. As such, the language as a resource orientation highlights the complexities and particularities of teaching and learning, and the need to enable teacher autonomy.

Acknowledgements

Many thanks to Pinkie Mthembu and Rachel Bowden for providing us with review feedback on the initial draft.

Notes

1 The other three criteria are for articulated language use, where awareness of language-use choices is evident. These criteria are not relevant for this discussion of actual spoken-/written-language use across various contexts.

References

Adler, J. (1999). The dilemma of transparency: Seeing and seeing through talk in the mathematics classroom. *Journal for research in Mathematics Education, 30*(1), 47–64.

Adler, J. (2001). *Teaching mathematics in multilingual classrooms.* Dordrecht: Kluwer Academic Publishers.

Aineamani, B. (2018). How learners communicate their mathematics reasoning in mathematics discourse. In J. Moschkovich, D. Wagner, A. Bose, J. Rodrigues Mendes, & M. Schütte (eds), *Language and communication in mathematics education.* ICME-13 Monographs (pp. 65–74). Cham: Springer. Doi: 10.1007/978-3-319-75055-2_6.

Barwell, R. (2009). Multilingualism in mathematics classrooms: An introductory discussion. In R. Barwell (ed.), *Multilingualism in mathematics classrooms: Global perspectives* (pp. 1–13). Bristol, Blue Ridge Summit: Multilingual Matters, 2009. Doi: 10.21832/9781847692061-003.

Barwell, R. (2018). From language as a resource to sources of meaning in multilingual mathematics classrooms. *Journal of Mathematical Behavior, 50,* 155–168.

Bialystok, E. (2006). The impact of bilingualism on language and literacy development. In T. K. Bhatia & W. E. Ritchie (eds), *The handbook of bilingualism* (pp. 577–601). Malden, MA: Blackwell Publishing.

Botes, H., & Mji, A. (2010). Language diversity in the mathematics classroom: Does a learner companion make a difference? *South African Journal of Education, 30*(1), 123–138.

Bunyi, G. (1997). Multilingualism and discourse in primary school mathematics in Kenya. *Language, Culture and Curriculum, 10*(1), 52–65. Doi: 10.1080/07908319709525240.

Canagarajah, S. (2011). Translanguaging in the classroom: Emerging issues for research and pedagogy. In L. Wei (ed.), *Applied Linguistics Review, 2: 2011* (1–28). Berlin and New York: De Gruyter Mouton. Available online: http://www.degruyter.com/view/j/alr.2011.2.issue-1/9783110239331.1/9783110239331.1.xml (accessed 20 May 2022).

Castro, M. (2015). Language practices in multilingual ecologies during mathematics instruction. PhD diss., University of Wisconsin-Madison, Wisconsin. Retrieved from ProQuest Dissertations & Theses Global. UMI Number: 3707126.

Chin, N. B., & Wigglesworth, G. (2007). *Bilingualism: An advanced resource book.* London: Routledge.

Creese, A., & Blackledge, A. (2010). Translanguaging in the bilingual classroom: A pedagogy for learning and teaching? *Modern Language Journal, 94*(1), 103–115. Doi: 10.1111/j.1540-4781.2009.00986.x.

Cummins, J. (2015). Translanguaging: What does it mean to teach for transfer in educating multilingual students? Conference on translanguaging – Practices, skills and pedagogy, Dalarna University, Falun, April 2015. PowerPoint presentation, slide 15.

Durkin, K. (1991). Language in mathematics education: An introduction. In K. Durkin & B. Shire (eds), *Language in mathematical education: Research and practice,* pp. 3–16. Milton Keynes: Open University Press.

Essien, A. (2010). Mathematics teacher educators' account of preparing pre-service teachers for teaching mathematics in multilingual classrooms: The case of South Africa. *International Journal of Interdisciplinary Social Sciences*, 5(2), 33–44.

Essien, A. (2013). Preparing pre-service mathematics teachers to teach in multilingual classrooms: A community of practice perspective. PhD diss., University of the Witwatersrand, Johannesburg.

Essien, A. (2018). The role of language in the learning and teaching of early grade mathematics: An 11-year account of research in Kenya, Malawi and South Africa. *African Journal of Research in Mathematics, Science and Technology Education*, 1–12. Doi: 10.1080/18117295.2018.1434453.

Essien, A. (2020). Norms of practices and pre-service teacher education for multilingual mathematics classrooms in South Africa. In I. Liyanage (ed.), *Multilingual yearbook 2020: Teacher education and multilingual contexts* (pp. 169–191). Cham: Springer.

Essien, A., and Sapire, I. (2022). Language policy implementation in early grade mathematics in South Africa: A 2010–2020 overview. In H. Venkat & R. Nicky (eds), *Early grade interventions in South Africa* (pp. 81–96). Cape Town: Oxford University Press.

García, O., & Otheguy, R. (2020). Plurilingualism and translanguaging: Commonalities and divergences. *International Journal of Bilingual Education and Bilingualism*, 23, 17–35. Doi: 10.1111/weng.12462.

García, O., & Wei, L. (2014). *Translanguaging: Language, bilingualism and education*. Basingstoke and New York: Palgrave Macmillan.

Halai, A. (2009). Politics and practice of learning mathematics in multilingual classrooms: Lessons from Pakistan. In R. Barwell (ed.), *Multilingual mathematics classrooms: Global perspective* (pp. 33–47). Bristol, Buffalo, NY, and Toronto: Multilingual Matters.

Halai, A., & Karuku, S. (2013). Implementing language-in-education policy in multilingual mathematics classrooms: Pedagogical implications. *Eurasia Journal of Mathematics, Science and Technology Education*, 9(1), 23–32.

Kajoro, P. (2016). Transition of the medium of instruction from English to Kiswahili in Tanzanian primary schools. In A. Anjum & P. Clarkson (eds), *Teaching and learning mathematics in multilingual classrooms: Issues for policy, practice and teacher education* (pp. 25–39). Rotterdam: Sense Publishers.

Kaphesi, E. S. (2002). The use of language in mathematics teaching in primary schools in Malawi: Bringing language to the surface as an explicit feature in the teaching of mathematics. PhD diss., University of Nottingham.

Kazima, M., Jakobsen, A., Mwadzaangati, L., & Gobede, F. (2023). Teaching the concept of zero in a Malawi primary school: Illuminating the language and resource challenge. *ZDM – Mathematics Education*. Doi: 10.1007/s11858-023-01473-8.

Khisty, L. L. (1995). 12 Making inequality: Issues of language and meanings in mathematics teaching with. In W. G. Secada, E. Fennema & l. Byrd Adajian (eds),

New Directions for Equity in Mathematics Education (pp. 279–297, at 297). Cambridge: Cambridge University Press.

Kovács, A., & Mehler, J. (2009). Flexible learning of multiple speech structures in bilingual infants. *Science, 325,* 5940, 611–612. Doi: 10.1126/science.1173947.

Langa, M. (2006). An investigation of learners' home language as a support for learning mathematics. Phd diss., University of the Witwatersrand, Johannesburg.

Langa, M., & Setati, M. (2006). Student's views on the use of home languages for learning mathematics. *Proceedings of the 14th annual meeting of the Southern African Association for Research for Mathematics, Science and Technology Education (SAARMSTE),* 9–12 January 2006, Groenkloof Campus, University of Pretoria, South Africa.

Lewis, G., Jones, B., & Baker, C. (2012). Translanguaging: Developing its conceptualisation and contextualisation. *Educational Research and Evaluation, 18*(7), 655–670. Doi: 10.1080/13803611.2012.718490.

Makalela, L. (2014). Teaching indigenous African languages to speakers of other African languages: The effects of translanguaging for multilingual development. In C. Van der Walt & L. Hibbert (eds), *Multilingual learning and teaching in higher education in South Africa* (pp. 88–104). Clevedon: Multilingual Matters.

Maluleke, M. J. (2019). Using code-switching as an empowerment strategy in teaching mathematics to learners with limited proficiency in English in South African schools. *South African Journal of Education, 39*(3), 1–9.

McLachlan, K., & Essien, A. A. (2022). Language and multilingualism in the teaching and learning of mathematics in South Africa: A review of literature in *Pythagoras* from 1994 to 2021. *Pythagoras, 43*(1), a669. Doi: 10.4102/pythagoras.v43i1.669.

Moschkovich, J. (1999). Supporting the participation of English language learners in mathematical discussions. *For the Learning of Mathematics, 19*(1), 11–19.

Moschkovich, J. (2007). Using two languages when learning mathematics. *Educational Studies in Mathematics, 64*(2), 121–144.

Mostert, I. (2019). Number names: Do they count? *African Journal of Research in Mathematics, Science and Technology Education, 23*(1), 64–74. Doi: 10.1080/18117295.2019.1589038.

Mostert, I., & Roberts, N. (2020). Diversity of mathematical expression: The language of comparison in English and isiXhosa early grade mathematics texts. *Research in Mathematics Education, 24*(1), 3–23. Doi: 10.1080/14794802.2020.1821757.

Msila, V. (2019). Rethinking Babylon: The language dilemma and the search for social justice in Africa. *English Academy Review: A Journal of English Studies, 36*(1), 100–112.

Owen-Smith, M. (2012). A set of multi-bilingual methodologies to address some current problems in education. *Strategies to overcome poverty and inequality: Towards Carnegie 111,* UCT Conference 3–7 September, supported by the National Planning Commission.

Pimm, D. (1991). Communicating mathematically. In K. Durkin & B. Shire (eds), *Language in mathematical education: Research and practice* (pp. 17–23). Milton Keynes: Open University Press.

Pitchford, N. J., Gulliford, A., Outhwaite, L. A., Davitt, L. J., Katabua, E., & Essien, A. A. (2021). Using interactive apps to support learning of elementary maths in multilingual contexts: Implications for practice and policy development in a digital age. In A. A. Essien & A. Msimanga (eds), *Multilingual education yearbook 2021: Policy and practice in STEM multilingual contexts*. Cham: Springer. Doi: 10.1007/978-3-030-72009-4_8.

Planas, N. (2011). Language identities in students' writings about group work in their mathematics classroom. *Language and Education*, 25(2), 129–146.

Planas, N., & Setati-Phakeng, M. (2014). On the process of gaining language as a resource in mathematics education. *ZDM – Mathematics Education*, 46, 883–893.

Poo, M., & Venkat, H. (2021). Approaches that leverage home language in multilingual classrooms. In A. A. Essien & A. Msimanga, A. (eds), *Multilingual education yearbook 2021: Policy and practice in STEM multilingual contexts*. Cham: Springer. Doi: 10.1007/978-3-030-72009-4_3.

Posel, D., & Casale, D. (2011). Language proficiency and language policy in South Africa: Findings from new data. *International Journal of Educational Development*, 31(5), 449–457.

Prediger, S., Kuzu, T., Schüler-Meyer, A., & Wagner, J. (2019). One mind, two languages – Separate conceptualisations? A case study of students' bilingual modes for dealing with language-related conceptualisations of fractions. *Research in Mathematics Education*, 21(2), 188–207. Doi: 10.1080/14794802.2019.1602561.

Robertson, S. A., & Graven, M. (2019). Exploratory mathematics talk in a second language: A sociolinguistic perspective. *Educational Studies in Mathematics*, 101(2), 215–232.

Ruiz, R. (1984). Orientations in language planning. *NABE Journal*, 8(2), 15–34.

Sapire, I. (2021). Language use in the learning and teaching of early grade mathematics in the context of multilingualism. PhD diss., University of the Witwatersrand, Johannesburg.

Sapire, I., & Essien, A. (2021). Multiple monolingualism versus multilingualism? Early grade mathematics teachers' and students' language use in multilingual classes in South Africa. In A. A. Essien & A. Msimanga (eds), *Multilingual education yearbook 2021: Policy and practice in STEM multilingual contexts*. Cham: Springer Nature, pp. 75–95. Doi: 10.1007/978-3-030-72009-4_5.

Setati, M. (2003). Language use in a multilingual mathematics classroom in South Africa: A different perspective. *International Group for the Psychology of Mathematics Education*, 4, 151–158.

Setati, M. (2005). Teaching mathematics in a primary multilingual classroom. *Journal for research in Mathematics Education*, 36(5), 447–466.

Setati, M. (2008). Access to mathematics versus access to the language of power: The struggle in multilingual mathematics classrooms. *South African Journal of Education, 28*(1), 103–116.

Sorto, M. A., Mejía Colindres, C. A., & Wilson, A. T. (2014). Uncovering and eliciting perceptions in linguistically diverse classrooms. *Mathematics Teaching in the Middle School, 20*(2), 72–75. Doi: 10.5951/mathteacmiddscho.20.2.0072.

Ticheloven, A., Blom, E., Leseman, P., & McMonagle, S. (2019). Translanguaging challenges in multilingual classrooms: Scholar, teacher and student perspectives. *International Journal of Multilingualism.* Doi: 10.1080/14790718.2019.1686002.

Vaish, V. (2019). Challenges and directions in implementing translanguaging pedagogy for low achieving students. *Classroom Discourse, 10*, 3–4, 274–289. Doi: 10.1080/19463014.2019.1628790.

Vogel, S., & García, O. (2017). Translanguaging. Published online, 19 December 2017. Doi: 10.1093/acrefore/9780190264093.013.181.

Zevenbergen, R. (2000). 'Cracking the code' of mathematics classrooms: School success as a function of linguistic, social and cultural background. In J. Boaler (ed.), *Multiple perspectives on mathematics teaching and learning* (pp. 201–223). London: Ablex Publishing.

Part One

Critical Engagement of Language Policies and Their Implementation or Reforms in Mathematics Education

2

Exploring the Implications of the Multilingual Turn in Mathematics Education Research for South African Policy-Makers, Researchers and Educators

Sally-Ann Robertson and Mellony Graven

Introduction

Issues bearing on language of learning and teaching (LoLT) in multilingual settings have increasingly attracted the attention of mathematics education researchers and teachers in Africa and elsewhere (see, for example, Sapire & Essien, 2021; Essien et al., 2016). Ironically, a great deal of research conducted around LoLT issues from Africa's many multilingual settings (see, for example, Heugh, 2000, 2005, 2011) appears to have failed to gain the traction it warrants in education practice. Internationally, however, unprecedented levels of migration of peoples away from their original homelands has created greater awareness of the need for more sustained and concerted attention to the challenge of how best to cater for learners from diverse linguistic backgrounds. Few countries today maintain whatever monolingual standing they might historically have had. Growing recognition of the crucial links between language and cognition has eroded the belief that it may be acceptable simply to gather learners together under a single (hegemonic) linguistic umbrella.

Lerman (2000) highlighted a 'social turn' in mathematics education whereby 'the traditional mathematical pedagogy of transmission of facts' was challenged and increasing recognition given to a more interactive view of mathematical knowledge building as a 'situated' 'product[s] of social activity' (pp. 22–23). So, too, May (2014) highlighted the emergence of a 'multilingual turn'. This has progressively challenged the 'monolingual bias' (ibid., p. 7) in the theory, research and practice around second-language teaching, learning and acquisition. A monolingual bias fails to adequately acknowledge the complex meaning-making potential contained in bi/multilingual speakers' linguistic repertoires. Instead, it assumes the desirability of linguistic 'purity' and a need to optimize ways for helping non-native users of a particular (usually dominant) language towards ever-closer native-like proficiency in that language. As Edwards (1994) noted: 'Multilingual settings provide a powerful incentive for prescriptive tendencies, especially where groups feel threatened by, or uneasy with, their linguistic neighbours,' often resulting in 'miseducation and prematurely curtailed education for many' (p. 12). Mohanty (2009) poignantly highlights the difficulties a marginalized or minoritized learner may face if he or she lacks proficiency in whatever language it is that happens to be prescribed for a particular schooling context:

> [Such a] ... child's first steps into school are steps into an alien world – a world she barely understands because, somewhere as she walks into her first classroom, the ties are snapped. Her resources, languages, means of communication, knowledge of her world and culture are set aside ... she has been pushed in, to be submersed (and pushed out later) in a system, the language of which she barely understands. It would take her three to five years just to comprehend the teacher and by then it would be too late.
>
> p. 4

The focus of this chapter is South Africa's evolving language in education history and how this has impacted teaching and learning in our primary-level mathematics classrooms. We share some insights into how the mathematics education community might work to better understand, and thence meet the cognitive and linguistic needs of learners from non-dominant language backgrounds. This is particularly the case for the millions of Black South African learners who, while representing a numerical majority in demographic terms, have, first under colonial rule and then under apartheid rule, experienced systematic marginalization, marginalization which, as we discuss in our next subsection, includes negation of the meaning-making potential of their first language (L1) in their encounters with classroom mathematics.

This chapter speaks to the merits of transdisciplinarity (see Robertson & Graven, 2018). The first author is an 'out-of-fielder'. Although she taught primary school mathematics in the early years of her career, her subsequent work as a teacher educator specialized in the fields of multicultural education, sociology of education and English second-language teaching and learning. It is these insights that she brings to discussions at the language/mathematics interface. The second author has worked extensively in the field of mathematics education (as teacher, lecturer, community-based educator, researcher and as the current incumbent of Rhodes University's South African Numeracy Chair, SANC). This is one of two national numeracy chairs tasked with finding solutions to some of the challenges facing South African primary mathematics education. Language is a key challenge both Chairs have identified as needing the ongoing attention of mathematics teachers, policy-makers and researchers. Independently of inequities deriving from failures to adequately address our country's linguistic diversity, however, our own research at the language/mathematics interface has given us an enhanced awareness of the inherently multimodal nature of mathematical meaning-making. So, while the focus for the present chapter is multilingualism, we recognize the future importance of our giving closer, research-based, attention to the meaning-making potential of other semiotic modes alongside the purely linguistic. Again, while not the focus of this paper, in our concluding remarks we note a welcome shift away from a monolingual bias that carries a purist emphasis on optimizing the effective use of 'boundaried', named languages rather than on optimizing effective communication using bi- and multilingual learners' full linguistic repertoire. Especially important in the mathematics classroom, we would welcome a broadening of the lens of classroom communication means from a focus on spoken multilingual languages to multimodal communication that looks to the communicative act as a jointly enacted communication act involving verbal, gestured and other modes of communication.

South Africa's Language in Education History

The Old: Oppressive and Inequitable Language Policy

South Africa's language in education history provides insight into how damaging a prescribed monolingual bias can be, and simultaneously shines light on the challenges in counteracting such bias. Language policy and practice within our educational institutions has, as Manyike and Lemmer (2014) note, 'been shaped ... by ideological and political interests rather than pedagogical considerations' (p. 251). This point has been raised earlier in the context of mathematics education by Setati and colleagues (e.g. Setati and Adler, 2000; Setati, 2005, 2008). For decades, in terms of the state provision of education first under British colonial rule, and subsequently in terms of the apartheid government's 1953 Bantu Education Act, a majority of South African children were deprived of access to their L1s in school. Instead, English and/or Afrikaans were the principal languages of teaching and learning. Under British rule, English dominated as LoLT. Under the Afrikaner Nationalist Party's rule, Afrikaans joined English as the dominant LoLT. This worked well for those for whom one or other of these languages was their L1. It did not work well for the majority of the Country's learners, however. They were forced, after an initial period of mother-tongue-based education (ranging between four and eight years of initial schooling), to transition across into instruction, and, more importantly, formal assessments, via a balance of English and Afrikaans. The fact that many Black learners lacked proficiency in these languages had a predictably negative effect on their educational (and other) prospects.

As resistance to the Nationalist government's apartheid system intensified, the imposition of Afrikaans in Black schools became a particular rallying point, and was a key factor in the uprising that began in Soweto on 16 June 1976 and, from there, spread countrywide. It would be another eighteen years before the Nationalist Party was voted out of power and South Africa's first fully democratic government was elected.

The New: Freedom of Choice Language Policy (perhaps too Free)

In recognition of the multilingual make-up of its people, South Africa's post-apartheid Constitution (1996) declared eleven languages as official (nine African languages, plus English, plus Afrikaans). In July of the following year, the Language in Education Policy (LiEP) was promulgated. Its 'underlying principle' was to 'maintain home language(s) while providing access to and ... acquisition of additional language(s)' (South Africa, DoE, 1997, p. 1), though individuals were accorded the right to choose their actual LoLT 'within the overall framework of the obligation on the education system to promote multilingualism' (ibid., p. 1).

An ongoing association of Afrikaans, and, similarly, of mother-tongue-based education, with Bantu Education, has caused profound scepticism about embracing the additive bilingual principles guiding South Africa's post-Apartheid LiEP. A potential flaw in this policy is that, in honouring the long-fought-for democratic right to freedom of choice, it perhaps erred 'on the side of allowing too much choice' (Desai, 1999, p. 46). Exercise of this freedom has tended, however inadvertently, to undermine the Policy's commitment to additive bilingualism.

So powerful is the perception that English is the language of opportunity that a majority of Black South African parents continue to choose an English-medium educational route (seen to provide also access to 'social goods' (Setati, 2008, p. 115)). However, choosing English when it is not a child's L1, adds an additional layer of cognitive struggle, and – potentially – thus reproduces the status quo. Black parents' faith in the power of English to advance their children's best educational (and socio-educational) interests is perhaps an example of the Bourdieu-ian notion of 'symbolic violence': 'the *violence which is exercised upon a social agent with his or her complicity* [italics in the original text]' (Bourdieu & Wacquant, 2002, p. 167).

Relatively early on, it was noted that parents, and – indeed – much of the educational community were inadequately informed of the potentially adverse consequences of choosing this subtractive form of bilingualism (Probyn et al., 2002). The current pre-eminence of English-medium schooling in South Africa, as Heugh notes, may be seen as an inevitable outcome of the either/or choices on offer (for example, schooling via either isiXhosa- or English-medium, or via either isiZulu- or English-medium): 'Asking parents to identify a single language "which language" is asking them to choose English' (email, 23 August 2021). Expanding further on this statement, she explained how, for the National Sociolinguistic Survey, respondents were provided a broader set of options ('Home language only'; 'Home language and English'; 'Good teaching of Home language and English'; 'English only'). Overwhelmingly, 94 per cent of respondents favoured a bilingual route for their children: 'Either Home language and English or Good Home language and English' (Heugh, email, 23 August 2021).

Language in Relation to Mathematics Learning Assessment Outcomes

Either/or school language policy choices have perpetuated a monolingual bias in South African schools. Despite less than 10 per cent of South Africans being native speakers of English (Statistics South Africa, 2012), by Grade 4 South Africa's Department of Basic Education reported that close on 80 per cent of children are taught through the medium of English (2010, p. 16). Learners who are not native English speakers have only limited opportunity to simultaneously continue with literacy development in their L1. Their L1 becomes a subject (paradoxically taught as either their second or third additional language, with an emphasis simply on learning the language, rather than learning how to *use* the language for academic purposes).

In working to access curriculum content, those who are learning through an L2 invariably face a doubling up of the cognitive load on them: they need first to process the language in order to process the discipline content. Inadequate subject-specific guidance to South Africa's teachers – mathematics teachers in the context of this chapter's discussion – on how to systematically mediate learners' capacity to learn through an L2 significantly compromises learners' opportunities to gain epistemological access to curriculum content. South African learners' poor performance on both national and international benchmarking assessments of mathematical proficiency bears testament to compromised epistemological access.

While, as Spaull (2016) cautioned, it is difficult to disaggregate language factors from other undoubted fault lines within South Africa's education system, language has been directly implicated as a factor in low levels of attainment. Although South Africa discontinued its strategy of Annual National Assessments (ANAs) in 2014, the attainment scores for Grade 4s in this final year of assessment provide bleak insight into learners' mathematical proficiencies. The average assessment score nationally was 37 per cent (South Africa, Department of Basic Education, 2014, pp. 9, 52). In her analysis of the linguistic complexity of the Grade 4 Mathematics ANAs, Sibanda (2017) noted that most learners 'had difficulties with both the linguistic and the mathematical demands of the test items [though] some learners ... managed the mathematical demands when linguistic mediation was provided' (p. 157). On the international front, South Africa participated in TIMSS 2015 and 2019, with South Africa's Grade 5 learners averaging achievement scores well below those of learners from most other participating countries (Reddy et al., 2022). The 2015 TIMSS report indicated that 61 per cent of South Africa's Grade 5 learners lacked basic mathematics knowledge and skills, with significantly better TIMSS outcomes for learners who 'always or almost always spoke the language of learning and teaching at home' as opposed to those whose home language was different from their school's LoLT (Reddy et al., 2016, p. 8). The 2019 TIMSS report noted that South Africa's Grade 5 performance level 'continues to be low, highly unequal and socially graded' (Reddy et al., 2022, p. xiv). Only 37 per cent of South African learners had acquired grade-appropriate mathematical knowledge and skills, with language again identified as an issue:

> Just over one in three learners (one in four in no-fee schools and one in two in fee-paying schools) spoke the language of the test at home. Learners who were more proficient in the language of the test achieved significantly higher mathematics ... achievement scores than those who were less proficient.
>
> Ibid., p. xiv

Such findings add strength to calls for closer attention to ways for actualizing the additive bi/multilingualism principles enshrined in South Africa's LiEP, a policy which, as Heugh (2000) stressed, was 'designed to guarantee pupils the best possible access to and proficiency in another language (English for the majority of pupils) alongside the language best known by pupils upon entry to school' (p. 3).

'Subtractive' versus 'Additive' Approaches to Bilingualism

The monolingual bias at play in South African classrooms represents, as noted, a *subtractive* form of bilingualism completely at odds with South Africa's post-apartheid Language in Education Policy (LiEP) (1997) advocacy of an *additive* approach to bilingualism. Here we briefly highlight some differences between 'subtractive' and 'additive' approaches to bilingualism to show that subtractive approaches are detrimental to learners' interests.

The terms 'additive' and 'subtractive' as applied to bilingualism were coined by Lambert, a Canadian psycho- and sociolinguist, sometimes dubbed 'the father of the psychological study of bilingualism' (Vaid et al., 2010, p. 290). The goal of the Canadian immersion programmes which Lambert was instrumental in setting up was that children should become equally fluent and academically proficient in both of Canada's official languages (French and English), that is, to become both bilingual and biliterate (Melikoff, 2018). This was wholly an *additive* approach to bilingualism. Figure 2.1 depicts five approaches to bilingual education, ranging from 'most subtractive' to 'most additive'. As the figure illustrates, in a subtractive bilingual approach learners' first language (L1) is 'taken away' and 'replaced by the second language' (Baker, 2011, p. 4). Additive approaches, by contrast, give learners the opportunity to achieve academic proficiency in a second language (L2) 'at no cost' to their L1 (ibid., p. 4).

While many sub-Saharan countries, including South Africa, advocate additive multilingualism (retention of L1 as an important teaching/learning resource throughout schooling: Models D and E of Figure 2.1), most learners across sub-Saharan Africa experience an 'early exit' *subtractive* bilingual approach (predominantly Model B of Figure 2.1: initial three years of schooling in L1, then a transition into a dominant (often former colonial) L2 in Year 4) (Heugh, 2005). The 'inherent design flaw' in this early exit model, as Heugh (2005) notes, is that it is 'almost impossible for learners to learn enough of the second language in three years to switch to a second-language medium of instruction in Grade 4' (pp. 6, 7). Ideally, in Heugh's view (2011) learners' L1

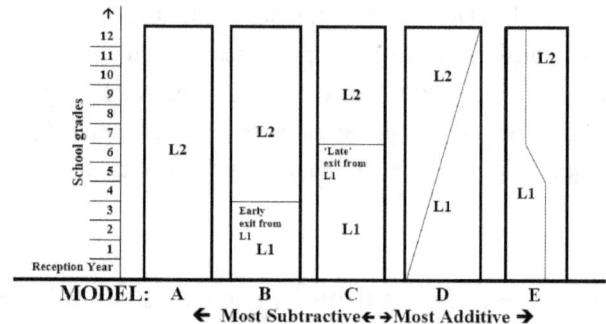

Figure 2.1 Some key models for bilingual education.
Source: Robertson (2017, p. 24), adapted.

needs to remain a key resource throughout their schooling; a poor second option being 6–8 years of L1 as the main LoLT. Based on her extensive participation over several decades in cross-national research on this issue, Heugh asserts that 'successful education requires mother-tongue-medium education throughout, but an absolute minimum of six to eight years of mother-tongue ... instruction' (2011, p. 154).

Two interrelated reasons for regarding the 'early exit' pattern (Models B and C of Figure 2.1) as particularly counter-productive are firstly, the points made by Chall and Jacobs (2003) about the 'fourth grade slump'; second, Cummins' explanations (e.g. 2005, 2008) about the importance of children's L1 for their early literacy development ('literacy' here interpreted in a broader sense than simply learning to read and write). The fourth-grade slump (occurring as relatively simple and carefully scaffolded texts encountered in earlier grades are replaced by 'more varied, complex, and challenging [both] linguistically and cognitively', texts) places particular strain on 'low-income children' (Chall & Jacobs, 2003, unpaged). It is made the more demanding when coupled with a switch into a new LoLT, with little or no ongoing systematic provision of meaning-making support mechanisms via the L1. Especially important here as contributory factors to the increase in cognitive and linguistic challenge are Vygotsky's distinctions (1986) between 'spontaneous' (everyday) and 'scientific' (more formal) conceptual understandings. Much of the curricular coverage in the initial years of schooling revolves around everyday concepts as children are introduced to basic literacy and numeracy skills. It is possible to conduct much of the teaching and learning here through the use of what Cummins (2008) has termed the children's 'basic interpersonal communication skills' (BICS) (a more everyday, informal sort of language). As the teaching and learning moves into more formalized and abstracted territory, the need arises for children to develop and use what Cummins (2008) called 'cognitive academic language proficiency' (CALP) (more formalized, precise, and often discipline-specific styles of language and discourse).

Figure 2.2 represents Cummins' (1984) linguistic interdependence hypothesis with minor adaptations to reflect the language circumstances of the majority of learners in the Eastern Cape region of South Africa. isiXhosa is one of South Africa's official languages, and the L1 for 78.8 per cent of people in the region (Statistics South Africa, 2012, p. 25). The linguistic interdependence hypothesis argues that, although surface features of two languages may differ, even quite significantly (in terms of their sound system and grammar, for instance), once acquired, many academic proficiencies (linguistic skills and/or knowledge) can transcend a particular language system. Assuming a relatively well-developed level of academic proficiency in using the L1, such proficiency can be transferred between the L1 and L2 as a bilingual learner's linguistic and conceptual development continues. So, for instance, at its most basic level this means that if a child can already read in his or her L1, s/he does not need to re-learn to read in the L2. Since that skill already exists, it is merely a matter of grappling with decoding a different set of lexico-grammatical linguistic input. Similarly, if a child already has some conceptual grasp of, for example, the relative sizes of different unit fractions in his/her L1, such understanding should be accessible also in the L2.

Cummins (1979) argued that 'under some conditions, access to two languages in early childhood can accelerate aspects of cognitive growth' (p. 229). He did, however, earlier stress (Cummins, 1976) that learners needed to have reached 'a threshold level of bilingual competence' in order for this to positively influence their cognitive functioning (p. 27).

A major difficulty in many of South Africa's primary mathematics classrooms is that both learners and teachers are operating in circumstances of subtractive bilingualism. Notwithstanding the Department of Basic Education's intention that learners entering Grade 4 should be 'reasonably proficient in their [L2] with regard to both interpersonal and cognitive academic skills', as the department has acknowledged, 'the reality is that many learners still cannot communicate well in [the L2] at this stage' (2016, p. 12). A point worth emphasizing in this regard is the unrealistic expectation that by Grade 4 learners will have become 'reasonably proficient in their L2', and able, therefore, to navigate the more linguistically and cognitively demanding subject matter they encounter. Independently of questions around the education system's capacity to mediate development of such proficiency, extensive research on what is involved in acquiring a second language, specifically acquiring academic language proficiencies in it, consistently shows

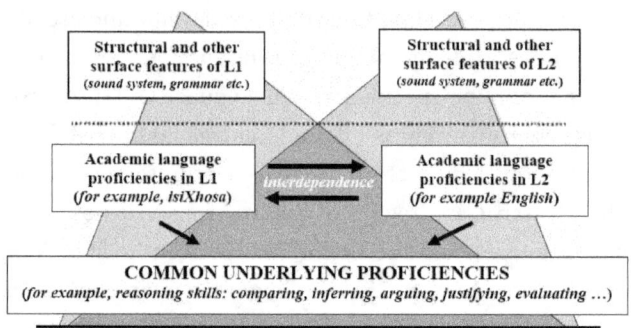

Figure 2.2 Representation of Cummins' linguistic interdependence hypothesis (1984) illustrating the potential for cross-lingual transfer of academic skills and knowledge. *Source*: Robertson (2017, p. 76), adapted with Cummins' permission.

that, while learners' interpersonal L2 linguistic skills may develop in a reasonably short time, it takes considerably longer to develop their academic linguistic skills. Cummins (1994) highlighted the importance of teachers distinguishing between 'the surface or conversational aspects of children's language and the deeper aspects of proficiency that are more closely related to conceptual and academic development' (p. 37). Elsewhere he reiterated that whereas everyday interpersonal fluency in L2 can be developed within two years, acquiring the 'specialized vocabulary and functions of language appropriate to [in the context of the present chapter, school mathematics]' (Cummins, 2008, p. 78) can – even in optimal circumstances – take anything from five to seven years. An aspect of mathematics teachers' work involves helping learners navigate what Gibbons (2003) termed the 'mode continuum' (2003, after Halliday). This involves helping learners move between common-sense, everyday ways of thinking, talking about, and using numbers and mathematical concepts to solve a problem and the more specialized, discipline-specific, formalized, and more cognitively challenging approaches to doing so (what, in Freudenthal's terms (1973), could be described as moving across from *horizontal* mathematization into *vertical* mathematization).

Addressing the Meaning-Making Challenge in Mathematics Classrooms

In this section, we theorize around some of the meaning-making challenges in South African mathematics classrooms that follow on from what we have discussed above. We draw on our experiences of our research and development work with teachers and communities in the Eastern Cape to exemplify these ideas.

The Rhodes University South African Numeracy Chair (SANC) runs a range of research-informed interventions in search of sustainable ways forward to addressing challenges facing South African primary learners and mathematics educators. Language is both a challenge and an opportunity explored across the various Chair projects which includes work with families (family math days and story-time programmes), after-school mathematics clubs, math and science camps and teacher professional development programmes. In each of these programmes, a key aim is supporting learners, families and teachers in using all language repertoires available, including gestural language, to explore mathematical ideas and as a meaning-making communication device.

Developing learner confidence in informal mathematical talk around ideas and concepts, in the classroom, at home, and in after-school clubs is a goal supported by activities such as number talks, mathematical games and storytelling (and re-telling and re-enacting). Across programmes developing exploratory talk in both the L1 and the L2 enables sense-making and interthinking (after Mercer, 2000) is modelled with an emphasis on highlighting the nature of progression towards more formalized subject-specific registers required for the development of mathematical CALP. Resources for classroom and take-home use are translated into multiple languages and made available to teachers, learners and families in their home language and English in order to encourage bilingualism in early mathematical talk and exploration. See Graven (2019) and Graven, et al. (2022) for further discussion of the model of projects and details of the family- and learner-focused programmes.

We noted in our introduction that language issues are receiving increasing attention from mathematics educators worldwide. This is partly because mathematical text has some inherently complex aspects, not least its multi-semiotic nature which calls for considerable 'semiotic integration' (Lemke, 2002, p. 22) across its mix of everyday and technical language, its system of symbols (e.g. $+/-/\times/\div/=/</>$) and its visual images (e.g. diagrams, graphs). Semiotic integration is made the more difficult when mathematical meaning has to be made through a learner's L2, a factor which severely challenges the millions of mathematics learners in South African classrooms. We have cited the following interview comment from one SANCP Grade 4 mathematics teacher in an earlier publication (Robertson & Graven, 2019, p. 223), but it bears repeating as it so clearly 'speaks to' this challenge. The teacher, Ms M (pseudonym), works at a school in the Eastern Cape province. The school's chosen language policy is 'straight for English' (Model A of Figure 2.1, above). The L1 of all of its learners is isiXhosa:

> Language is very important, because maths isn't only about numbers: 'add this', 'subtract this'. There's lots of language involved. There's English language first of all: that is a challenge to these learners. And also the maths language itself. So, if one doesn't have English as a language and also the maths language, then [...] there's no learning and teaching that is taking place. And what frustrates - I'm in the Grade 4 class - it's as though I am teaching to the Grade 2s. [...] I think I'm going nowhere. I'm doing nothing. Because I think, 'How can I move on when they don't understand?' Sometimes I think it's easy. But to them, it's not easy.
>
> Robertson, 2017, p. 276

Research data (ibid.) show that what routinely transpired in Ms M's observed lessons was extremely limited, extremely formulaic learner talk (i.e. reciting back sound chunks that had gone before). Learners' lack of proficiency in the L2 prevented any sort of substantive mathematical meaning-making via exploratory engagement with a particular concept. Were it not for Ms M's school's enforced 'straight for English' policy, and long-held anxiety of many South African teachers about the legitimacy of code-switching (see, for example, Probyn, 2009), Ms M's way forward would have lain in making systematic use of isiXhosa alongside English in helping her and her learners' towards more effective negotiation of mathematical meaning.

Research data (Robertson, 2017) from another SANCP Grade 4 teacher, Ms P (pseudonym) show the feasibility of such a way forward. Ms P teaches at another school in the same township area as Ms M. This school practises a more flexible approach towards having English as the dominant language medium from Grade 4, so, while Ms P was of the opinion that she was '*supposed* to teach [her learners] in English' (Robertson, 2017, p. 286; see also Robertson & Graven, 2020a, 2020b), she felt free to exercise her initiative by using something of an additive approach. 'Languaging' is a term coined by Swain (2006) to describe the 'process of making meaning and shaping knowledge and experience through language' (p. 98). In Ms P's mathematics lessons languaging was via a mix of English and Ms P's and her learners' shared L1 (isiXhosa). In several of Ms P's observed lessons, she would invite individual learners to come to the front of the classroom and share their mathematical thinking with the rest of the class. In one such instance, the task was to complete a numeric flow diagram Ms P had drawn on the chalkboard (Figure 2.3).

Ms. P called on individual children to complete a line of the numeric flow, and she would ask some of them to explain how they had arrived at their answers.

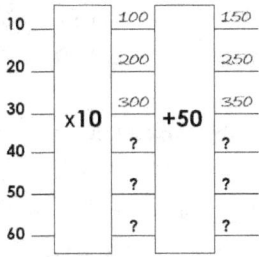

Figure 2.3 Ms P's numeric flow diagram. *Source*: Robertson (2017, p. 103).

Thus, instead of letting a child simply indicate that the final answer to the penultimate calculation (50x10)+50 was 550, Ms P pressed for an explanation: 'Wenze njani ndifuna uqonda apha kwenzeke ntoni' (How did you get the answer? I want to know). Some learners responded simply by gesturing (pointing, in sequence, to their answer for the multiplication action and then to their addition one; see Robertson & Graven, 2021a, 2021b). That any one child showed hesitancy, neither gesturing nor articulating how an answer was derived, is irrelevant in the context of the present discussion. What to us is relevant is that a subsequent child appeared to have benefitted from the interthinking opportunities afforded by Ms P's prior requests for explanation. When this child was asked to complete the last line of the numeric flow diagram (60x10)+50, and Ms P asked, 'Ngubani impendulo? (What's the answer?), the child voluntarily included an explanation of the steps *she* had taken in arriving at the answer, responding (in English): 'It's six hundred. And six hundred plus fifty, it's six hundred and fifty.'

There are encouraging signs that the language mixing flexibility observed in Ms P's class is being encouraged in our Eastern Cape region. Indeed, Ms P's school is amongst the 2015 primary schools selected to participate in a mother-tongue pilot project in the Eastern Cape. Depending on the main L1 in the particular area, either isiXhosa or Sesotho is being piloted as the main LoLT for the teaching of mathematics, natural science and technology for Grades 4, 5 and 6. On the basis of the apparent success of this extension, it has been announced that similar piloting will be conducted in other provinces. In this same announcement the Minister of Education is quoted as saying, 'The bottom line is that we need to adopt mother-tongue instruction in South Africa' (Big language changes planned for schools in South Africa, 2022). On a cautionary note, we reiterate here Heugh's point about bilingual routes being preferred to 'either/or' monolingual routes.

'Translanguaging' as a Vehicle for Legitimizing Mixed Language Use in Classrooms

Various terms are used to describe mixed language practices in classrooms. 'Code-switching' is perhaps the term most familiar to South Africa's teachers. It has, however, and as noted earlier, something of a 'forbidden aura'. While generations of South African teachers have covertly practised code-switching to scaffold their learners' L2 meaning-making endeavours, this may invoke a sense of transgressing official policy. This we see in Ms P's poignant admission alluded to earlier: 'I'm supposed to teach them in English, but they don't understand.... So – most of the time, I speak Xhosa – the one that they understand.... They are supposed to be taught in English ... so I'm supposed to speak English, but I can't do otherwise' (Robertson, 2017, p. 286).

'Translanguaging' is increasingly used as an alternative term for mixed language use in multilingual classrooms. Advocates for translanguaging are motivated largely by concerns for educational equity. Such practices are seen to contribute towards the social justice imperative of challenging the hegemony of a single dominant language in a multilingual schooling setting. Endorsing minoritized learners' right to use their L1 alongside an officially designated language in the classroom also broadens the linguistic base from which learners can potentially draw in their meaning-making endeavours, and, thereby, their opportunities for enhanced epistemic access.

Concerns have been expressed that some interpretations of and strategies for implementing translanguaging are under-researched, thus threatening to undermine the concept's transformative possibilities. Jaspers (2017) writes that, while he supports the positive intent underpinning translanguaging initiatives, he fears, as often happens with 'popular new concepts' the danger of 'discursive drift', a phrase Jaspers attributes to Deborah Cameron (1995). Cameron (as quoted by Jaspers, 2017, p. 2) explains that 'discursive drift' is the process whereby new terms begin 'to drift away from [their] ... earlier (and usually narrower) sense [and] ... in the process ... lose their precision, acquire connotations they did not have before, and start to overlap with other terms from which they were once distinguished'. In an attempt to guard against discursive drifting in the interpretation and implementation of translanguaging practices, in our own work with it and in multilingual mathematics classrooms, we now briefly explore aspects of this term's origins, and subsequent evolution.

'Translanguaging' is a translation of the Welsh word '*trawsieithu*'. It was coined by Cen Williams, a Welsh educator, to describe the systematic classroom use of two languages within a single lesson (Lewis et al., 2012). This might, for example, involve initial discussion of a topic in Welsh, and the writing up about it then being done in English. More current uses of the term are widely ascribed to the advocacy work done by, principally, in the first instance, Ofelia García, a Cuban-born American bilingual education professor (see, for example, García, 2009). This newer use of the term describes the fluid ways in which bilingual speakers communicate, deploying their 'full linguistic repertoire without regard for watchful adherence to the socially and politically defined boundaries of named (and usually national and state) languages' (Otheguy et al., 2015, p. 281).

In the same way that Freudenthal spoke of horizontal and vertical mathematization, Heugh (2019) makes a useful distinction between horizontal and vertical translanguaging. She notes that the Welsh–English bilingual model outlined by Williams is geared towards vertical bilingual development (high levels of academic bilingual proficiency across both languages). The model envisaged by García, by contrast, offers a more informal (horizontal) vision of bilingualism geared towards more inclusive, equitable, classroom (and everyday) interaction. Heugh acknowledges that the two models are 'not mutually exclusive' and both the horizontal and the vertical are necessary components of classroom discourse. She cautions, however, that 'the long-term educational efficacy' is under-researched, and that current research on ways for improving educational outcomes in multilingual setting points to the desirability of learners attaining high levels of oral and written academic proficiency in both their named L1 and in the – and what is invariably a dominant – named L2.

Figure 2.4 is a synthesized diagrammatic representation of Cummins' BICS/CALP distinction, on which we have overlaid both Freudenthal's horizontal/vertical mathematization and Heugh's horizontal/vertical translanguaging ideas. As shown in the figure, movement across the Quadrants involves starting with everyday, more BICS-like, languaging, but with a gradual progression in the direction of the kind of more formal, CALP-like pattern of languaging.

Take, for example, the shape ☐ being named by an isiXhosa-speaking local person as 'four corners' which in everyday terms describes it simply and clearly as it is indeed a shape with four corners. This description would belong in Quadrant A. There are, of course, other shapes with four corners such as rhombi, rectangles, quadrilaterals and parallelograms. So, this shape is given a specific formal name in mathematics and in school 'isqueri' ('square' in English). As children progress up the grades they will learn that this square is indeed also a rectangle because even while in everyday terms it looks very different from most commonly seen rectangles (doors, windows, ceilings) it satisfies the formal property of having opposite sides equal, and it has four right angles. This kind of

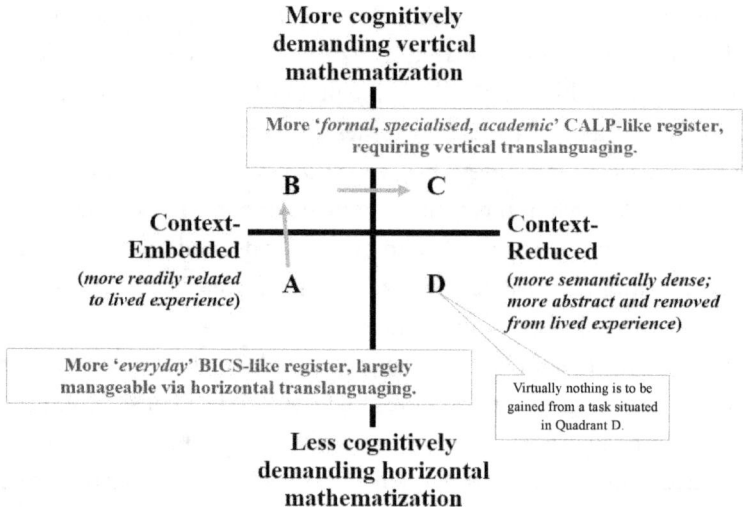

Figure 2.4 Synthesis of Cummins' BICS/CALP distinction with Freudenthal's and Heugh's ideas around horizontality and verticality in relation to mathematization and (trans-)languaging, respectively.
Source: After Freudenthal (1973), Cummins (1984), Heugh (2019).

mathematical insight and reasoning would belong in Quadrant B. Furthermore, as learners come to recognize both squares and rectangles are also parallelograms and quadrilaterals because they share specific properties with these larger categories of shapes, this then would move them towards Quadrant C type mathematization. Getting to this point involves ongoing movement back and forth between the horizontal and the vertical planes as learners engage with new mathematical ideas and concepts and related language. In multilingual settings, it will also involve significant amounts of fluid horizontal translanguaging, mainly at the oral level, as learners make meaning of new mathematical content and engage in basic descriptive forms of reasoning as they are prepared for translanguaging of the more systematic, vertical and abstract language and forms of reasoning needed to build and promote their academic bilingual proficiency.

Becoming a skilled user of any named language can be a lifelong process, required, even, of native speakers of that language. Inducting learners into the types of language best suited to exploring mathematical concepts and ideas is seen as an integral part of a mathematics teacher's job. This is what allows learners to take advantage of the increasing precision afforded by specialized mathematical vocabulary and discourse structures. As Freudenthal (1973) commented, 'the more abstract, that is the further away from intuition, a subject matter is [or, could we here say, 'becomes'?], the more is careful linguistic expression required. ... perfecting mathematical language is a continuous process' (pp. 28–29).

Becoming a skilled user of a named, but as yet frequently un-standardized language, as is the case with many African indigenous languages, poses a different set of challenges. There are those who argue that many of the indigenous African languages are currently not adequately developed to handle the demands of 'academic' (as opposed to 'everyday') discourse. Rhodes University's African Language Studies division has a research chair explicitly set up to address this issue. Its principal brief is to develop and promote research relating to the ongoing intellectualization of African languages, multilingualism, and education. The Research Chair has invited all those working in education to contribute towards the realization of these goals, emphasizing the importance of ensuring that South African teachers are well-versed in 'the notion of mother-tongue and mother-tongue-based-bilingual-education' (Kaschula & Maseko, 2014, p. 11).

Language theorists such as Krashen (1981, 1982) view perfecting one's second language as akin to perfecting one's L1. It is an often unconscious process. Krashen contrasts this with the more formal, conscious kind of learning that happens in language classrooms (learning the grammar of a named language, for example). This latter process Krashen describes as *learning*; the unconscious kind as *acquisition*. Krashen sees acquisition as important in the sense that it enables people to actually *use* a language. While Krashen is a controversial figure in the field of second-language teaching and learning, his theories are popular with language teachers because they are accessible and intuitively appealing. However, aspects of his theories (e.g. his acquisition/learning distinction) have been criticized. Most language acquisition theorists believe both conscious and unconscious processes are involved in learning a language and these terms are often used interchangeably. Perhaps what is useful about Krashen's theory is that it reminds us that a lot of our language learning is unconscious and not the direct result of teaching. This sits well with the fact that, although mathematics teachers are charged with the task of teaching their learners the 'language of mathematics', they are *not* qualified language teachers as such. To expect them to be so is placing an additional, and frequently unacceptable burden on them. A point stressed by Krashen and many other language theorists is that whatever the second-language input, it should be both authentic and used for an important and genuine purpose. Many language theorists (Krashen amongst them) argue that the best way to learn a language is by using it as the LoLT. This may perhaps be one of the factors that fuelled South African Education Department policy option regarding learners learning through their L2 (predominantly English, as noted earlier) from Grade 4 onwards. By the same token, therefore, there is equal validity in assigning LoLT status to learners' L1 alongside the L2, as illustrated in Models D and E of Figure 2.1. Our own view is that Model D is the better of these two. Whichever model is used, it remains vital that induction into academic language discourse be explicitly undertaken, not assumed to be a (largely unconscious) 'osmotic' process. The same principle applies for subject-specific teachers beyond mathematics. They too need explicit guidance in developing the kinds of linguistic insights and pedagogical skills that will enable them to provide the necessary language learning support to their learners.

Concluding Thoughts

In concluding this chapter, we emphasize two points. First, while we have not included discussion on the power of multimodality as another semiotic source for mathematical meaning-making, we note that attention to other modes has the potential to add to what Gibbons so aptly described as 'message abundancy' (2015, p. 44). These other modes might, for example, include the use of physical artefacts; gesturing and other forms of body language (tone of voice, facial expression); various sources of audio-visual materials; inscriptions (by both teacher and learners). Such message abundancy has the potential to enhance all learners', but especially L2 learners', opportunities to become genuine participants in mathematical sense-making. Further research should look to expand attention from multilingual verbal communication to multilingual and multimodal communication.

Our second and final point is that perceptions about the power of English as providing access to social and economic goods has created a conflation between becoming a proficient user of English and using English as the main linguistic vehicle through which to become a proficient learner of mathematics. This conflation is highly problematic in that, as we have indicated, it places an enormous additional burden on both the mathematics teacher and the mathematics learner. This said, there is no escaping that English represents a language of international 'opportunity'. This behoves the mathematics education community therefore to contribute towards ensuring that mathematics teachers are equipped to support their L2 students towards becoming proficient users not only of their L1, but of English too. In other words, researchers and policymakers need to coordinate their efforts to devise and put in place strategies to assist mathematics teachers in playing their part towards the development of learners who are able to perform in both bilingual and biliterate ways in their mathematics classrooms. In this respect, further research is needed in mathematics classrooms where teachers, across differentially resourced contexts, successfully draw on multilingual and multimodal repertoires of communication to develop their learners' mathematical understanding and means of communication.

References

Baker, C. (2011). *Foundations of bilingual education*. 5th ed. Clevedon: Multilingual Matters.

Big language changes planned for schools in South Africa. (2022, 10 March). *BusinessTech.* Available online: https://businesstech.co.za/news/government/566738/big-language-changes-planned-for-schools-in-south-africa/ (accessed 29 March 2022).

Bourdieu, P., & Wacquant, L. J. D. (2002). *An invitation to reflexive sociology*. Cambridge: Polity Press.

Chall, J. S., & Jacobs, V. A. (2003). The classic study on poor children's fourth-grade slump. Available online: http://www.aft.org/periodical/american-educator/spring-2003/classic-study-poor-childrens-fourth-grade-slump (accessed 24 April 2023).

Cummins, J. (1976). *The influence of bilingualism on cognitive growth: Synthesis of research findings and explanatory hypotheses.* Working Papers on Bilingualism, No. 9: Bilingual Education Project, The Ontario Institute for Studies in Education (OISE) (pp. 1–44). Toronto: OISE.

Cummins, J. (1979). *Cognitive/academic language proficiency, linguistic interdependence, the optimum age question and some other matters.* Working Papers on Bilingualism, No. 19: Bilingual Education Project, The Ontario Institute for Studies in Education (pp. 198–205). Toronto: OISE.

Cummins, J. (1984). The role of primary language development in promoting educational success for language minority students. In Office of Bilingual Bicultural Education, *Schooling and language minority students: A theoretical framework* (pp. 3–49). Sacramento, CA: California State Department of Education.

Cummins, J. (1994). The acquisition of English as a second language. In K. Spangenberg-Urnschat & R. Pritchard (eds), *Kids come in all languages: Reading instruction for ESL students.* 13th printing, 2005 (pp. 36–62). Newark, DE: International Reading Association.

Cummins, J. (2005). Teaching for cross-language transfer in dual language education: Possibilities and pitfalls. *TESOL Symposium on dual language education: Teaching and learning two languages in the EFL setting,* Bogazici University, Istanbul.

Cummins, J. (2008). BICS and CALP: Empirical and theoretical status of the distinction. In B. Street and N. H. Hornberger (eds), *Encyclopedia of language and education, Volume 2: Literacy.* 2nd edn (pp. 71–83). New York: Springer.

Desai, Z. (1999). Enabling policies, disabling practices. *Per Linguam*, *15*(1), 42–53.

Edwards, J. (1994). *Multilingualism*. London: Routledge.

Essien, A. A., Chitera, N., & Planas, N. (2016). Language diversity in mathematics teacher education: Challenges across three countries. In R. Barwell, P. Clarkson, A. Halai, M. Kazima, J. Moschkovich, N. Planas & M. V. Ubillús (eds), *Mathematics education and language diversity: The 21st ICMI Study* (pp. 103–119). Cham: Springer. Doi: 10.1007/978-3-319-14511-2_6.

Freudenthal, H. (1973). *Mathematics as an educational task*. Dordrecht: D. Reidel.

García, O. (2009). Education, multilingualism and translanguaging in the 21st century. In T. Skutnabb-Kangas, R. Phillipson, A. K. Mohanty, & M. Panda (eds), *Social justice through multilingual education* (pp. 128–145). Bristol: Multilingual Matters. Doi. org/10.21832/9781847691910-011.

Gibbons, P. (2003). Mediating language learning: Teacher interactions with ESL students in a content-based classroom. *TESOL Quarterly*, *37*(2), 247–273.

Gibbons, P. (2015). *Scaffolding language scaffolding learning: Teaching English Language Learners in the mainstream classroom*. 2nd edn. Portsmouth: Heinemann.

Graven, M. (2019). Building multidirectional learning opportunities between researcher, teacher, and teacher educator communities. In G. M. Lloyd & O. Chapman (eds), *International handbook of mathematics teacher education: Volume 3* (pp. 241–264). Leiden: Brill Sense.

Graven, M., Hokonya, W., Long, R., & Vale, P. (2022). A decade of the South African Numeracy Chair learner intervention projects. In H. Venkat & N. Roberts (eds), *Early grade mathematics in South Africa* (pp. 134–151). Cape Town: Oxford University Press.

Heugh, K. (2000). *The case against bilingual and multilingual education in South Africa*. PRAESA Occasional Papers No. 6. Cape Town: PRAESA, UCT.

Heugh, K. (2005). Mother-tongue education is best. *HSRC Review*, *3*(3), 6–7.

Heugh, K. (2011). Theory and practice – language education models in Africa: Research, design, decision-making and outcomes. In A. Ouane & C. Glanz (eds.), *Optimising learning, education and publishing in Africa: The language factor: A review and analysis of theory and practice in mother-tongue and bilingual education in sub-Saharan Africa* (pp. 105–157). Hamburg, Germany & Tunis Belvédère, Tunisia: UNESCO Institute for Lifelong Learning (UIL) & Association for the Development of Education in Africa (ADEA).

Heugh, K. (2019). *The place of translanguaging in multilingual education and assessment*. Available online: https://www.timss-sa.org/blog/the-place-of-translanguaging-in-multilingual-education-and-assessment (accessed 19 February 2022).

Jaspers, J. (2017). The transformative limits of translanguaging. *Working Papers in Urban Language & Literacies 226*.

Kaschula, R. H., & Maseko, P. (2014). The intellectualisation of African languages, multilingualism and education: A Research-based approach. *Alternation*, Special Edition, *13*, 8–35.

Krashen, S. D. (1981). *Second language acquisition and second language learning.* Oxford: Pergamon.

Krashen, S. D. (1982). *Principles and practice in second language acquisition.* Oxford: Pergamon.

Lemke, J. L. (2002). *Mathematics in the middle: Measure, picture, gesture, sign, and word.* Available online: https://www.researchgate.net/profile/Jay_Lemke/publication/267853726_Mathematics_in_the_middle_Measure_picture_gesture_sign_and_word/links/54bfe3c30cf28eae4a663acb/Mathematics-in-the-middle-Measure-picture-gesture-sign-and-word.pdf (accessed 11 April 2014).

Lerman, S. (2000). The social turn in mathematics education research. In J. Boaler (ed.), *Multiple perspectives on the teaching and learning of mathematics* (pp. 19–44). Westport, CT: Ablex.

Lewis, G., Jones, B., & Baker, C. (2012). Translanguaging: Origins and development from school to street and beyond. *Educational Research and Evaluation, 18*(7), 641–654.

Manyike, T. V., & Lemmer, E. M. (2014). Research in language education in South Africa: Problems and prospects. *Mediterranean Journal of Social Sciences, 5*(8), 251–258.

May, S. (2014). Disciplinary divides, knowledge construction and the multilingual turn. In S. May (ed.), *The multilingual turn: Implications for SLA, TESOL and bilingual education* (pp. 7–31). New York: Routledge.

Melikoff, O. (2018). *The St. Lambert experiment in French immersion revisited: Fifty years later.* Available online: https://olgamelikoff.com/the-st-lambert-experiment-in-french-immersion-revisited-fifty-years-later/ (accessed 5 August 2019).

Mercer, N. (2000). *Words and minds: How we use language to think together.* London: Routledge.

Mohanty, A. K. (2009). Multilingual education: A bridge too far? In T. Skutnabb-Kangas, R. Phillipson, A. K. Mohanty & M. Panda (eds), *Social justice through multilingual education* (pp. 3–18). Bristol: Multilingual Matters.

Otheguy, R., García, O., & Reid, W. (2015). Clarifying translanguaging and deconstructing named languages: A perspective from linguistics. *Applied Linguistics Review, 6*(3), 281–307.

Probyn, M. (2009). 'Smuggling the vernacular into the classroom': Conflicts and tensions in classroom codeswitching in township/rural schools in South Africa. *International Journal of Bilingual Education and Bilingualism, 12*(2), 123–136.

Probyn, M., Murray, S., Botha, L. Botya, P., Brooks, M., & Westphal, V. (2002). Minding the gaps: An investigation into language policy and practice in four Eastern Cape districts. *Perspectives in Education, 20*(1), 29–46.

Reddy, V., Isdale, K., Juan, A., Visser, M., Winnaar, L., & Arends, F. (2016). *TIMSS 2015: Highlights of mathematics achievement of Grade 5 South African learners.* Pretoria: Department of Basic Education / Human Sciences Research Council.

Reddy, V., Winnaar, L., Harvey, J., Hannan, S., Isdale, K., Arends, F., & Juan, A. (2022). *The South African TIMSS 2019 Grade 5 results: Building achievement and bridging achievement gaps*. Pretoria: Department of Basic Education / Human Sciences Research Council.

Robertson, S.-A. (2017). The place of language in supporting children's mathematical development: Grade 4 teachers' use of classroom talk. PhD diss., Rhodes University, Grahamstown.

Robertson, S.-A., & Graven, M. (2018). Using a transdisciplinary framework to examine mathematics classroom talk taking place in and through a second language. *ZDM: The International Journal on Mathematics Education, 50*(6), 1013–1027.

Robertson, S.-A., & Graven, M. (2019). Exploratory mathematics talk in a second language: A sociolinguistic perspective. *Educational Studies in Mathematics, 101*(2), 215–232. Doi: 10.1007/s10649-018-9840-5.

Robertson, S.-A., & Graven, M. (2020a). A mathematics teacher's response to a dilemma: 'I'm supposed to teach them in English but they don't understand.' *South African Journal of Childhood Education, 10*(1), 1–11.

Robertson, S-A., & Graven, M. (2020b). Language as an including or excluding factor in mathematics teaching and learning. *Mathematics Education Research Journal, 32*(1), 77–101. Doi: 10.1007/s13394-019-00302-0.

Robertson, S.-A., & Graven, M. (2021a). Delaying demands for formal verbal articulation in early encounters with mathematical ideas. (Oral communication). In M. Inprasitha, N. Changsri & N. Boonsena (eds), *Proceedings of the 44th Conference of the International Group for the Psychology of Mathematics Education* (PME). Vol. 1 (p. 173). Khon Kaen: PME.

Robertson, S.-A., & Graven, M. (2021b). Tuning-in to non-linguistic resources during collective problem-solving in a second language context. (Short communication). In Y. H. Leong, B. Kaur, B. H. Choy, J. B. W. Yeo & S. L. Chin (eds), *Excellence in mathematics education: Foundations and pathways*. Proceedings of the 43rd Annual Conference of the Mathematics Education Research Group of Australasia (p. 444). Singapore: MERGA.

Robertson, S.-A., & Graven, M. (2022). Working on and with verbal, visual and gestured confluences in mathematical meaning-making (short communication). In N. Fitzallen, C. Murphy, V. Hatisaru & N. Maher (eds), *Mathematical confluences and journeys: Proceedings of the 44th Annual Conference of the Mathematics Education Research Group of Australasia, Launceston, Tasmania, 3–7 July* (p. 610). Adelaide: MERGA (Mathematics Education Research Group of Australasia).

Sapire, I., & Essien, A. A. (2021). Multiple monolingualism versus Multilingualism? Early grade mathematics teachers' and students' language use in multilingual classes in South Africa. In A. A. Essien and A. Msimanga (eds), *Multilingual education yearbook 2021: Policy and practice in STEM multilingual contexts* (pp. 75–95). Cham: Springer. Doi: 10.1007/978-3-030-72009-4_5.

Setati, M. (2005). Teaching mathematics in a primary multilingual classroom. *Journal for Research in Mathematics Education, 36*(5), 447–466.

Setati, M. (2008). Access to mathematics versus access to the language of power: The struggle in multilingual mathematics classrooms. *South African Journal of Education*, 28(1), 103–116.

Setati, M., & Adler, J. (2000). Between languages and discourses: Language practices in primary multilingual mathematics classrooms in South Africa. *Educational Studies in Mathematics*, 43(3), 243–269.

Sibanda, L. (2017). Do the Annual National Assessments in mathematics unfairly assess English language competence at the expense of mathematical competence? In M. Graven & H. Venkat (eds), *Improving primary mathematics education, teaching and learning: Research for development in resource-constrained contexts* (pp. 147–159). Basingstoke: Palgrave Macmillan.

South Africa (1996). *The Constitution of the Republic of South Africa (Act 108 of 1996)*. Pretoria: Government Printer.

South Africa, Department of Basic Education (2010). *The Status of the Language of Learning and Teaching (LoLT) in South African public schools: A qualitative overview*. Pretoria: Government Printer.

South Africa, Department of Basic Education (2014). *Report on the Annual National Assessments of 2014: Grades 1 to 6 & 9*. Pretoria: Government Printer.

South Africa, Department of Basic Education (2016). *Curriculum and Assessment Policy Statement: Foundation Phase: Grades 1–3 (English Second Additional Language)*. Pretoria: Government Printer.

South Africa, Department of Education (DoE) (1997). *Language in Education Policy*. Pretoria: Government Printer.

Spaull, N. (2016). Disentangling the language effect in South African schools: Measuring the impact of 'language of assessment' in Grade 3 literacy and numeracy. *South African Journal of Childhood Education*, 6(1), 1–20.

Statistics South Africa (2012). *Census 2011: Census in brief*. Pretoria: Statistics South Africa.

Swain M. (2006). Languaging, agency and collaboration in advanced second language proficiency. In H. Byrnes (ed.), *Advanced language learning: The contribution of Halliday and Vygotsky* (pp. 95–108). London: Continuum.

Vaid, J., Paivio, A., Gardner, R. C., & Genesee, F. (2010). Wallace E. Lambert (1922–2009). *American Psychologist*, 65(4), 290–291.

Vygotsky, L. S. (1986). *Thought and language*. Edited translation, A. Kozulin. Cambridge, MA: Massachusetts Institute of Technology Press. Original work published in Russian in 1934.

3

Teaching and Learning Mathematics in Algeria as a Multilingual Country: Difficulties, Challenges and Hints for Future Research Studies

Nadia Azrou

Introduction

It is hard to find an African country which has not been a place or a passage for an outside civilization, culture, or colonization, over history. It is very common in African countries that most indigenous peoples speak one or more languages. During colonization, some European languages (such as French, English, Portuguese or Italian) have been imposed as the official languages in one or another African country, and this continued even after independence. When the official language, in an African country, is not a European language, as with Arabic countries, English or French was frequently the language of instruction in school or at university, and certainly, these become part of the culture. Factors of power, culture, history, ethnicity, politics and others created a situation in which many languages co-exist at the same time, influencing each other, and more importantly shaping the life of the people through their use in thinking and learning.

While this multilingual situation may appear advantageous for people to communicate with the rest of the world, to have more opportunities to get a job and to be open to diversity, in some cases it is also disadvantageous, particularly when there are difficulties for the different languages to coexist together or difficulties for people to adopt and use one or more languages, due to reasons of identity, of poor mastery or simply of deep language differences, as we will see later.

In this chapter, I will present the multilingual situation of Algeria in its whole complexity, of which some aspects are common with other African countries. Through different research steps, I will illustrate some of these aspects and provide evidence for some delicate points which should be taken into consideration when studying a multilingual situation in the teaching and learning of mathematics at different school levels and at university level.

The Situation of Algeria

Being in a strategic position on the Mediterranean Sea, in North Africa, and very close to southern Europe, Algeria was a region subject to many influences and invasions across history: Phoenician traders (from 900 BCE through 146 BCE); the Romans (from 98 BCE through 117 CE); in 429 CE, Vandals arrived from Spain; in 533 CE, the Byzantines; from 642 CE, Arabs armies invaded North Africa bringing Islam to the Berber autochthones; the Spanish (from 1504 through 1792), the Ottomans (from 1554 through 1830) and the French (from 1830 through 1962). Of all of those invaders, those who had the strongest impact were the Arabs and the French. Traces of their influence that were left in Algerian culture are clearly apparent in the languages spoken in Algeria.

The Languages of Algeria

Arabic

Algeria is usually considered as a Muslim and an Arabic country, which results in the dominating role of the Arabic language as it is the 'lingua franca' of the Arab world. However, it has only been the official language since independence, in 1962. It is the language of instruction at different school levels; it is the language of formal contexts and the language of literature, official documents, formal written media news bulletins and official discourses (political discourses, religious discourses in the mosques and prayers, discourses in the courts, etc.). But at present, only people who have attended school for several years can understand it and speak it on particular occasions; indeed, it is not the daily spoken language of Algerians. It is important to mention that Arabic is a rich and sophisticated language: it is the language of the Quran and the language of Arabic poetry, known for its high level of expression, precision and beauty, and consequently, the learning of this delicate language requires years of practice.

Algerian Spoken Language

Algerian Arabic (Darija or Algerian dialect), which is the mother language of most Algerians (a Berber language, named Tamazight, is the mother language for the rest), is derived from Arabic, has many French words and expressions, and also contains Spanish, Italian and Turkish words, and even English words, which were brought by the US Army during the Second World War to the northwestern of the country. Darija is close to the dialects spoken in Tunisia and Morocco but less understood by other Arabic peoples. This vernacular language has different accents in different regions and some foreign words are expressed differently in these regions; for example, Spanish and English words are present in the dialect in the north-west where Spanish and American presence was located, while Italian words are present in the northeast, which is closer to Italy. This colloquial language, full of code-switching, was not written down, until the recent emergence of social media, which allowed for an increasing amount of online writing that results in short texts in Latin letters (from left to right) or in Arabic letters (from right to left).

Tamazight

The Berber language (Tamazight) is the mother language of the Berber people, the indigenous people of North Africa; it is widely spoken in the Kabylian region (east of the capital Algiers, in the north central part of Algeria), while it is spoken only in Berber families in the rest of Algeria. The Berber language is both a written and an oral language; it has many oral derivate dialects spoken in North Africa, many of them are spoken in Algeria: *Tashawith* is spoken in the Awrass in the northeast by Shawi people; *Tashenwith* is spoken in Mount Chenoua in the west of Algeria *Tamzabith* is spoken in the Mzab region in the north central part of the Algerian Sahara; *Tamahaq* is spoken by Tuareg people in the south. The Berber language was recognized as a second national language in 2002, and only in 2016 was it recognized as the second official language, a long period during which an official status for it had been demanded by the Berber people; since then, it has been taught in schools in the Berber Area.

French

French is the language that was brought by the French colonizers and used for 132 years, it has been imposed in instruction and administration during this period. It continued to be used as the language of instruction during a decade after the independence (1962), before being replaced by Arabic. Since the Arabization of instruction (in the seventies), French has been taught from Grade 3 onwards. French is the second language for literature (along with Arabic) and has the same dispersion as Arabic; there have always been newspapers in French, radio channel and TV channel in French.

English

Since the eighties, English has been the only foreign language (except French) taught in Algeria from middle school (6th to 9th Grade) onwards. Before this decision, other foreign languages could also be taught to middle school students, according to local choices: Spanish, Italian, German, etc. The English language could not compete with the French language, which was strongly present in society for a long time, until the 2000 decade where the French language has become less mastered by the population:

> Even though Algerian people recognize the strong presence of French in the Algerian society, however, they welcome the expansion of English perceived not only as a simpler language with a wider scope but also as a real asset in professional development. The English language benefits from a modern image; it is felt as an adaptable and non-fixed language unlike French which suffers from its image of a rigid language which contributes to making it not very accessible.
>
> Abid-Hocine, 2007, p. 143

Moreover, Algerian scientists and researchers have realized that most scientific papers are published in English, which has made English the key language for publication and access to recent research at the international level (Abid-Hocine, 2007).

Recently, in August 2022, the Algerian president decided that English will be taught together with French from the 3rd Grade starting from September 2022, a decision that not only reinforces the status of English but also weakens the position of French.

In the image in Figure 3.1, one can see that almost all public signs in Algeria are written in Arabic and in French.

Figure 3.1 Street names and signs written in both Arabic and French.
Source: Nadia Azrou.

The Coexistence of Four Languages

The relation between these four languages (Arabic, Algerian language, French and Tamazight) has not been always peaceful. Arabic is related to the religious identity, being the liturgical language of Islam. It is supported and maintained by the Islamic religion but also by the Arabic identity brought to this non-Arabic country and justified by the introduction of Islam (as is the case for several Arabic countries). It has always been claimed by those who defend the Arabic language that Algeria is a Berber country Arabized by Islam. French has been, since independence, the language of science, modernity, and openness to the world. After Arabization, in the seventies, two trends developed among cultivated people – the Arabic-speakers and the French-speakers – who are in opposite positions, representing two faces of the Algerian identity which are in continuous conflict. In reality, there is also a conflictual situation between school, and industry and trade society, as the former uses Arabic and the latter uses French. In other words, two worlds coexist in Algeria, obeying two opposite logics: an identity logic, maintained and supported by the nationalistic ideological education valued by the conservative elite, and an economic pragmatic logic advocated by the modernist elite (Taleb Ibrahimi, 2015).

The Berber people, particularly the Kabyle people, have battled since the independence in favour of the use of their language, by regular manifestations, which did not always have peaceful outcomes. Most of the time, the government's response was repression through the deployment of forces according to the principle of law and order. This conflictual situation lasted until 2016. Nowadays, four languages are taught in the Berber area: Arabic is still the language of school instruction, while Tamazight, French and English are taught as additional languages. Kabyle and other Berber people also speak the Algerian language as it is the spoken 'lingua Franca' of Algerians all over the country. It is important to mention here an important issue in the Berber area, which is the regular use of French in the daily life (code switching with Tamazight) and the success of using French in universities by students (Saoud, 2017).

The Algerian dialect is gaining more influence with time, due to the decreasing use of the Arabic language, through the use of social media, which has allowed for the first time its writing, and due to the affirmation of Algerian identity. Many people in Algeria claim to be Algerian and not Arabic anymore. Consequently, to gain people's confidence and closeness, the Algerian language is used more and more in politics, in religious discourses, in universities and on TV programmes. Recently advertisements have begun to use expressions written in the Algerian language using either French letters or Arabic letters.

Teaching Mathematics and Sciences

As concerns the language of teaching mathematics and sciences, it has also undergone many changes: from 1962 to 1976, the teaching was in French (like before the independence), then after 1976, it began progressively to be in Arabic in schools; all three school levels (primary, middle and high school) were completely functioning in Arabic in 1986, but at university, the teaching of mathematics and technical and experimental sciences has always been in French (which is different from the humanities that are taught in Arabic). However, in 2005, there was a change brought by a new reform: in the three school levels, regarding the language of teaching mathematics, Latin symbols were adopted for mathematical symbols (written from left to right) but Arabic was kept for written verbal expressions and mathematical terms (written from right to left), while discussion in the classrooms was still supposed to be in Arabic as before. This situation is still in use so far.

My Completed Studies

The First Study

The research performed for my PhD thesis (which concerned some difficulties with proof and proving at the undergraduate level), together with the findings of

Azrou and Khelladi (2019) revealed linguistic difficulties of Algerian students caused by the fact that they learn mathematics in a second language (French). In particular, in the study reported in Azrou and Khelladi (2019), difficulties concerned producing mathematical proof texts. In revising the data collected for that study, two needs emerged in order to move from emerging difficulties to their interpretation: finding a suitable framework to deal with the level of mastery of the language, which is needed for advanced mathematical activities; and identifying salient differences between languages, that might result in obstacles when students must move (due to institutional constraints) from one language to another in those activities, particularly as it concerns the ways of expressing logical relationships.

The Second Study

This subsequent study (Azrou, 2019) concerned Algerian university students who entered the university and started to learn mathematics completely in French after having learnt mathematics, in all previous school levels, with verbal expressions in Arabic and written formulas in French. Linguistic difficulties were investigated, as students used three different languages: French to write and read, Arabic and Algerian language for discussions between teachers and students, and among students, and also for thinking. Findings from interviews of students showed a complete dependence of students' learning mathematics on translation to Arabic (to think) and from Arabic (to write in French). To understand mathematics when translating from one language to another, students had to translate the mathematical statements from one language and express them in the other language. If this translation was hindered by different logico-linguistic structures of the three languages, the students would meet problems when understanding and expressing mathematical statements.

The Third Study

To identify the differences between the languages used in university mathematics, an in-depth investigation of the linguistic structures of some logical aspects, very important in mathematical reasoning, in the three languages was necessary. This was done in the study (Azrou, 2020), where the conditional reasoning, usually expressed by: 'if ... then ...' and logical negation in mathematics were examined and compared in the three languages (French, Arabic and Algerian dialect), concerning the way these are expressed and the meanings they uncover. The results revealed relevant differences between how the conditional expressions and their negations are expressed in the three languages. In French, as in English, the conditional reasoning is expressed by 'si..., alors...'; more precisely 'si... *protasis* ..., alors ... apodosis...' (particularly for mathematics) or *si ... protasis ..., apodosis ...* (more frequent in common language). The degree of possibility of a conditional in French – as in English, relies upon the modes and tenses of the verbs within *protasis* and *apodosis*. We have four main types or degrees of possibility of the conditional:

1. Type 0 (always possible conditional)
   If you <u>heat</u> ice, it <u>melts</u> (present simple – present simple).
   Si tu chauffe de la glace, elle fond (présent – présent).
2. Type 1 (possible conditional referring to the future)
   If you <u>do</u> not hurry, you <u>will miss</u> the train (present simple – future simple).
   Si tu ne fais pas vite, tu rateras le train (présent – future simple).
3. Type 2 (a not so likely to be realized conditional)
   If you <u>went</u> to bed earlier, you <u>would</u> not <u>be</u> so tired (past simple – present conditional).
   Si tu dormais tôt, tu ne serais pas fatigué (imparfait – conditionnel présent).
4. Type 3 (past not realized conditional)
   If you <u>had studied</u> harder, you <u>would have passed</u> the exam (past perfect – perfect conditional).
   Si tu avais travaillé plus dur, tu aurais réussi à l'examen (plus que parfait – conditionnel passé).

In Arabic, the conditional sentence also has two parts: protasis is called *the condition* (الشرط) and apodosis is called *the response of the condition* (جواب الشرط). However, there are three main differences in French (and English):

1. There are many conjunctions for the equivalent of 'si' (if) and many for 'alors' (then).
2. The degree of possibility of the conditional is not expressed by the mode and the tense of the verb.
3. The conjunction for a conditional that has not been realized are different from the conjunction used for a possible or a probable conditional.

More importantly, the teaching of the conditional reasoning in an Arabic language course presents all the conjunctions analogous to 'if', which are: law

لو lawla لولا, idha إذا, emma إما (either), koulama كلما (everytime), lamma لما (when), In إن, idhma اذما, man من (whoever), ma ما, mahma مهما (whatever), mata متى (when), ayyana أيّان, anna أنّا, ayna أين (where), aynama أينما (wherever), haythuma حيثما, kayfama كيفما, ay أي (which), and those analogous to 'then', which are: ma ما, fa ف, la ل, nothing. The conjunctions used for a conditional not realized are: law لو ..., la ل .... But the teaching does not involve the degree of possibility, which can be understood from the meaning and the context of the sentence. In mathematics, the conditional sentence is expressed only in one conventional form: **idhakana** إذا كان ... protasis ... **fainna** فإن ... apodosis ..., which is not currently used in common language, which is analogous to the French form (si ... alors ...) in the type 0 situation.

For the Algerian language, things are also different, even though the degree of possibility of the conditional is also not expressed by the mode and the tense of the verb, as in Arabic.

In the Algerian language, the conjunctions are different, the analog of 'if' is 'ki' and there are no words for 'then' in the possible conditional; while for a conditional that has not been satisfied, the analog for 'if' is 'lukane' and for 'then', there are no words, or 'lukane' is used. So, we say: 'lukane ... (nothing) ...', or 'lukane ... lukane ...'.

For the negation, in French it is expressed by: '...ne verbe...pas...'; for example: la voiture **n**'est **pas** blanche (the car is not white). In Arabic, in the natural language, we negate verbs by using only 'la' before the verb (la+verb), ('la' is also the opposite of 'yes' in Arabic) when the verb is in the present. When the verb is in the past, the negation is made with 'lam' لم, and when the verb is in the future, the negation is made with 'lan' لن. We also negate a nominative sentence by using 'laysa' which comes before a noun, while 'la' comes before a verb and forms the negation of a verbal sentence. It is important to note that when we negate by 'laysa' a nominative sentence which contains 'all' (as in English when we say: not all students came today), the negation is partial (as in mathematics) and when we negate by 'la' a verbal sentence containing 'all', the negation is total (as when we say in English: all students did not come today). To negate an adjective, we use either 'lasysa' ليس or 'ghayr' غير.

In the Algerian language, it is different: when we negate, we use a prefix 'ma' attached to the verb followed by a suffix 'esh' (ma+verb+esh: ma+eat+esh which means 'I do not eat'), while a nominative sentence is negated by putting 'mashi' before the noun. For example: *mashi hamra* means 'it is not red', *mayektebesh* means 'it does not write'. As in Arabic when we negate a sentence containing 'all', we can either negate the verb or the noun; when we negate the verb ('all did not come'), it means there is no exception and the negation is total, and when we negate the noun, we put 'mashi' before 'all' ('not all came') and in this case, the negation is partial (with exceptions).

The Fourth Study

The previous study provided evidence for some important differences between the languages used at school and in university and raised a question about whether teachers are conscious about these important differences and their impact on students' learning. This fourth study explored, through semi-structured interviews, high school mathematics teachers' awareness of those differences and their consequences on students' learning of mathematics both in school, and in the transition to university (see Azrou, 2023). The interviews questions were:

Q1. You know that in high school mathematics textbooks, and in the official Arabic language for mathematics, there is only one expression for conditional statement: 'idha kana ... fa inna ...'. But students know other expressions for the conditional statement in Arabic, and they currently express conditional statements in Algerian language, which also is different from 'idha kana ... fa inna ...'. Have you observed students' shifting from one expression of conditional statement to another, by using other words than (idha kana ... fa inna ...), or by using expressions in the Algerian language?
Q1a. For instance, how can a student express in Arabic the meaning of the sentence '*si la fonction était derivable, alors elle serait continue*' ('if the function were differentiable, it would be continuous')?
Q1b. At university, we observed that several students have big difficulties when moving from their usual conditional statement in Arabic in high school mathematics, to the conditional statement in French. Have you any idea about the reasons for these difficulties?
Q1c. What do you think about the possibility of preventing these difficulties in the classroom?
Q2. Do you think that students would have problems when negating mathematical expressions in the translation from Arabic to French or vice versa, for instance in negating '*all the balls are red*'? What kind of difficulties do you anticipate?
Q2a. Does it happen that students use dialect to negate in mathematics?

According to their responses, teachers acknowledged that they should explain the mathematical meaning of the conventional conditional statement but did not realize that it would be necessary to make links and comparisons with other different (non-conventional) conditional statements in Arabic and the Algerian language. They neglected these different conditional forms and avoided using and explaining their meaning, thus leaving students in doubt when they use them orally in mathematical discourses. The same situation occurred with negation: students usually translated the standard Arabic expression of negation into the Algerian language with the possibility of getting two sentences with two different meanings. Moreover, it is clear to teachers that students need to use Algerian language, and teachers try to help students by using Algerian language themselves, but their responses showed that they are not aware of students' difficulties when shifting from one language to another (between oral Algerian language and written Arabic), that have different structures (Azrou, 2020). This might be a sign of teachers' lack of awareness of the deep structural differences between the three languages, as it concerns the expression of a conditional statement and its negation. This interpretation is supported by the fact that teachers considered lack of Arabic mastery and French mastery as the only reason for students' difficulties with conditional statements and their negations in high school and at university, instead of considering structural linguistic differences. Some teachers insisted on students' weak *mathematical understanding* of a conditional statement and its negation, in other words, of how these logical aspects are considered in mathematics (without considering the relevance of students' mastery of linguistic expressions for them, and the possible consequences of it on understanding, when mastery is weak).

The Fifth Study

The fifth study concerned some integrations of high school and university mathematics textbooks (written in Arabic in school, in French at the university) for coping with the need to help students (and teachers, too!) to deal with the logical-structural differences between the three languages (Arabic, French, Algerian language) (see Azrou, 2023). For example, regarding the conditional form, it is very helpful to remind students that the form used in mathematics in school, in Arabic, is a conventional one and that other forms are available, including the one used in Algerian language. It would be very helpful to remind them that in Arabic, there are two ways of negating a sentence, which contains 'all', the total negation and the partial negation; and in mathematics, it is the partial negation which is adopted.

Here are some examples:

- For a textbook of probability (first year of university), we might include the following messages in bubbles:

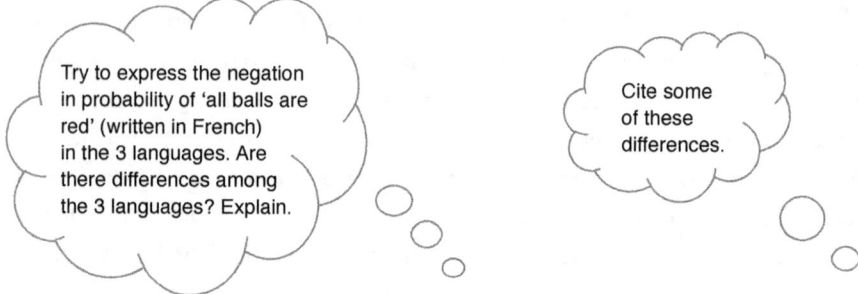

- For a high school textbook:

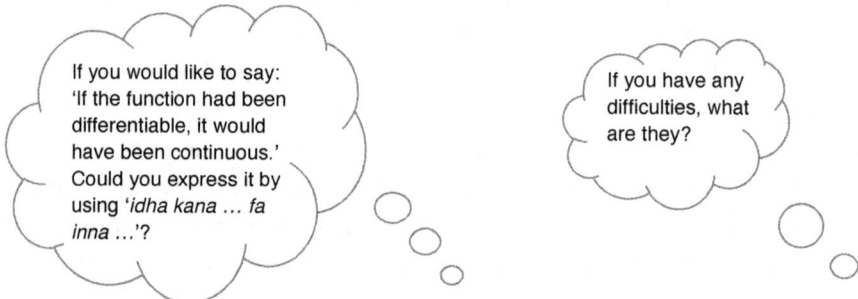

- Exercises of translation

Systematic exercises of translation into the three languages can be proposed, in order to make students aware of the delicate issues that were discovered in the fourth study (i.e. the linguistic differences) and how to deal with them. The first step might be, in high school, to ask for simple translations from Arabic into the Algerian language (and vice versa) of sentences like 'If two numbers are negative, then their product is positive', and sentences with other conjunctions different from the conventional one (i.e. idhakana ... fainna).

The Sixth Study (in Preparation)

The aim of this study is to find out which languages students use when they are engaged in a mathematical activity together, and whether and how they use different languages at once. In other words, they might use one language for thinking and another for speaking and another for writing, or they could use a mixture of two or more languages in a way similar to code-switching (Adler, 2001), and when and how they use the code-switching.

We have proposed three tasks for university students of different levels (bachelor and master) who were gathered in groups of two or three students. We have asked them to solve one task and write down the solution, we have recorded their discussion. The tasks necessitated discussion and could not be solved by a procedural process; this was meant to make students discuss. We know that they would use French, Arabic and Algerian language, but we aimed to find out which language they use with which activity. In other words, when and how do they use each language when solving the problems and writing down the solutions and what difficulties they encounter that could originate from the linguistic situation at the university.

The previous studies described a problematic situation at many levels that calls for understanding and intervention. However, several studies are needed to investigate the multiple factors operating in the teaching and learning mathematics in a country where many languages are used.

Important Issues for Future Research in Algeria and Other Multilingual African Countries

Through the description of the example of Algeria and of the planning of my research projects (and of some of their results), many delicate issues have been discovered that suggest future research in Algeria specifically, and more generally in other African multilingual countries. Through what I have discovered in the previous parts of this chapter, I hope to make a contribution that might be useful for the study of the situation in other multilingual African countries.

Studies Deriving from Performed Studies in Algeria

The Roots *of* Multilingualism

Understanding multilingualism is a crucial point, particularly understanding political decisions, power, conflicts, and resistances that concern the adoption of one language or another in instruction, but also in the culture. It happens that a population or a group of people, in a country, may resist learning or using a language, which is an official language or a language of instruction, for some reasons (identity, history, politics, etc). It is important to understand these delicate situations to find out the reasons and the origins of difficulties with learning or using some languages, because these difficulties are not always of linguistic nature. Similarly, it is also important to understand what are the factors that favour a language and thus create a predisposition among the population to prefer it and adopt it over another coexisting language. For example, in Algeria like in many Arabic countries, the religion of Islam supports and maintains the use of Arabic, while French has been weakened by the instability of the political relationship with France over the last two decades. Moreover, concerning French, while it is normally used in different places like the capital Algiers and the Berber region, in other parts of Algeria, French is viewed as a sign of superiority and opposition to one's identity. As a consequence, in these places, people tend to resist learning and using French.

Concerning local languages (which in several cases, are the mother language of the population) and the official or institutional languages, it is important to understand how they are considered by the population and by the official authorities. It can happen that a local language might not be allowed in school or in official institutions, and some populations might have claimed an official status for their local language for a long time (as happened for Tamazight in Algeria); these phenomena could create embarrassment for a local language and decrease in using it, or a proud and increasing use of it. Consequently, how and where a local language is used and what are the relationship with the official languages are indicators for favouring or resisting against some languages. For example, in Algeria, the Algerian language is a deviation from Arabic that is full of French words, which favours the learning of French, more than the Egyptian language or the Syrian language. In the past, more than forty years ago, using the Algerian language in Algeria, was not allowed in the classroom and was a sign of a low scientific level; however, now using it is becoming a sign of integrity and identity.

The Differences between the Used Languages

Research is needed to study the deep differences (concerning the elaboration and the expression of thoughts) between languages that occur, not only in official documents, but also in the daily life of the society (including the spoken languages) and in the teaching and learning of mathematics, technology, and sciences at different instruction levels, as was done by comparing Arabic, French and the Algerian language in the third study. Studies should focus on expressions used in scientific thinking, in particular, how to express and understand conditional thinking, the negation, the generality and the particularity expressed by articles, contradiction, conclusion, etc; in the currently used languages, and in the language used for mathematics. For instance, in Algeria, the translation from French to Arabic of some mathematical terms has caused difficulties for students understanding them: for example, a rational number, in Arabic is called a 'talking number', and the irrational number is called 'dumb number'. Also, the negation of a statement with 'all', in the Algerian language, might be total or partial depending on the position of the negation, whether it is on the verb or on the substantive, while in mathematics it is always a partial negation. Concerning this issue, the research literature is abundant with comparison between several languages regarding mathematics (e.g. Edmonds-Wathen et al., 2016). In multilinguistic countries, for most people, the local language may be the language of thinking. It would be helpful to understand if a local language can replace a language of instruction, particularly by expressing important logical constructions (regarding negation, conditional statements, etc.), or if this has limitations, and what kind of limitations that could hinder students' mathematical understanding when moving from a local language to the language of instruction, to mathematical language. Studies are needed, particularly to understand how the mathematical register (Halliday, 1985) is formed from the existing languages.

Students' Practices

It is important to understand the reality of the use of different languages when students engage in mathematical problem solving, as was planned for the sixth ongoing study, mentioned above.

In each country, research should examine which languages students use when they are engaged alone or in group mathematical activities, how do they use the languages, if they use different languages all together and why. In other words, they might use one language for thinking and another for speaking and another for writing, or they could use a mixture of two or more languages for some activities. This would show the limits of their linguistic performances in the different languages, the direction of translation (from which language to which language), the effect of the language used for thinking (and also for talking and for writing) on their mathematical understanding. It would also reveal their mathematical difficulties related to language switching and code-switching. It is important to point out that this is not a simple issue to investigate when students work together, because they might not 'show' the teacher what they do, for different reasons (like the favoured language in instruction, the need to save one's self-image (Azrou & Khelladi, 2019) or to hide the low mastery of the language they should use, etc). In general, it is also difficult to guess the language of thinking used by the student (but also used by the teacher). It is even more complicated to guess it when the thinking process occurs in more than one language. The analysis of a situation of students' collaborative work (but also that of teachers, for example for a task design) could allow overcoming, or at least, limiting such difficulties of investigation.

Studies are also needed to enhance the ways in which multilingual learners positively utilize available resources during their mathematics learning (e.g. Moschkovich, 2002; Gutiérrez et al., 2010), to help students productively use their native language competences to support their communication and understanding in the language of teaching mathematics (e.g. Moschkovich, 2002, 2010) (cited in Langer-Osuna et al., 2016, p. 164). Such work begins to illuminate the productive use of resources that educators could strategically build on during instruction (Langer-Osuna et al., 2016, p. 164).

Teachers' Practices in the Classroom

The practices of teachers in the classroom in a multilingual context is an indicator of how the teaching occurs. They might reveal some students' difficulties created by these practices, or possible opportunities to promote students' learning. The research findings of Chitera (2009) show that the mathematics teacher educators consider multilingualism and the language practices that come with it such as code-switching more as a problem rather than a resource for teaching and learning. In the case of Algerian universities, teachers tend to use the Algerian language to help students understanding mathematics written in French, but this does not always seem helpful for students. Moreover, in many cases, some teachers value the use of French to help students' learning in French, but in this case, many students with low linguistic competences in French, argue that they are not eager to learn in French. It is important to understand actual teachers' practices in the classroom, first by identifying which languages teachers use, how and why. But also examining the languages favoured and disfavoured by teachers and by students seems important. This would clarify whether these uses promote mathematics students' learning, according to the intention of the teachers.

For instance, responses to how teachers make their choices to use one language or another during mathematical activities (explaining, discussing, writing, translating, recording, etc.), and how they orchestrate the linguistic practice in the classroom (do they respond in the same language used by students, or do they impose on them the language of instruction?) might be very helpful to better understand the situation in the classroom. The reasons for their choices could be the linguistic limitations of teachers, their beliefs, their culture, their preparation and practice of teaching mathematics, or something else worth investigating. Studies are also needed to evaluate the range of strategies and methods employed by teachers and learners in multilingual classrooms for their efficiency and effectiveness.

Difficulties of Students and Teachers

The various ways in which teachers and learners use and produce language depend on the social structure and the multilingual settings in which they find themselves. A teacher's use of code-switching in a multilingual mathematics class is therefore not simply cognitive or pedagogical but is also a social product arising from the particular political and social context (Setati, 2002, p.18).

It would be very useful to make explicit the kinds of difficulties faced both by students and teachers in teaching and learning mathematics in the presence of more than one language. In two similar contexts of multilingualism, students and teachers might have different kinds of difficulties. For instance, in Algeria, some university teachers who master French speak in French and do not use the Algerian language because they think it is inappropriate and does not help students to learn and be familiar with practicing (speaking, writing, thinking, and reading) mathematics in French. Students generally complain about these teachers. Do they encounter more difficulties compared to teachers who speak and allow students to speak the Algerian language in the classroom? Teachers at university also face the difficulty of translating (often asked by students) in Arabic some mathematical terms which do not exist in Arabic (because university mathematics is not completely translated into Arabic) or are not known by the teachers (as the textbooks are in French). Other university teachers, like students, do not master French, or refuse to use French, orally for some reason. As one can see, the difficulties are not the same in all situations and they depend on different aspects of the context: they go from weak mastery of a language, to resisting and refusing a language, to translating from a language to another, to speaking a language and writing in another language. Difficulties of teachers might cause difficulties for students (when teachers know nothing about the languages used by students), might increase difficulties of students (when teachers do not master the language of instruction as students do), and might cause an unawareness of students' situation. Difficulties of students might extend from a weak mastery of one or more languages needed to learn mathematics, to a problem of translation from one language to another, to shame or refusal to learn or use a language. These issues are very important to investigate in order to understand the nature of the linguistic context in different countries.

Mathematics Textbooks in a Multilingual Context

Research should contribute to the improvement of mathematics textbooks for students in a multilingual context. We cannot continue to use, for multilingual students, textbooks designed for monolingual students. How can we improve actual textbooks to help students cope with their linguistic and mathematical difficulties? In addition, interventions using present textbooks, in order to help students and teachers to meet the challenge of multilingualism in instruction would be very useful. Unfortunately, according to my knowledge a systematic research effort is lacking on this issue.

Further Suggested Studies in Multilingual Countries

The Kind of Mathematics Taught and Learned in a Multilingual Context

Research has provided evidence that there is a relationship between the level of mastery of the language of instruction, when it is not the mother language of students, and the nature of the mathematical activities engaged in. Barton and his collaborators (Barton et al., 2005), who conducted a study for three years with university students in Australia, showed that second language students performed better than native language students in the first and the second years with procedural mathematics, while in the third year, with more cognitively demanding mathematical activities, they performed less well than the native language students. In her study, Setati (2003) has shown that in a context like South Africa, where mathematics and English both have symbolic power, and where procedural discourse dominates over conceptual discourse in school mathematics teaching and learning, a practice is forged wherein it is difficult to move the teaching of mathematics beyond procedural discourse.

As we have seen in the fourth study (see Azrou, 2023), high school teachers' awareness about the differences between Arabic, French and dialect was investigated by interviews. The following question was asked:

> For instance, how can a student express in Arabic the meaning of the sentence '*si la fonction était derivable, alors elle serait continue*' ('if the function is differentiable, would it be continuous')?

Teachers responded that they do not use the corresponding conditional form in Arabic because there is no need for it, which indicates an absence of argumentation and of questioning the existence and the role of the mathematical conditions. This fact indicates the kind and the nature of mathematical activity in classrooms, which is more about executing processes and direct calculations using known procedures and rules. It seems 'natural' to teach 'easy' mathematics when the linguistic performances of students are weak or superficial; while it looks possible to move to argumentative activities of advanced mathematical thinking only when the linguistic performances of students are high enough and reach some level of mastery that would make this possible. On the other side, dealing only with easy mathematical activity prevents students' linguistic performances developing and does not challenge their thinking.

Given this situation, further research is needed to investigate the relationship between the level of mastery of the language of instruction and the complexity of the mathematical activities proposed to the students. Moreover, we need to know why students do not sufficiently develop their level of the language of instruction when dealing with the mathematical activities proposed to them. And given the level of students' language, why do they not develop their mathematical thinking to the level needed to deal with cognitively demanding mathematical activities?

Positive Aspects of Multilingualism

It has been noted in Algeria that the situation in the Berber region, and particularly in the Kabylia (a part formed mainly from the east of Algiers to Bejaia city) regarding learning technical and experimental sciences, at the university, in French is not a problematic issue (Saoud, 2017). Moreover, learning in French or in Arabic, in this region with a different culture and ethnicity, has never been a problem. The good results of the national exam baccalaureate (at the end of high school and prior to entrance to university), in this region, show that it came first, in the national ranking for all the Algerian regions for the last nine years (Said, 2020). In the case of Kabylia, investigations (Afir, 2022) show that education is considered by parents as the only means of making a future for their children, in a socially and particularly economically disadvantaged region. The French language is viewed as the language of success and access to the modern world (Outaleb, 2013), particularly in the perspective of further education in France. Said (2022) investigated why the Kabylia region came first in the national exam by interviewing Tessa Ahmed, a pedagogue, and a former councilor in the Algerian ministry of education who claimed that the opportunities of personal fulfilment are rare in the mountain regions, like the Kabylia region; he also argued that: 'it is this context that has made Kabylia, at all times, the largest reservoir of internal and external emigration. Since the independence, parents have made it their duty to stimulate and push their children to succeed in their studies to escape the constraints of this harsh mountain life' (Said, 2022). This context, clearly, boosts children and seems to help them overcome problems with learning in many languages.

This suggests that there is a multilingual context, which is positive and successful. It raises the question of understanding the factors of strength and of weaknesses which make a multilingual context either successful or problematic. Studies are needed to identify such factors.

Teacher Education

A multilingual context, as we have seen, is a rather complicated context in which many delicate issues are intertwined. Certainly, a heavy weight of responsibility is placed on the shoulders of teachers in terms of being aware of, and understanding the situation, of making choices, and of behaving accordingly. This consequently sets the bar for teacher preparation very high in order to teach mathematics in such contexts. At the teacher training level, a course that attends to the complexities of teaching and learning in multilingual classrooms is essential (Essien, 2014). Research is indeed needed to define the kind of training needed in these particular situations, both for pre-service teachers and for the professional development of teachers as the linguistic context changes over time.

We may observe that in Algeria, as in many countries, teacher education, if it ever exists, focuses more on mathematics content teaching for future teachers, without considering the problems of the linguistic context in which they will teach and thus missing the development of classroom practices which would be beneficial. This fact has been documented by many studies (e.g. Ngu, 2004; Essien et al., 2016; Chitera, 2011), showing that teacher education programmes in multilingual countries are not well adapted to teaching mathematics to students' speaking and learning in more than one language, even in the cases in which there is a clear awareness about the need for this aspect of teacher education. Studies of teacher education should focus on multiple issues. The following are a few examples:

- Creating programmes which consider a 'bi-cultural focus' in the curriculum that legitimizes the culture of the school and of the community (Halai & Barwell, 2015, p. 541) and developing instruction which is sensitive to the needs of minority students and 'equitable strategies' that encourage collaborative knowledge production, student authority, ownership of knowledge and mutual respect (ibid., p. 542).
- Creating teachers' awareness of the specificity of the multilingual context because 'creating awareness of the multilingual context of teaching and what it entails should be a thread that runs through the entire (mathematics) teacher education curriculum' (Essien et al., 2016, p. 117). Teachers' awareness is a very crucial factor to investigate in multilingual contexts; it is important as concerns: the structural differences of the languages used in education (Arabic, Algerian language, Tamazight and French), the related students' difficulties when learning mathematics, the different links between the existing languages (the dominant language, the preferred language by students, the reasons behind resisting use of a language, the level of competence of students of the language of instruction, how the teaching of a language occurred, etc.), and the consequences on students' mathematical performances. It is important to understand if teachers are aware of these issues; and if not, it would be useful to understand why, particularly in the case where they live in the same context of their students and talk the same languages. Studies that examine teachers' awareness of the different aspects concerning the languages used in the teaching and learning of mathematics in Algeria (as was done in the fourth study) and in other African countries are necessary.
- Identifying teachers' practices in the classroom to empower mathematics learning: for instance, (1) empowering learners to take responsibility for their learning in small groups, and looking at the outcomes of group work, could be strategies that teachers could employ in such multilingual settings (Halai & Barwell, 2015, p. 541); (2) ensuring 'respect' for learners in multiethnic classrooms by creating ample space to listen to them and guide their thinking (ibid., p. 541); and (3) developing competence in children's native languages, but also understanding how children can productively

draw on native and emergent languages to support communication in the language of instruction (Gort, 2006; Moschkovich, 2002, in Langer-Osuna et al., 2016, p. 164).

- Dealing with the multiple tensions emerging from language diversity. When instruction occurs in one language and students speak in many other languages outside of school, this creates tension, and it is clear that teachers play a key role in navigating this tension, according to Barwell and his collaborators (2016). Teachers' mediation on this tension takes several forms. In some cases, it involves translating, code-switching or using language mixtures to provide additional forms of mathematical meaning making for students (ibid., p. 190).

Concluding Thoughts

We have presented many aspects of the teaching and learning mathematics in the multilingual situation of Algeria by focusing on some aspects linked to the teaching and learning of mathematics, which have been discovered by a few studies. These studies have shown that university students' difficulties in writing an understandable, clearly expressed proof were caused by low linguistic performance in French, the need for first university mathematics students to translate from French into Arabic or Algerian language into French (when they start studying mathematics in French), the logical aspects of the structural differences between the three languages present in the classroom (Arabic, Algerian language and French), the high school teachers' poor awareness of the consequences on learning of the particular multilingual context, some propositions of how to improve mathematics textbooks to help students cope with some difficulties rooted in the differences between the used languages, and finally on how students use code-switching when they deal with a problem solving activity in a group. These studies revealed lacks and difficulties: difficulties of students in learning mathematics effectively using the three languages and lacks in teachers' awareness about many important language-related issues. Consequently, being inspired by the results of the performed studies, we have suggested studies to promote research in order to deal with delicate issues like teacher education, mathematics textbooks and teachers' practices in the classroom. We have also suggested investigating the roots of multilingualism and the position of different languages in the society, in the history and in the culture of a country, in order to understand better what happens in classrooms as we consider a classroom an important part of the larger society.

References

Abid-Houcine, S. (2007). Enseignement et éducation en langues étrangères en Algérie: La compétition entre le français et l'anglais. *Droit et cultures*, 54, 143–56. Doi: 10.4000/droitcultures.1860.

Adler, J. (2001). *Teaching mathematics in multilingual classrooms*. Dordrecht: Kluwer Academic Publishers.

Afir, A. (2022). Voilà pourquoi la Kabylie arrive toujours en tête des résultats du baccalauréat. ObservAlgérie.com, 24 July. Available online: https://observalgerie.com/2022/07/24/societe/kabylie-resultats-bac-2022/ (accessed 30 July 2022).

Azrou, N. (2020). Linguistic difficulties in the transition to the university: learning mathematics in three structurally different languages. In J. Ingram, K. Erath, F. Rønning, & A. Schüler-Meyer (eds), *Proceedings of the Seventh ERME Topic Conference on language in the mathematics classroom* (pp. 15–22). Montpellier: Université de Montpellier. hal-02970540.

Azrou, N. (2023). Teaching and learning mathematics in a multilingual context: which language mastery for which mathematics? In A. Schüler-Meyer, J. Ingram & K. Erath (eds), *Proceedings of the Twelfth ERME Topic Conference on language in the mathematics classroom*, Oxford University and ERME (European Society for Research in Mathematics (pp. 6–13). ERME / HAL Archive. hal-03992500.

Azrou, N., & Khelladi, A. (2019). Why do students write poor proof texts? A case study on undergraduates' proof writing. *Educational Studies in Mathematics*, 102(2), 257–274. Doi: 10.1007/s10649-019-09911-9.

Azrou, N. (2019). Learning mathematics in French at the undergraduate level in Algeria. In U. T. Jankvist, M. Van den Heuvel-Panhuizen & M. Veldhuis (eds), *Proceedings of the Eleventh Congress of the European Society for Research in Mathematics Education* (pp. 1598–1605). Utrecht: Freudenthal Group & Freudenthal Institute, Utrecht University and ERME. hal-02435231.

Azrou, N. (2023). Mathematics textbooks in a multilingual country: The case of Algeria. *Proceedings of the 16th* IARTEM *Conference disciplinary and trans-disciplinary knowledge and skills for an uncertain future: Are educational media up to it?* IUL Research.

Barton, B., Chan, R., King, C., Neville-Barton, P., & Sneddon, J. (2005). EAL undergraduates learning mathematics. *International Journal of Mathematical Education in Science and Technology*, 36(7), 721–729. Available online: Doi: 10.1080/00207390500270950.

Barwell, R., Chapsam, L., Nkambule, T., & Setati M. Phakeng (2016). Tensions in teaching mathematics in contexts of language diversity. In R. Barwell, P. Clarkson, A. Halai, M. Kazima, J. Moschkovich, N. Planas, M. Setati-Phakeng, P. Valero and M. Villavicencio Ubillús (eds), *Mathematics education and linguistic diversity: The 21st ICMI study*. New ICMI Study Series (pp. 175–192). Cham: Springer. Doi: 10.1007/978-3-319-14511-2_10.

Chitera, N. (2009). Code-switching in a college mathematics classroom. *International Journal of Multilingualism*, 6(4), 426–442.

Chitera, N. (2011). Language of learning and teaching in schools: Am issue for research in mathematics teacher education? *Journal of Mathematics Teacher Education*, 14(3), 231–246. Doi: 10.1007/s10857-010-9167-3.

Edmonds-Wathen, C., Trinick, T., & Durand-Guerrier, V. (2016). Impact of differing grammatical structures in mathematics teaching and learning. In R. Barwell, P. Clarkson, A. Halai, M. Kazima, J. Moschkovich, N. Planas, M. Setati-Phakeng, P. Valero and M. Villavicencio Ubillús (eds), *Mathematics education and linguistic diversity: The 21st ICMI study*. New ICMI Study Series (pp. 23–46). Cham: Springer.

Essien, A. A. (2014). Examining the opportunities for the development of interacting identities within pre-service teacher education mathematics classroom. *Perspectives in Education*, 32(3), 62–70.

Essien, A. A., Planas, N., & Chitera, N. (2016). Language diversity in mathematics teacher education: Challenges across three countries. In R. Barwell, P. Clarkson, A. Halai, M. Kazima, J. Moschkovich, N. Planas, M. Setati-Phakeng, P. Valero and M. Villavicencio Ubillús (eds), *Mathematics education and linguistic diversity: The 21st ICMI study*. New ICMI Study Series (pp. 103–119). Cham: Springer.

Gort, M. (2006). Strategic codeswitching, interliteracy, and other phenomena of emergent bilingual writing: Lessons from first grade dual language classrooms. *Journal of Early Childhood Literacy*, 6(3), 323–354.

Gutiérrez, K. D., Sengupta-Irving, T., & Dieckmann, J. (2010). Developing a mathematical vision. In J. Moschkovich (ed.), *Language and mathematics education: Multiple perspectives and directions for research* (pp. 29–71). Charlotte, NC: Information Age Publishing.

Halai, A., & Barwell, R. (2015). Mathematics education in a multilingual and multicultural environment. In S. J. Cho (ed.), *The proceedings of the 12th International Congress on Mathematical Education: Intellectual and attitudinal challenges* (pp. 539–545). Cham: Springer. Doi: 10.1007/978-3-319-12688-3.

Halliday, M. A. K. (1985). *An introduction to functional grammar*. London: Arnold.

Langer-Osuna, J. M., Moschkovich, J., Norén, E., Powell, A. B., & Vazquez, S. (2016). Student agency and counter-narratives in diverse multilingual mathematics classrooms: Challenging deficit perspectives. In R. Barwell, P. Clarkson, A. Halai, M. Kazima, J. Moschkovich, N. Planas, M. Setati-Phakeng, P. Valero & M. Villavicencio Ubillús (eds), *Mathematics education and linguistic diversity: The 21st ICMI study*. New ICMI Study Series (pp. 163–173). Cham: Springer.

Moschkovich, J. (2002). A situated and sociocultural perspective on bilingual mathematics learners. *Mathematical Thinking and Learning*, 4(2–3): 189–212.

Ngu, J. (2004). *Initiative teacher education in sub-Saharan Africa*. Paris: UNESCO.

Official Diary of the Government of Catalonia. (2003). *Law 1/2003 of Universities* (Reference No. 3826). Barcelona: Department of Universities, Research and Information Society.

Outaleb, A. (2013). Pratiques et représentations du français au sein de deux familles kabyles. In C. Sini (dir.), *Les langues dans l'espace familial algérien* (pp. 95–109). Oran: CRASC (Centre de recherche en anthropologie sociale et culturelle).

Said, A. (2022). Algérie: Pourquoi la Kabylie arrive toujours en tête des résultats du bac? Jeuneafrique.com, 23 July. Available online: https://www.jeuneafrique.com/1364318/politique/algerie-pourquoi-la-kabylie-arrive-toujours-en-tete-des-resultats-du-bac/ (accessed 30 July 2022).

Saoud, T. (2017). L'identité linguistique des jeunes étudiants en Kabylie entre transmission et préservation. *Insaniyat / إنسانيات*77–78, 193–206. Doi: 10.4000/insaniyat.18033.

Setati, M. (2002). Researching mathematics education and language in multilingual South Africa. *Mathematics Educator*, 12(2), 6–20.

Setati, M. (2003). Language use in a multilingual mathematics classroom in South Africa: A different perspective. *International Group for the Psychology of Mathematics Education*, 4, 151–158.

Taleb Ibrahimi, K. (2015). L'école algérienne au prisme des langues de scolarisation. *Revue internationale d'éducation de Sèvres*, 70, 53–63. Doi: 10.4000/ries.4493.

4

Novice Teachers' Use of the Mother Tongue in Mathematics Junior Primary Multilingual Classrooms in Northern Namibia

Tulonga T. Shuukwanyama, Caroline Long and Jeremiah S. Maseko

Introduction

The teaching of mathematics in the mother tongue at primary level has been consistently supported by various studies claiming that it allows young learners to both comprehend mathematical concepts and develop personal identities (Setati, 2008; Chitera, 2010; Makonye, 2015). Various African countries, including Namibia, have considered adapting their language policy to ensure that learners in the early grades of schooling are instructed in the mother tongue. In a systematic review of research, Essien (2018) found that learners whose language is Afrikaans or English were mostly advantaged with regards to their performance compared to children whose home language was an indigenous South African language. According to Planas and Setati-Phakeng (2014), language policies are used for the purpose of addressing social inclusion, although in various ways and with various consequences. After independence in 1990, Namibia implemented a language policy for the first time. This new language policy aimed to preserve and revive the cultural heritage of the national languages in Namibia which the government felt had been lost during the colonial era. It further aimed at promoting English as the official language (Ministry of Basic Education, Sports and Culture (MBESC), 1993). The language policy stresses the importance of learning in the mother tongue to achieve equity and to redress the past imbalances. This policy implementation meant that Grades 1 to 3 would be taught either through the mother tongue or through the predominant local language.

From Grades 4 to 12, the medium of instruction is English, which is the official language through to tertiary education. Grade 4 is the transitional grade where learners are transitioned to being taught in English, while the mother tongue is used as a supportive language to teaching in English. However, this policy was viewed as problematic for both teachers and learners, according to the Ministry of Basic Education Sport and Culture (MBESC) (2003), as the policy did not explicitly state how local languages should be used in schools. Hence, there were discrepancies on how the language policy was implemented from region to region. In 2002, the Namibian government decided to revise this language policy in order to meet the current demands and emerging changes. In addition, the revised edition intends to make sure the policy intentions are clear and that every citizen of the country has access to education in their mother tongue as a human right. This revision is in line with what Planas and Setati-Phakeng (2014) indicated in their study, that language policies can be used as a means to address social inclusion, to help with integration, to ease historical tensions and to address the overvaluing of other languages.

Major changes that were made to the existing policy include the strengthening of mother-tongue instruction in pre-primary (Grades 1, 2 and 3) through material development, and pre- and in-service teacher training. However, the emphasis on a school, school board and parent community decision to offer English as the medium of instruction from Grade 1 must receive ministerial approval (MBESC, 2003, p. 3).

In 2008, a further language policy was drafted, and then implemented in 2010. This language policy reflects the same language policy as the original of 1992; however, schools wanting to offer English-medium instruction from Grade 1 upwards need ministerial approval and in addition, two languages should be included in the curriculum (Tötemeyer, 2010). Most schools in Namibia, especially those in urban areas, are multilingual and this factor has led to these schools requesting English as a language of learning and teaching (LoLT). According to Planas and Setati-Phakeng (2014), pedagogical and didactical challenges may occur in mathematics classrooms for learners who are deprived of using their mother tongue (home language). Implications are that this choice may reduce learner classroom participation and learning opportunities (ibid.), and also undermine their mother tongue and its culture. However, other schools, although multilingual, opted for the predominant local language.

Although after its introduction the policy stressed material development and pre- and in-service training in the mother tongue, junior primary teachers at the University of Namibia are trained in English. This issue is similar to Malawi, where the policy is silent on teacher educators using the local language in a college mathematics classroom, whereas teachers are required to use the local languages in their mathematics classroom (Chitera, 2010). In Namibia, this issue still prevails, despite the fact that teachers are required to teach in the mother tongue, including subjects such as mathematics, which to some extent has a unique terminology, some terms of which have not been explained nor translated into the mother tongue (Oshiwambo), and therefore are not recorded in the literature. Furthermore, most of the mathematics education and numeracy lecturers at the University of Namibia are non-Oshiwambo-speakers, while others are not fluent in the mother tongue, especially with regard to mathematics terminology. As a result, they may not have the knowledge to adequately teach the mathematical concepts in the mother tongue. In a study by Trewby et al. (2000), it emerged that most Namibian lower primary school teachers' knowledge of their mother tongue was limited, a situation that may lead to poor transmission of mathematical concepts.

This poor knowledge of the language has created a point of concern as one is faced with the question of how newly qualified teachers from the University of Namibia, whose formal mathematics education had been completed in English, find it possible to effectively implement the policy and teach mathematical concepts in Oshindonga, when they opt to teach at lower primary during their first few years of teaching. The paucity of literature on the challenges of teaching mathematics in the mother tongue is a concern, with most research reports focused on experienced teachers rather than on novice teachers, the latter being the focus of this study. With migration of people across regions in the country, classrooms are becoming multilingual and newly qualified teachers need to find ways to ensure all learner languages are considered without focusing only on a predominant local language (MBESC, 2003) which according to policy should be used. Teaching in a multilingual classroom requires pre-service teachers to acquire skills not only obtained through experience but also through some kind of formal enculturation (Essien, 2010, 2021). The skill acquired has an impact on how teachers successfully respond to the implementation of language policy in multilingual classrooms and how they position multilingualism. This situation demands further research as to how teacher training can improve mother-tongue competency in teachers, especially in the Namibian context in order to effectively use learner home language in teaching mathematics in multilingual classrooms. The present study contributes to this pertinent research issue in Namibia by investigating how newly qualified teachers view the implementation of the language policy when teaching mathematics without compromising quality teaching and learning, especially in multilingual classrooms. The research questions that informed this study were:

1. To what extent do newly qualified teachers use the mother tongue to teach mathematics at the lower primary level?
2. What challenges do junior primary novice teachers experience when using the mother tongue in their mathematics classroom?
3. What mechanisms do the newly qualified teachers employ to alleviate these challenges?

The above questions assisted in establishing what further research is required in the area of language in teaching and learning mathematics in the Namibian context, particularly with regard to multilingual classrooms and to the lessons that exist for teaching mathematics globally in the context of language diversity. In relation to this, Planas and Setati-Phakeng (2014) have argued that if priority is given to language-as-resource rather than language-as-problem and/or language-as-right, there might be a reduction in some of the unequal conditions of learning mathematics in multilingual classrooms. In answering these questions, we examined how the newly qualified teachers value the language policy and how they implemented it in their mathematics classroom.

Teaching and Learning of Mathematics in the Mother Tongue

The importance of teaching in the mother tongue has been emphasized in the Namibia language policy and in the literature, especially in teaching junior primary learners. However, language difficulties can hinder learner ability to solve mathematical word problems (Kazima, 2008). In addition, unclear, ambiguous language can impede learning of mathematical concepts. Setati et al. (2008) found that in most cases, learning becomes difficult when one is taught in a language that one does not understand well, and in this case, learners resort to learning by memorising facts, rather than engaging conceptually. This situation is more likely to occur in multilingual classrooms where some learners' mother tongue is not considered, especially in cases when a predominant language is used. Chitera (2010) avers that when a colonial language (foreign language) is used, learners in the classroom become quiet, obedient, learn to memorize, learn survival strategies and also learn that they are unlikely to succeed. Thus, language can bring education closer to people or drive them away from education (ibid.); that is to say, competency in a language removes some barriers to learning. In the same study, Chitera (ibid.) further explained that it is not only learners who face challenges when a foreign language is used but also teachers. Teachers are likely to encounter more challenges when explaining themselves in a foreign language than when using their mother tongue. According to Chauma (2012), it is thus of importance that the vocabulary and a glossary of mathematics in the mother tongue, as the medium of instruction, is available to teachers for them to become knowledgeable in teaching mathematical concepts. Furthermore, if a teacher has poor linguistic resources, it may lead to diminished developmental thinking and concept formation in learners. It is therefore important for teachers to be competent in a language of instruction to avoid such barriers. However, the question of how such mathematics teachers with poor linguistic resources assist learners in multilingual classroom, is a topic of concern since Essien (2018) has also emphasized that learners' mathematics sense-making is determined by various issues as many are influenced by the teacher's linguistic resources. These issues include: how learners understand the usage and structure of the language, how mathematics learning is shaped by the use of everyday language, how learners express mathematical thinking in their own language and how textbook language matches the language the teacher uses.

Despite the many advantages of teaching mathematics in a local language, there are also accompanying challenges such as the lack of a mathematics vocabulary in the mother tongue and difficulties with translations (Phatudi & Moletsane, 2013; Khejeri, 2014; Umar, 2018). The Khejeri (2014) study indicated that mother-tongue languages in the Hamisi District, Kenya, lack vocabulary, especially in mathematics and the arts, and this limitation has consequential effects on content processing, the quality of lessons, the pace of knowledge transfer and, importantly, the learning impact of mathematics. Chitera (2010) and Umar (2018) report that most teachers find translation and code-switching a challenge, particularly as they have to ensure that mathematical concepts are not misinterpreted or diluted. However, although code-switching was identified as a challenge, Setati (2002) has stressed the importance of code-switching as a relevant resource in teaching and learning in bilingual mathematics classrooms. Interestingly, research by Mouton (2007) has shown that a low level of language proficiency is one of the reasons why code-switching is widespread in Namibian classrooms, and because of poor linguistic levels in English, and/or the mother tongue, teachers tend to switch between languages. This view is supported by the McLachlan and Essien (2022) review of literature where it is argued that poor linguistic skills can have an effect on mathematical learning. McLachlan and Essien (2022) therefore suggest that further research be conducted to determine the effective use of code-switching in Namibian classrooms, particularly in multilingual mathematics classrooms and especially when teachers are reported to have poor language proficiency. However, Planas (2014) has observed that various research studies on language diversity and the learning of mathematics focus mostly on problems experienced by some linguistically diverse students rather than the opportunities offered and experienced. Other studies (Setati et al., 2008; de Jong et al., 2016) have argued for a shift to looking at language as a resource rather than language as a problem in order to facilitate the learning of mathematics.

Theoretical Framework

In this study, we draw on the work of the Ruiz (1984) on orientations to language, in order to guide our analysis and reflection on the implementation of the language policy by newly qualified teachers. Ruiz (ibid.) outlined three orientations to language planning which include language-as-problem, language-as-right and language-as-resource. These are a 'complex of dispositions toward language and its role, and towards languages and their role in society' (ibid., p. 16). All orientations have different perceptions toward language. The language-as-problem orientation considers the use of one dominant language by individuals for economic, political and social integration in their society, it does not support bi/multilingualism but rather sees it as a problem (ibid.; de Jong et al., 2016; McLachlan & Essien, 2022). In Namibia, this is evident in the language policy where schools are encouraged to opt for a predominant local language or English in cases where learners speak different mother-tongue languages, which then becomes difficult for the teacher to effectively ensure all learners understand because of diverse mother-tongue languages in the classroom. On the other hand, language-as-right encourages linguistic inclusion and guards against discrimination of individuals on the basis of language and that every citizen has the right to be taught in their mother tongue. Article 3 (1) of the Namibian Constitution states that: 'Namibia's official language shall be English,' but people who do not speak the official language are not denied the use of their mother tongue in administration, justice, education and public service. However, although this has been a matter of research in South Africa (McLachlan & Essien, 2022), it still needs to be established in Namibia with respect to multilingual classrooms as to how inclusion of various mother-tongue languages is being implemented.

Language-as-resource, simply put, focuses on the advancement of the marginalized language resources and on the preservation of the dominant language resource (de Jong et al., 2016). Planas (2018, p. 216) defines language-as-resource as: 'the potential of language to function in ways that dialectically produce and resolve tensions between languages of learners in cultures of school mathematics and the official language of instruction'. Thus, language-as-resource encourages multilingualism mainly to enrich classroom discussion (McLachlan & Essien, 2022), which brings out more learning. Various studies have called for multilingual classrooms to embrace instructional approaches that consider learners' home languages as resources for mathematics learning rather than as problems, because of the various benefits that the language-as-resource orientation has for learners (Planas & Setati-Phakeng, 2014; de Jong et al., 2016; Prediger & Uribe, 2021).

By examining the perceptions of newly qualified teachers with regard to the implementation of the language policy, this framework is necessary to allow researchers to see and explain how these teachers view the role of different languages in their mathematics classrooms as either an asset, problem or right. This view not only determines the effective implementation of the policy, but it could also be used to see how they position the LoLT as emphasized in the language policy.

Data Collection and Procedures

This study took place at ten primary schools located in the Oshana region of northern Namibia. Two schools with junior primary grades which use the mother tongue as a medium of instruction and which have a newly qualified teacher, were randomly selected from each of the five circuits. Among the schools that instruct in Oshiwambo, the researchers focused on schools that use the local language Oshindonga as the medium of instruction. Schools were located either in rural or urban environments. From each school, one novice teacher formed the sample of ten newly qualified junior primary school teachers. All schools selected had only one newly qualified teacher, which facilitated the selection. All teachers are university graduates and hold various teaching qualifications, with teaching experiences ranging from one year to three years.

Data for this study were collected by means of classroom observations as well as semi-structured interviews. Non-participant observation was used to observe all teachers while teaching mathematics in the vernacular/mother language for a period of five days, thus, one lesson per day. The choice of the language helped with the classroom observation in identifying how teachers were implementing the language policy, and the difficulties they experienced. In the case of non-participant observations, field notes were used for daily data records and other observations encountered in the field setting.

A semi-structured interview schedule with key questions was used during interviews to obtain in-depth insights into the participant's thoughts and beliefs and thus generate data, and thereby provide rich and explanatory responses. The individual interviews lasted roughly 40 minutes and were recorded using a voice recorder.

This research used thematic analysis which focuses on identifying important information from the data through a coding process and categorising it to identify the emerging themes which relate to the research questions. The aim of the analysis was to understand the data gathered and make sense of the collected data in relation to Ruiz's (1984) orientations to language, and answer the research questions.

Findings

Teachers' Perceptions of Teaching Mathematics in the Mother Tongue

Perceptions on policies has an influence on how teachers respond to their implementation. The study established two predominant views from the participants responses; positive views in teaching mathematics in the mother tongue and negative views. Another interesting finding indicates that teachers from different settings valued English and Oshindonga differently in relation to its benefit of enhancing the learning of mathematics in that particular setting. Positive perceptions were reported mostly by teachers teaching in rural areas, while negative views were reported by participants predominantly teaching in urban areas. These views are discussed in the next sections.

Positive Views on Teaching Mathematics in the Mother Tongue

A number of teachers agreed that teaching mathematics in the mother tongue can be beneficial to both the learners and the teachers. The main benefit that emerged from the interviews was the ease with which learners grasped concepts when the mother tongue is used. Participants believe that because familiar vocabularies are used in the mathematics classroom, it makes it easier for learners to understand concepts and relate them to everyday use. This indicates that learners are thus able to make connections between what they already know and what they are learning in the classroom. According to Planas and Ngoepe (2020), learners tend to participate meaningfully in mathematics content when talking in their home language, a language with which they are familiar. Participants reported that learning is enhanced since learners are using the language that they understand and commonly use. One participant indicated that teaching in the mother tongue really enhances understanding because if you are teaching the child about addition, for example, (given the sum 3+4) then you say to the learner '*gwe dha ko ne ku ndatu*' (add four to three), so the child will know and understand that now I have to '*gwe dha ko*' (I have to add four items to three items) because the learners are familiar with the word 'gwe dha ko' (add).

Another participant commented that it becomes easy for learners to read and understand mathematics problems when in Oshindonga. This promotes positive attitudes towards the learning of mathematics since the language used is familiar to learners, although there may be concepts that would be new to them and may require further explanation:

> It is the same language that they are using at home and it is the same language they use in the classroom, which means (most of) the vocabulary will be the same.
>
> T03

Participants further specified that teaching in the mother tongue provides learners with a chance to become confident and express their views without fear of being judged if they use poor language. The arguments were that learners in most cases, create their thinking in the mother tongue but when a foreign language is used, learners have to translate from their mother tongue into the foreign language. This translation may not always come out correctly, and hence they may be inclined to hold back on their participation. As observed during lesson presentations, there was more engaging participation within classrooms in rural areas since all learners speak the same mother tongue compared to classrooms in urban areas where classrooms are multilingual. However, in the urban classroom, this engaging participation only occurred after the teacher has code-switched or translated into the learners' language. This example indicates how language can be used to maximize discussions in the classrooms. Looking at all the benefits from the findings, one can see that teachers, although unknowingly, view the mother tongue as a pedagogical resource in enhancing learning in classroom.

Negative Views of Teaching Mathematics in the Mother Tongue

Participants also indicated concerns and fears of teaching mathematics in the mother tongue; these concerns are the negative effects on learners' learning. Emerged concerns include: concern about learners who do not understand the mother tongue being used in the classroom, concern about transmitting unclear concepts to learners, concern about disadvantaging learners in acquiring mathematical concepts in English for the next grade, concern about lack of a well-developed vocabulary and concern about the lack of a relationship between school mathematics vocabulary and home vocabulary.

Participants indicated that teaching in the mother tongue could disadvantage those learners who do not speak the mother tongue which is the LoLT at the school. Participants stressed that with multilingual classrooms in the Oshana region, the use of the local language as the LoLT might cause learning difficulties for learners who do not speak the language, and therefore may result in their understanding of mathematical concepts not being well developed. This concern sees language-as-problem and discriminatory towards leaners who do not speak the LoLT; however, the use of English here does not guarantee learning either as learners may not have developed English proficiency.

Another emergent concern related to the transmission of imprecise concepts to learners. Participants feared that since some mathematical concepts are not well defined in the mother tongue, teachers may wrongly explain concepts to learners as it may need translation into a language that the learners will understand. Some participants were concerned that because of a lack of properly developed vocabulary in the mother tongue, teachers may use different terms within the same mother tongue to teach the mathematical concepts:

> My concern is, you find two teachers from various schools using two mathematical terms which may be confusing to learners, for example for the shape cone, some teachers use the terms they were taught at their junior schools, some refers to it as 'oshubu (fish trap)' others as 'ombako (funnel)' and it is not clear which concept is acceptable.
>
> T02

Participants also felt that teaching learners in the mother tongue at junior primary level may have a negative effect for when they move into the upper grades where learners transition to a different language such as English which becomes the LoLT. This is because mathematical concepts in the mother tongue are not always similar to those in English and may bring about confusion in later grades. This relates to Setati's (2008) findings on teachers' language choices where most teachers preferred to use English as it was seen as an international language and thus could be used to prepare learners for participation in the international world. This aspect indicates how different languages can be concurrently located differently as resources within the same context (de Jong et al., 2016). In this study, although teachers recognize learners' mother tongue which in this case points to language-as-right, they use English as a resource for future learning.

Some participants indicated that one concern is a lack of alignment or congruence between the home language and the classroom language of mathematics. The teachers explained that some of the mathematical vocabulary used at home is not the same as that being used in the classroom or that appearing in the textbooks. Hence this is seen as a challenge in convincing learners as to why the other term is more appropriate to use at school. T01 stated that:

> At home kids are told is 'osipenitha' (five cents), at school they are taught 'oosenda ntano' (five cents), so there is not much connection between the words.

Concerns raised by the teachers on the use of the mother tongue can be placed under the influence of language-as-problem in the multilingual classroom rather than language-as-resource or as-right.

Challenges Experienced in Teaching Mathematics in the Mother Tongue

The findings emerging from the study uncovered various challenges that teachers in this study experience while teaching mathematics in the mother tongue to junior primary learners. Challenges differ from concerns because the participants have experienced these challenges, but not all concerns have been experienced by the teachers. Challenges include difficulty with Oshindonga mathematical concepts, lack of terminology in Oshindonga and challenges of translation between languages.

Most participants indicated that they experience difficulties explaining mathematical concepts in the mother tongue stating that certain mathematical concepts in the Oshindonga language were difficult to explain as they were not familiar with them. This aspect was also detected during observation where some teachers struggled to create well-structured word sums during the lesson. One of the word sums read: '*Tate okwa pendje oongaku omi29, meme ta gwedha po omu12, kumwe adhihe odhili ngapi?*' (My father gave me 29 shoes, my mother added 12 more how many shoes do I have all together?). The word '*omapando*' (*pairs*) was not considered here which affected how learners answered the question. Some learners considered 29 as 29 pairs of shoes so they doubled the number of shoes while others took this as 29 individual shoes. Another teacher who was teaching about adding two-digit numbers which suggests '*oonomola mbali + oonomola mbali*' (two numbers plus two numbers). Confusion about this arose amongst learners as some seem to understand it to mean digits that have a number 2, because when the teachers asked for a two-digit number, learners gave 12, 22, 42 and 62. In addition, there were those that gave examples such as 3 and 44, because these represent two numbers.

Another related challenge was that some mathematical concepts that do not have an exact translation to the mother tongue: some of these words are borrowed directly from English and do not exist in the mother tongue. Teachers have to explain these concepts in English, the language in which they were trained, to help develop understanding for their learners. The participant explained this at length:

> Let me say you are teaching about shapes, we have different shapes that we teach in Grade 1 and some of those shapes their names are directly translated from English to mother tongue, it is difficult to explain it to learners because sometimes a learner can ask 'Ms, what is oprisma yo lee' (what is a rectangular prism)? The word prism is in English but here we are using it as a mother tongue word, which it is not, while yo lee is in mother tongue, so to make learners understand you just do it in English.
>
> T03

According to Setati et al. (2008), there is a dichotomy created between the mother tongue and English that creates an impression that the use of the mother tongue for teaching and learning must necessarily exclude and be in opposition to English and vice versa. This has not been clearly specified in the language policy.

An additional challenge that emerged from the findings was translating concepts from English to Oshindonga as most teaching resources are written in English. Participants established that they do not have experience in translations since their use of the mother tongue, Oshindonga, is not well advanced to do an appropriate translation. Some concepts appear to have terminology in the mother tongue which leads to teachers not having a clear idea of which is appropriate to use since there is no common mathematics register in the mother tongue. The researchers observed that lack of textbooks in the mother tongue was evident in classrooms as the majority were in English. Hence, in these observed lessons, most teachers would make copies of activities from these English books and give it to learners without translating them into the mother tongue. Teachers would attempt to translate the activities to Oshindonga while learners were working on the activity. However, many struggled with the translation of concepts which in some cases, misled learners and led to wrong answers. Chitera (2010) also concluded that a major challenge with translation is ensuring that the mathematical content or concept is not diluted in the process or that the entire meaning is not lost. One of the examples observed was when a teacher asked: 'Which of the following has the similar height?' the teachers translated as '*Oyini ya faathana?*' '*faathana*' which can be translated to mean 'Which of the following are the same/alike?' This may not only refer to the height, and so a child may focus on other attributes other than height, which is the focus of the question. Another instruction asked learners to 'arrange the following in order', which the teacher translated as, '*tula me landulathano ewanawa*'. *Ewanawa* refers to beautiful/nice, so the teacher literally means 'arrange the following in a beautiful or nice order', which again led some learners to interpret the question differently. According to Chauma (2012), translation does not only involve the transferring of meaning from one language to another, it also involves the transferring of conceptual knowledge and thus it is a specialist skill that teachers need to be taught at their training institution. Thus, from the above observation, conceptual knowledge is lost due to poor knowledge of translation.

Some participants raised the challenge of teaching mathematical concepts in a multilingual classroom. Participants teaching in urban schools indicated that since classrooms have learners from various tribes and backgrounds, teaching in a mother tongue such as Oshindonga specifically, does not assist all learners in developing understanding of mathematical concepts. One participant, T08, indicated there are fewer Oshindonga-speaking learners in comparison to learners who speak other languages as the mother tongue. It is thus appropriate for them to use both languages, Oshindonga and English, to accommodate all learners:

> For me Oshindonga is not a problem, I was taught in Oshindonga for (most) of my life, the problem is when you say something in mother tongue and the whole class ask you what is that Sir? We don't understand anything. So then firstly, the terms used are already a problem, and secondly, the language of instructions is also a problem.
>
> T08

Although this may be a solution to the challenges, participants reported that when planning for lessons, they have to consider setting activities in both

English and Oshindonga, which is time-consuming. We have observed that most teachers preferred to use English rather than the mother tongue, particularly as English becomes the LoLT in the upper grades, it is easier to use in explaining concepts and also to include other learners in the learning process whose mother tongue is not the LoLT. This language decision is despite the fact that teachers know what is required by policy and the benefits of teaching in the mother tongue. This aspect was emphasized by de Jong et al. (2016) that English is still seen as the only resource for economic success at national level, despite the repositioning of local languages as intellectual, civil and cultural resource at regional level.

Another challenge observed that resulted from multilingualism was the use of informal language or commonly used home language. The researchers observed a case when a teacher using a poster during the introduction to the lesson, asked learners to name the pictures. Surprisingly, learners had various names which differed to those used in the classroom. As it appears, most of these challenges are a result of viewing language as a problem instead of viewing language as a resource as described by Planas and Setati-Phakeng (2014).

Coping Mechanisms

Participants were also probed to reflect on how they dealt with the challenges. Some participants were hesitant in explaining how they coped with the challenges, which could be the fear of being judged or perhaps it is just a lack of coping strategies to deal with such challenges. Coping strategies that emerged from the findings include the use of code-switching, assistance from colleagues, use of drawings and manipulatives, avoidance of difficult terminologies and the use of a range of textbooks.

Almost all teachers, except for two, reported to have used code-switching from Oshindonga to English as a coping mechanism. Code-switching was used for example when teaching topics such as measurement and geometry, where some terms directly translated into the mother tongue or do not have proper terms in the mother tongue. It means that some concepts are not easy to explain or teach in the mother tongue. Participant T01 indicated that code-switching was seen as a solution when they could not clearly express themselves in the mother tongue, particularly in teaching topics such as place value and money. Some teachers indicated that they practised code-switching to English to develop their learners' English mathematics vocabulary to prepare them for the next grade where they transition to being taught in English. Code-switching was observed as a common method in most classrooms but most prevalent in urban schools.

In some cases, teachers were observed using code-switching as a way of accommodating all learners in the learning process, since urban classrooms were mostly multilingual. This finding is supported by Phakeng (2016) who recognizes that most teachers use code-switching to ensure that they did not disadvantage their learners by depriving them of learning and knowing English and only focusing on the use of the mother tongue. It seems that only two languages were used by the teachers in their classrooms, Oshindonga and English, although they reported to have multilingual classrooms especially in urban areas. This implies other learners' mother-tongue languages were not considered which in a way deprives them of their rights. In addition, these learners whose mother tongue is not Oshindonga might not always understand English when the teachers translate or code-switch which creates a further problem for them.

Setati (2002) argued for the importance of code-switching as a relevant resource in teaching and learning in bilingual mathematics classrooms. Setati suggested that the learners' first language can act as a support needed to develop proficiency in the LoLT when learning mathematics, especially when the LoLT is not their first language. In a study by Essien (2010), findings indicated that teacher educators have encouraged pre-service teachers to code-switch as a teaching strategy on condition that learners are benefitting from it, but it should not be used as a strategy to enable pre-service teachers to switch to their comfortable language to communicate. Instead, we argue that code-switching should rather be used as a pedagogical resource to support the learning of mathematics and to preserve or sustain the mother tongue of learners whose mother tongue is not the LoLT.

A method that was observed as a coping mechanism was translation. Translation into English helped teachers ensure that learners who understand English and whose mother tongue was not Oshindonga, understand the mathematics content. It was also observed that most urban schools used English more frequently than Oshindonga.

Apart from code-switching and translation, all participants identified that they relied on their senior colleagues who have been in the field for a longer time, for assistance on how to teach some mathematical concepts in the mother tongue.

Teacher T08 also indicated her appreciation to colleagues:

> Honestly I feel like, coming to an Oshindonga medium of instruction school I really didn't think I would be at this stage, but I was helped by the colleagues, we plan together and they helped with language and when I am having difficulties then I can go there and ask questions like I don't understand this how do you put it in English or how do you put it in Oshindonga.

It is interesting to note that at times, most participants were more focused on getting the vocabulary right in Oshindonga than on how they could help learners understand the content.

Participants suggested that a good strategy is the use of drawings or pictures and concrete materials or manipulatives, to demonstrate mathematical concepts that they found challenging to explain. Using this as a teaching strategy helped the teachers overcome mathematical language challenges experienced in both English and/or in the mother tongue. T01 explained that she prepares the relevant teaching materials taking into account learners' context, using familiar pictures and also obtaining or constructing teaching aids that are from learners' environment that she knows would be effective to assist them in understanding the topic or the concept better, particularly if she is challenged in explaining it in the mother tongue. According to Moschkovich (2012), the use of aids encourages teachers not only to focus on developing conceptual understanding by giving definitions or by describing a procedure, but also in using multiple pictorial representations such as pictures, objects, symbols, tables and graphs. Moschkovich (ibid.), for example, used a picture of a rectangle as an area model to demonstrate how two fractions are equivalent or how multiplying a positive fraction by one makes the product smaller.

One interesting coping strategy that emerged from data is that when teachers were confronted with difficult or unfamiliar concepts, they avoided teaching the concepts until they could get assistance. Others reported that sometimes they would just entirely avoid teaching the concepts and hoped that learners would learn it in the next grades to avoid experiencing the embarrassment of their inexperience.

The last strategy was consulting a range of resources especially textbooks for various explanations of concepts. The teachers indicated that apart from consulting senior or veteran teachers, they resorted to consulting different mathematics textbooks. Most books are written differently and some have clearer information than others. Some textbooks use easier and have more understandable language than others. Thus, if teachers are not getting what they are looking for in one textbook, they would consult others which would give them an extensive understanding of that specific concept and a variety of ways to teach it.

Concluding Thoughts

Language plays a crucial role in the teaching and learning of mathematics and it is considered as a great resource that can help advance the learning and teaching of mathematics (Setati et al., 2008), as long as teachers are prepared to effectively use language for instruction. Although language can be considered as a resource in the advancement of the learning of mathematics, it was also observed as not being straightforward. One of the challenges teachers expressed in the implementation of the language policy was translation, which they use in an attempt to accommodate all learners in the learning of mathematics and also to comprehend content written in English. Despite this partly being a challenge, it also indicates how language is used as a resource and not as language as a problem.

Translation was mostly pertinent in urban area where the LoLT was not shared by all learners. However, translation remains a concern since participants were not exposed to the translation practices during their tertiary education.

Further research could look at the effectiveness of translation by teachers in teaching mathematics content. Our analysis indicates that some teachers were concerned about the lack of relationship between school mathematics vocabularies while others indicated the similarity between home language and school language which helps in the teaching of mathematics. Teachers need to understand that learning mathematics advances from informal language to more mathematically structured language and ultimately to academic mathematical language as they progress in the learning of mathematics (McLachlan & Essien, 2022). Thus, teachers need to understand the importance of the informal language as a starting point in the learning and teaching of mathematics, especially at lower primary level.

It is evident from our analysis that English and the language of the mother tongue are simultaneously positioned differently as a resource in the same context (de Jong et al., 2016). The mother tongue was positioned by the participants as a culture and intellectual resource while English as an international resource. Hence, this had an influence on how teachers used the two languages in teaching mathematics.

Using the language orientations framework, we have noticed that some novice teachers in urban area consider the LoLT as language-as-problem as it seems to bring about problems in their classrooms especially its lack of vocabulary in mathematics. Other than that, they see English as a language that brings benefits to their learners' learning of mathematics when explaining concepts (during code-switching) or when accommodating other learners with different mother-tongue languages in the lesson. However, in these multilingual classrooms, these 'other learners' mother-tongue languages remain unused as a resource since teachers only tend to use English or the LoLT. In relation to language-as-right, teachers also talk about teaching learners in English, which is the language of higher grades for which learners need to be prepared.

The findings of the study point to the restructuring of university teacher education for prospective junior primary teachers. A further recommendation is that a bilingual dictionary with the mathematical concepts for this phase be developed in Oshindonga and English. To implement each of these recommendations requires the involvement of experienced teachers, university lecturers and language specialists. The design of such a project, and its implementation, is seen as the way forward for mathematics education in Namibia. In addition, McLachlan and Essien (2022) have pointed to the use of translanguaging to serve the needs of multilingual classrooms instead of code-switching as it suggests that the languages with which leaners and teachers come to school are fluid and flexible.

References

Chauma, A. (2012). Teaching primary mathematical concepts in Chitumbuka: A quest for teacher education. *South African Journal of Higher Education, 26*(6): 1280–1295.

Chitera, N. (2010). Languages of learning and teaching in schools: An issue for research in mathematics teacher education? *Journal of Mathematics Teacher Education,* 14:231–246.

de Jong, E. J., Li, E., Zafar, A. M., & Wu, C. (2016). Language policy in multilingual contexts: Revisiting Ruiz's 'language-as-resource' orientation. *Bilingual Research Journal, 39*(3–4), 200–212.

Essien, A. A. (2010). What teacher educators consider as best practices in preparing pre-service teachers for teaching mathematics in multilingual classrooms. *Perspectives in Education, 28*(4), 32–42.

Essien, A. A. (2018). The role of language in the teaching and learning of early grade mathematics: An 11-year account of research in Kenya, Malawi and South Africa. *African Journal of Research in Mathematics, Science and Technology Education, 22*(1), 48–59. Doi: 10.1080/18117295.2018.1434453.

Essien, A. A. (2021). Understanding the choice and use of examples in mathematics teacher education multilingual classrooms. *ZDM – Mathematics Education, 53,* 475–488. Doi: 10.1007/s11858-021-01241-6.

Kazima, M. (2008). Mother tongue policies and mathematical terminology in the teaching of mathematics. *Pythagoras, 67,* 56–63. Doi: 10.4102/pythagoras.v0i67.74.

Khejeri, M. (2014). Teachers' attitudes towards the use of mother tongue as a language of instruction in lower primary schools in Hamisi District, Kenya. *International Journal of Humanities and Social Sciences, 4*(1), 75–85.

Makonye, J. P. (2015). What are student teachers' perceptions in the use of home languages in the teaching and learning of mathematics? *Journal Communication, 6*(1), 28–37.

McLachlan, K., & Essien, A. A. (2022). Language and multilingualism in the teaching of mathematics in South Africa: A review of literature in *Pythagoras* from 1994 to 2021. *Pythagoras, 43*(1), 1–11. Doi: 10.4102/pythagoras.v43i1.669.

Ministry of Basic Education, Sport and Culture (MBESC) (1993). *The language policy for schools, 1992–1996 and beyond.* Windhoek: Ministry of Education and Culture.

Ministry of Basic Education, Sport and Culture (MBESC) (2003). *The language policy for schools in Namibia.* Okahandja: NIED (National Institute for Educational Development).

Moschkovich, J. (2012). Mathematics, the common core, and language: Recommendations for mathematics instruction for ELs aligned with the common core. Presented at the Understanding Language Conference. University of California, Santa Cruz, CA. *Student Learning and Related Factors: Research Reports,* 304–310. Available online: https://files.eric.ed.gov/fulltext/ED584919.pdf (accessed 24 October 2018).

Mouton, B. D. (2007). The simultaneous use of two or more media of instruction in upper primary classes in the Khomas Educational Region. MA thesis, University of Namibia, Windhoek.

Phakeng, M. S. (2016). Mathematics education and language diversity. In A. Halai & P. Clarkson (eds), *Teaching and learning mathematics in multilingual classrooms: Issues for policy, practice and teacher education* (pp. 11–23). Rotterdam: Sense Publishers. Doi: 10.1007/978-94-6300-229-5_2.

Phatudi, N., & Moletsane, M. (2013). Mother tongue teaching through the eyes of primary school teachers in the North West Province of South Africa. *Journal of Educational Studies, 12*(1), 157–171.

Planas, N. (2014). One speaker, two languages: Learning opportunities in the mathematics classroom. *Educational Studies in Mathematics, 81,* 51–66.

Planas, N. (2018). Language as resource: A key notion for understanding the complexity of mathematics learning. *Educational Studies in Mathematics, 98*(3): 215–229.

Planas, N., & Ngoepe, M. (2020). From language as right to language as resources in mathematics. HAL Id: hal-02569003. https://hal.archives-ouvertes.fr/hal-02569003 (accessed 24 October 2021).

Planas, N., & Setati-Phakeng, M. (2014). On the process of gaining language as a resource in mathematics education. *ZDM – Mathematics Education, 46,* 883–893.

Prediger, S., & Uribe, Á. (2021). Exploiting the epistemic role of multilingual resources in superdiverse mathematics classrooms: Design principles and insights into students' learning processes. In A. Fritz, E. Gürsoy & M. Herzog (eds), Diversity dimensions in mathematics and language learning: Perspectives on culture, education and multilingualism (pp. 80–97). Berlin and Boston, MA: De Gruyter. Doi: 10.1515/9783110661941.

Ruiz, R. (1984). Orientations in language planning. *NABE Journal, 8*(2): 15–34.

Setati, M. (2002). Research mathematics education and language in multilingual South Africa. *Mathematics Educator, 12*(2), 6–20.

Setati, M. (2008). Access to mathematics verses to the language of power: The struggle in multilingual mathematics classrooms. *South African Journal of Education, 28*, 103–116.

Setati, M., Molefe, T., & Langa, M. (2008). Using language as a transparent resource in the teaching and learning of mathematics in a Grade 11 multilingual classroom. *Pythagoras, 67*, 14–25.

Tötemeyer, A. (2010). Multilingualism and language policy for Namibian schools. *PRAESA Occasional Papers* No. 37. Project for the Study of Alternative Education in South Africa (PRAESA), University of Cape Town. Cape Town: PRAESA.

Trewby, R., Van Graan, M., & Legere, K. (2000). *The implementation of the Namibian language policy in education: Lower primary grades and pre-service teacher education.* Windhoek: Namibia Educational Research Publication.

Umar, F. A. (2018). Teacher factors influencing use of mother tongue in teaching of Mathematics in lower primary schools in Yola south local government. MA thesis, Kenyatta University.

Part Two

Curriculum and Pedagogy Issues in Multilingual Education within Mathematics in Africa

5

Multilingualism Challenges in Mathematics Education in Morocco

Moulay Driss Aqil

Introduction

According to Sadiqi (2003) 'Morocco is a Berber, Arab, Muslim, Mediterranean and African country' (p. 17). Sitting as it does at the intersection of the Middle East, Europe and Africa, a multitude of languages have impacted on Morocco's culture throughout history. The Country's linguistic heritage includes Greek, French, Arabic, Spanish and Portuguese (Zouhir, 2013). As Calvet (1998) argues, despite a number of minority dominant languages, 'the languages that are statistically dominant are in fact languages that are politically and culturally subordinate' (p. 40). Zouhir (2013) has identified two categories in the Moroccan language 'arena': first, Moroccan Arabic and Berber, which comprise weak social and symbolic capital; and second, French, Standard Arabic and English, which have become institutional languages with strong social capital. Not surprisingly, there is a competitive struggle for dominance among all the languages, whether it is within each category or across categories (Boukous, 2009).

This chapter specifically engages with how aspects of this struggle have impacted mathematics education in Morocco since 1912, when it became a French Protectorate before becoming fully independent in 1956. The research informing this chapter supports a scholarly foundation for how mathematics is taught and studied in Morocco through a lens of cultural diversity. The particular focus for the chapter is on Arabization alongside the Arabic–French bilingual education tradition. Specifically, this chapter examines secondary mathematics textbooks with respect to the Arabization and Arabic-French bilingual education. New interpretations of this gaze on textbooks contribute to a deeper understanding of vital issues around mathematics education reforms centring on multilingualism and cultural diversity.

Early Learning in Morocco

One reason for the poor academic performance of children in schools in Morocco dates back to the years before a child even starts school – the lack of understanding and general neglect (by both parents and policymakers) of children's cognitive development (Young, 2009). How children develop is regarded as a private family concern throughout the Middle East and North Africa (MENA) region, resulting in extremely limited public investment in how children develop intellectually, cognitively and academically (Zellman et al., 2009; Zellman et al., 2011). Early childhood programmes are also limited, and those that exist may not offer high-quality care (Faour, 2010; Young, 2009). Faour (2010) noted that Pre-K programme enrollments are generally low in the Arab countries. One consequence of this, and a general lack of investment in pre-school provision is that important research on how the brain develops, and how critical a child's preschool years are to establish the foundation for future education, is under-recognized (Fox et al., 2010; Heckman, 2011).

Qualitative research in Casablanca, Morocco revealed that parents often do not consider the first years of a child's life as fertile ground for learning and development (Zellman et al., 2014). These researchers found that parents even believed that it was inappropriate to expose children to great amounts of stimulation in their first few years after birth because they felt their young, immature brains could not handle processing all that information. Parental beliefs such as this directly contradict a large body of research that supports the idea that parents have a critical role in molding their young children's capabilities, in terms of developing the kind of cognitive and non-cognitive skills (i.e. self-control, perseverance, self-esteem) that impact overall academic success and even later adult achievement (e.g. Heckman, 2011; Duckworth & Quinn, 2009; Peterson & Seligman, 2004). Brain research has also identified that the first years of a child's existence lay the groundwork and support for learning throughout the child's life (Fox et al., 2010; Melhuish, 2004; Sylva et al., 2010). Growing up in a home that values reading and exposes the child to books lends to improved literacy outcomes (Totsika & Sylva, 2004). Although research on these topics in Morocco is limited, local findings have echoed all of these realities. Wagner and Spratt (1988), for example, conducted a longitudinal study tracking parental involvement and child achievement in Morocco. They found that parents who acted as teachers of their children in the early years and whose attitudes about their involvement were positive produced better readers, even at ages 6 and 7. Hence, early learning and parenting among other influences play a major role in how children deal with the linguistic challenges in school and in their daily lives.

The Conflict between Arabization and French-Standard Arabic Bilingualism

Many scholars argue that language and culture are intimately intertwined, even inseparable. Fairclough (1992) affirmed, for example, that 'language use reflects culture and it is impossible to dissociate the two in any real sense' (p. 6). Others have also addressed the concept of the reflectivity of culture through language. For example, Tsui and Tollefson (2007) argued that 'the relationship between language policy and national cultural identity is dialectical' (p. 7). That is to say, any change in language policy – which is an interdisciplinary academic field – may have a decisive impact on national and cultural identities. Given the connection among Standard Arabic, Islam and nationalism, recent moves towards Arabization may be viewed as a sign that the Arabic language and culture have been revived.

Currently, Morocco is confronting the need to become bilingual, whether by choice or mandate. Like many other emerging nations, Morocco as a matter of choice or not, is working to integrate bilingual education programmes into its secondary school system. However, an inevitable conflict has arisen between the country's desire to preserve its authentically Arab identity through that language and culture versus the powerful call to enter the 21st-century world by retaining a modern foreign language, specifically, in this instance, French.

The complications underlying the issue of Arabization are not only about language but also about politics and ideology. Opposition parties and Islamists use Arabization as a tool to gain power in the political arena. Scholars addressing the ideological connections argue that the policy of Arabization will create unequal opportunities for students. According to Moustaoui (2007), choosing Arabic as the official language of the country is thus, principally a political act (p. 129). Fitouri (1983) claimed that until the idea of Arabization is fully adopted, bilingualism and biculturalism will remain controversial issues and moreover, that such a narrow system will lead to school failures and, ultimately, the recreation of the kind of elitism that was prevalent under the French colonial rule. The debate focused on language in fact thus reverberates with implications for citizenship, government policy, religion, national identity and culture. Political opponents, religious leaders and those in the lower social classes – dubbed Arabizants – have all utilized Arabization as part of a hidden agenda to re-establish collective rights, social justice and equal opportunities for all. However, French-educated Moroccans hold positive attitudes toward French-Standard Arabic bilingualism, arguing that Arabizants wish to uphold 'traditional ideas that perpetuate backward and irrational thinking in the country' (Ennaji, 2005, p. 2). French-educated Moroccans also believe that French-Arabic bilingualism will add new vocabulary through the act of translation or transfer that will in fact make Arabization stronger. To this end, Ahmed Lakhdar-Ghazal (1976), a lexicographer and former director of the Institute of Arabization in Rabat, argued that bilingualism is key if Standard Arabic is to become a modern language. As he wrote, Arabic 'should ideally be modeled on French and follow its example as a language of modernity' (p. 64). As a reflection on this idea, Ennaji (2002) observed the following:

> A linguistic conflict exists between Classical/Standard Arabic and French, the two prestigious languages in the country. The predominance of French is manifested essentially in education, administration, industry, banking, and commerce. French has been maintained for instrumental purposes and for building contacts with the West in general. It is the vehicle of science, technology, and modern culture. The predominance of French implies that the chances of strengthening the place of Classical/Standard Arabic are reduced; as a matter of fact, it is still confined to restricted domains like formal traditional speeches, religious discourse, as well as literary and cultural aspects.... The supremacy of French in the modern sector has not resulted in negative reactions by the Moroccans, most of whom believe the French-Standard Arabic bilingualism is the best option for the development of the country.
>
> p. 3

Even the late king of Morocco Hassan II believed firmly that bilingualism would assure the success of Arabization, stating in a 1978 speech in Ifrane that 'if Arabization is a duty, bilingualism is a necessity'. Ennaji (2009) pointed out the ubiquity of French even in the shadow of Arabization efforts:

> Despite decades of Arabisation, French is still used in education, administration, and the private sector. The efforts of Arabising the educational system have not succeeded for three main reasons: (i) the place of French is still very strong in key socioeconomic sectors; (ii) the ruling elite holds negative attitudes toward Arabisation and the way it has been politicised and implemented, and (iii) the official language policy has been inconsistent, and as a result there seems to be no plan to Arabise higher education.
>
> p. 17

Efforts were made by the Moroccan government for Standard Arabic to compete with French; however, some feared that 'French will always be predominant, and Standard Arabic marginalized' (Ennaji, 2002, p. 8). Along these lines, Chakrani's (2013) study of language attitudes showed that:

> The higher the social class, the more likely respondents are to hold favorable attitudes towards French and the increasing use of English and move away from the local code of Moroccan Arabic, Standard Arabic, and Berber.
>
> p. 431

Considering all these expressed reservations about Arabization and the negative attitudes of students and teachers towards Arabization, I believe it will be worthwhile to get a closer look in the next section at how this manifests in the Arabized mathematics textbooks used in the secondary schools. Some excerpts from selected textbooks are briefly analysed in an effort to assess how they might impact students' learning of mathematics.

Analysis of Secondary Mathematics Textbooks and Mathematical Symbols

Using one language as the medium of instruction is successful in some countries. However, in historically multilingual societies such as Morocco, education based on one medium of instruction can ultimately be problematic. While the goal of Arabization was to spread Arabic by suppressing French and other local languages, such as colloquial Arabic and Tamazight, its weakness was clear: Policymakers had not considered that Arabic required a completely new terminology to teach Mathematics, science and technology before even trying to implement Arabization.

To exemplify the lack of mathematical symbols and key terms in Arabic, I provide illustrations from secondary mathematics textbooks (see Figures 5.1 and 5.2). The motivation behind selecting these textbooks is the difficulty of making sense of the mathematical content written with two languages that read in opposite directions, especially when mathematical symbols are involved. Involving mirrored symbols make the task even harder. The high school textbook (Figure 5.1a), for example, reveals that most of the content and illustrations are expressed in the French language. Such an examination of just a few pages of secondary-level mathematics books uncovers a number of anomalies. Arabic is read from right to left and French from left to right. This so-called 'Arabized' secondary mathematics contains code switching and symbol borrowing. Furthermore, Arabic is used descriptively as connection words, while most of the mathematical content is in French. Note that equations and functions appear as they are typically rendered in French. This is a total aberration. Both teacher and student must read the Arabic from right to left and the French in the reverse order. How is this Arabization?

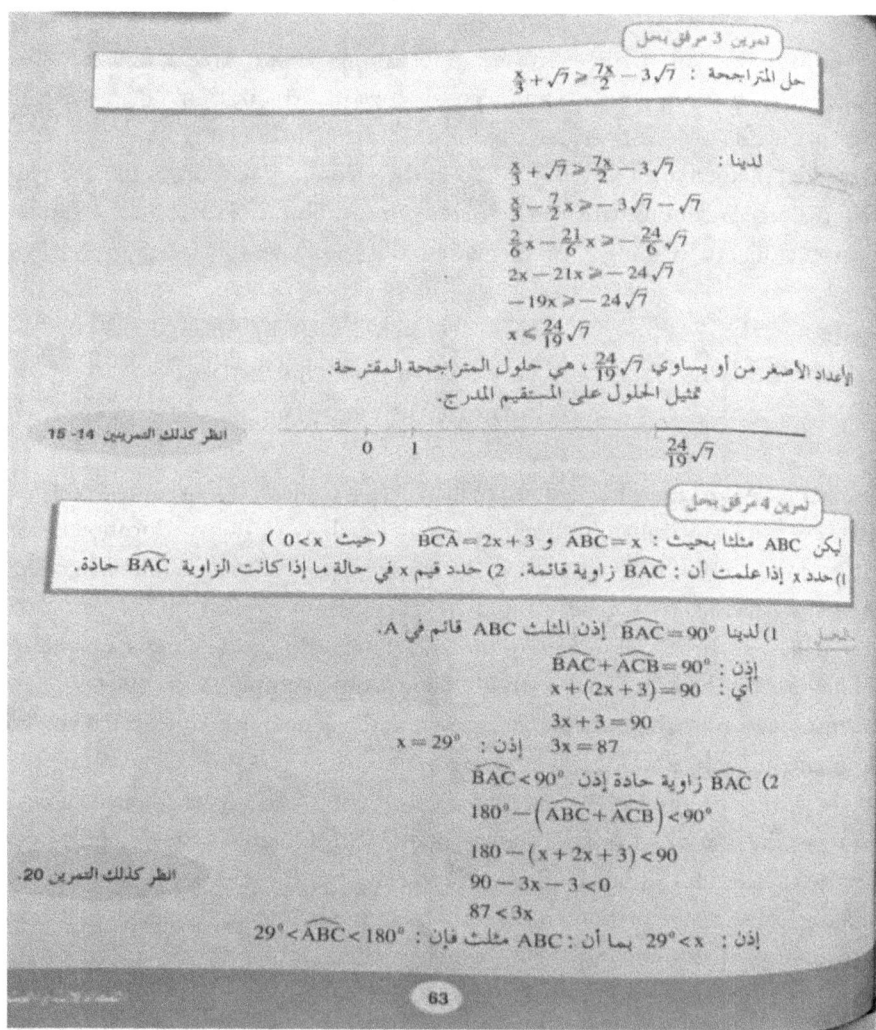

Figure 5.1a Jayid (2012 edition) الرياضيات كتاب التلميذ (ة) السنة الثالثة من التعليم الثانوي المفيد في الإعدادي (What's interesting in mathematics, the book of the student, third year secondary preparatory). *Source*: Hakani, Fahmi, Ghazaili and Bouzite (2012, p. 63). Reproduced with permission of Dar Attakafa.

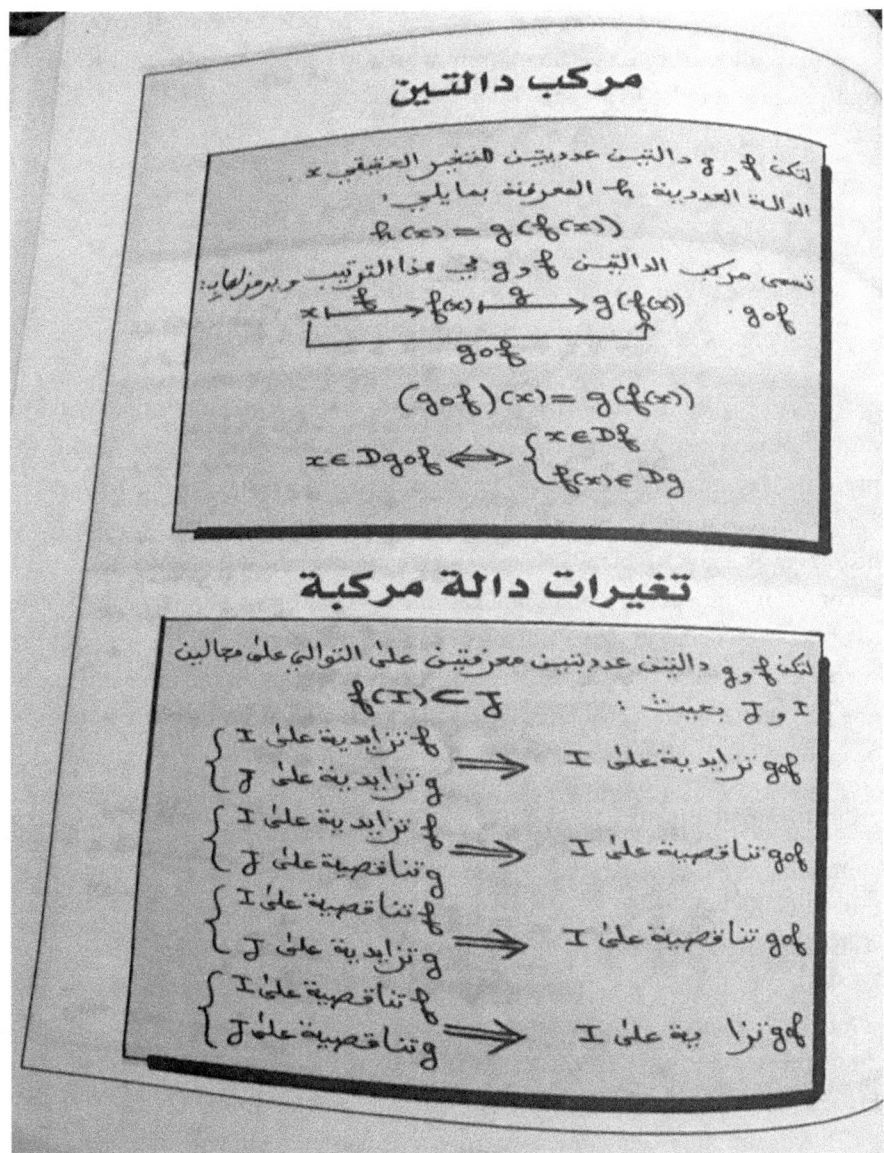

Figure 5.1b (Mathematics analysis, problems and solutions, first year of baccalaureate). *Source*: Hakani and Ghazaili (2012 edn, p. 123). Reproduced with permission of Dar Attakafa.

Let us read the last sentence in Figure 5.1a. To help the reader, arrows have been placed to indicate the direction in which to read this sentence (LR: left to right; RL: right to left):

29<ABC<180	مثلث فإن	ABC:	أن بما	29 < x:	إذن
⟶	⟵	⟶	⟵	⟶	⟵
LR	RL	LR	RL	LR	RL

If the same sentence were written in English, it would be:

Therefore: 29<x since ABC a triangle then 29<ABC<180

To read this sentence, which is considered Arabic Mathematics, we need to move from right to left. In between, if the word(s) is(are) written in Arabic, we must read from right to left. But if the word(s) is(are) written in French, we must read from left to right. This means that a back-and-forth movement is required just to cover a few Arabic words to describe mathematical French content. This becomes an unnecessary and cumbersome process that a student would have to undergo in order to figure out a way to read the material and reason out the correlation between the two languages. Unfortunately, this is but one sentence of one page; it becomes a challenge for teachers and students to apply this method of reading to each topic and, essentially, the entire book in each mathematics class the student must undertake in his educational career – both primary and secondary levels. This chapter highlights only a few random pages from different commonly used secondary mathematics textbooks in public schools to illustrate this challenge (Figures 5.1 and 5.2).

In Figure 5.1b, the beginning of the sentence reads from right to left. Upon reaching the braces, we must read from left to right because of the 'imply' symbol. Mathematically, this is sensible, yet it is a violation of Arabic reading direction (right to left). In this case, it seems that whenever Arabic is between French mathematical words, one needs to read from left to right.

This is another illustration of the inconsistency inherent in so-called Arabization. This 'search' for how to read the languages on the page prevents both student and teacher from focusing on the content and concept. To avoid this type of literacy problem, I contend that the text should be rendered in only one language, not both.

Now, consider another inconsistency in Figure 5.2a.

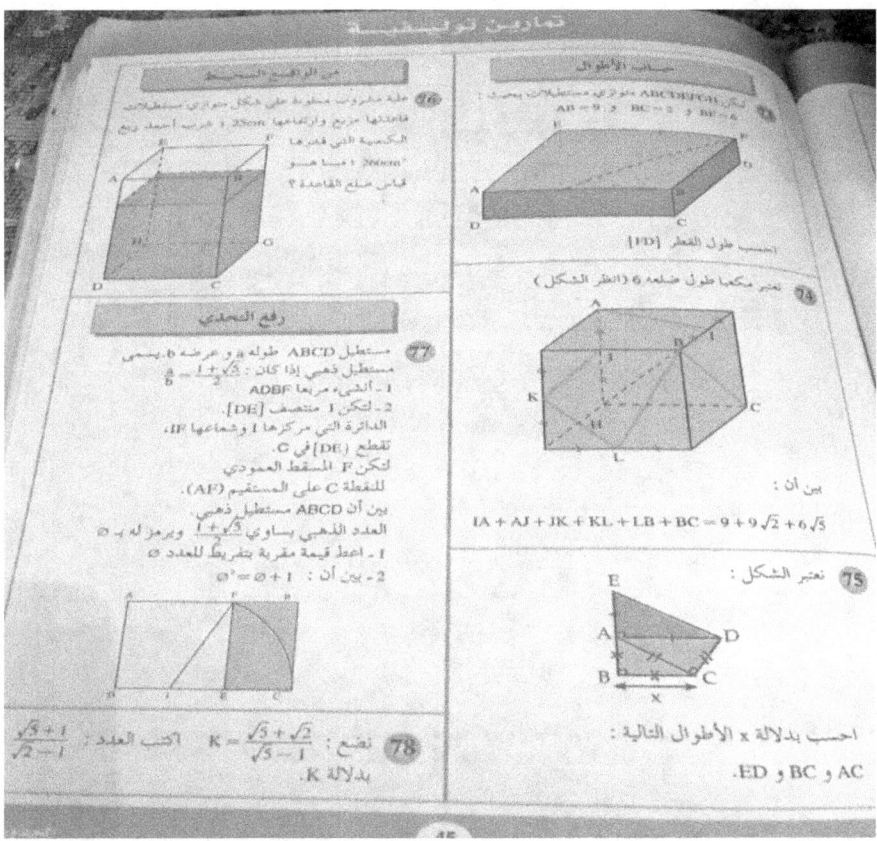

Figure 5.2a المفيد في الرياضيات كتاب التلميذ (ة) السنة الثالثة من التعليم الثانوي الاعدادي (What's interesting in mathematics, the book of the student, third year secondary preparatory). *Source*: Hakani, Fahmi, Ghazaili, Bouzite and Jayid (2012 edn, p. 45). Reproduced with permission of Dar Attakafa.

In the exercise labelled #75 in Figure 5.2a, Arabic is again read from right to left and French from left to right, but Arabic commas are inserted between the sides AC, BC and ED, with a period at the end of ED. This forces the reader to read the full question from right to left, including the French parts – thereby violating the reading of French. It becomes apparent how these inconsistencies can confuse and hinder learning and instruction. Exercises 5 and 6 in Figure 5.2b seem easier to decipher, even though French and Arabic are typically used jointly.

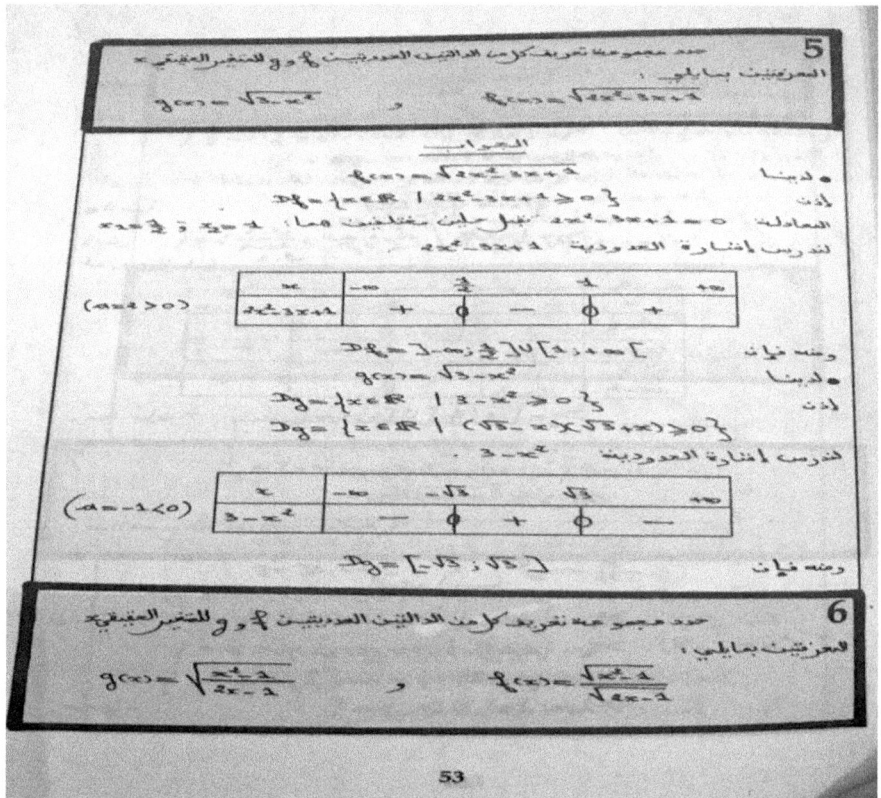

Figure 5.2b الرياضيات التحليل تمارين وحلول السنة الأولى من سلك البكالوريا (Mathematics analysis, problems and solutions, first year of baccalaureate). *Source*: Hakani, Ghazaili (2012 edn, p. 53). Reproduced with permission of Dar Attakafa.

Mathematical Symbols and Notations Mirroring

Right-to-left mathematical directionality is related to mirroring, as noted above with the Latin notations. Mirroring means that mathematical symbols and notations, as a result of right-to-left writing, are adapted accordingly. An example is below:

LTR symbol	Mirrored RTL symbol
∈	∋
→	←
≤	≥
∫	∫

Σ		Ƹ
LTR symbol	Incorrect RTL Mirroring	Mirrored RTL symbol
¢	₽	₫

Below is an example of mathematics in Arabic using mirrored symbols, which allows all the lines to be read from right to left, as Arabic reads:

$$\left. \begin{array}{c} \text{Ƹ}_{\text{س}=1}^{\text{س}} \quad \text{س} \cdot \text{ س} \mid \text{إذاكان} \mid > 0 \\ \text{ظٰπ} \quad \text{س}^{\text{س}} \text{دس} \mid \text{إذاكان} \mid \text{س} \text{ع} \text{3م} \end{array} \right\} = \text{ات}(\text{س}) $$
$$ \text{غير ذلك } (\text{س}| \pi \geq 2,141) $$

Other Arab countries have progressed in the realm of Arabized mathematical notations. Saudi Arabia, for example uses Arabic-Indic numerals and Arabic alphabets but borrows Latin symbols and switch their direction (creating a 'mirror' image of the symbol) so that reading right to left for the Arabic can be maintained. This is a good step toward efficiency, but for Arabization to succeed for its students in the complex area of mathematics, much more thoughtful research should be done. For Arabization to be complete and essential 'self-sufficient' as a language of mathematical instruction, it should have its own symbolic language and vocabulary, free of any Latin notations – even mirrored ones (see Table 5.1).

Table 5.1 Different forms of sums of cubic roots

Latin	Arabic	mirrored Latin
$\sum_{x=0}^{n} \sqrt[3]{x}$	$\underset{\text{س}=\cdot}{\overset{\text{ن}}{\text{جــ}}} \sqrt{\text{س}}$	$\underset{\text{س}=0}{\overset{\text{ن}}{\text{Ƹ}}} \sqrt[3]{\text{س}}$

Table 5.2 depicts some Arabic mathematical notations for limits, functions, partial derivatives and integrals, including mirrored symbols for the last two. Table 5.3 shows Latin inverse trigonometric functions and Arabic inverse trigonometric functions, which are free of mirrored Latin notations. However, in the case of Morocco French, the use of the mathematical language works in conjunction with Arabic.

Table 5.2 Arabic mathematical limits, functions, derivatives and integrals notations

Description	Arabic
Limit	نهــا
Function	د(س)
Derivatives	د'(س) ، ص' ، ص'ّ ، د⁶ص/دس⁶
Integrals	∫ . ∬ . ∭ . ∮

Table 5.3 Arabic inverse trigonometric functions

Latin	sin⁻¹	cos⁻¹	tan⁻¹	cot⁻¹	sec⁻¹	csc⁻¹
Arabic	جا⁻¹	جتا⁻¹	ظا⁻¹	ظتا⁻¹	قا⁻¹	قتا⁻¹

While modern Standard Arabic is the official or national language in most Arabic countries and presents a uniform writing system, writing formulas is not well standardized. For example, in Morocco, formulas are written left to right while in other Arabic countries they are right to left, as seen below:

Saudi Arabia	Morocco
― ٣س + ٣	-3x + 3
√س + ٣	x + 3

Notice that Morocco uses European numerals while Saudi Arabia uses Arabic-Indic numerals. The three set of numbers are considered in Table 5.4.

Table 5.4 Three sets of numbers

	European	0	1	2	3	4	5	6	7	8	9
	Arabic-Indic	٠	١	٢	٣	٤	٥	٦	٧	٨	٩
	Eastern Arabic-Indic	٠	١	٢	٣	۴	۵	۶	٧	٨	٩

Discussions

Arabic's limitation in filling the educational needs of Morocco's students led the populace to maintain the use of French in conjunction with Arabic. In the same vein, by the time the Arabized student reached higher education, the only language used in the universities is strictly the French language. Consequently, researchers attempted to improve Arabic's terminology, but Arabic often requires the use of numerous words to convey one word in French. This translation issue only stirred up more confusion and vagueness in the precision of the language and diluted the intended power of the Arabization policy.

If the issue of Arabization concerns preserving cultural identity, certainly Figures 5.1 and 5.2 do not represent such. Policymakers are well aware that prior to Arabization students were thriving, well informed bilinguals. Why not return to a time when French was dedicated to mathematics and Arabic to the humanities and social sciences. Learning mathematics with a hybrid of Arabic and French seems counterproductive in many ways, not the least of which is that their opposite directions, symbolically and literally, cancel each other out.

The confusion was magnified by the undercurrent of this movement – that students were unprepared to handle French in school. They were restricted from becoming adequately proficient in French to pursue it in more complex fields of scientific study, such as mathematics. Consequently, educational standards weakened significantly as students grappled primarily with French and then with scientific subject matter.

It is a long-held Moroccan custom to speak French more fluently than Arabic because of its social resources. Thus, financially comfortable parents ascertained that their children would be more skilled in French than Arabic, given that French has always been the prevalent language of business and trade in Morocco. Arabization was also intended to restore the Moroccan Arab-Islamic cultural identity free of all Western contamination. As pointed out at the outset of this paper, Arabization policymakers have always ignored the historical linguistic diversity of Morocco. This compelled Tamazight speakers, for example, to emerge as a force to preserve their language and winning this battle in 2011.

As an increasing number of dual language schools emerge, demand for bilingual education researchers who can steer programme-evaluation research and enhance more effective forms of dual language programmes are needed. Such an evolution of the model may lead to even higher achievement, but researchers may also detect less effective forms of implementation.

Concluding Thoughts

Recommendations

Several recommendations arise from the points made in this chapter which I now offer policy-makers and professional educators and teachers.

Recommendations to Policymakers and Reformers

As this chapter has sought to reveal, Arabization of mathematics in Morocco has many shortcomings. Without any plan to extend Arabization beyond postsecondary or provide mathematical terminology in Arabic, French seemed to be permanently in place. However, in this global age, language barriers only isolate cultures from each other and shut the door on increasingly broadening education and employment opportunities. The flow of information today is governed by world knowledge, not by one ruling power or one language. Most importantly, adopting French in Morocco will help reinstate a generation of Moroccan intellectuals proficient in French to contribute to the Moroccan educational system.

At the same time, the continued use of the national language of Arabic in Moroccan schools should be fostered to preserve national culture and heritage. My own recommendation would be to return to teaching mathematics in French as prevailed during the 1960s and 1970s, while the Arabic language at the time was used primarily for the humanities. If, however, the decision is that Arabic be used in the teaching of mathematics, then the following steps would need to be achieved simultaneously:

1. Terminology and mathematical symbols in Arabic (as well as the Amazigh language) need to be created. The indigenous language must not only be taught and used in primary and secondary levels, but also taught properly at all educational levels. An Arabization policy impacting scientific topics can only apply to the Moroccan educational system when Arabic is equipped with a total set of mathematical terminology and symbols that are free of French, borrowed symbols, switched codes, mirroring, both verbally and in print.
2. More research is needed in the Arabic language to cope with all levels of education, including the tertiary level. To bring this about, it is important to learn from the Golden Islamic Middle Age era when Greek mathematics was translated into Arabic. The new focus should be translating Western

scientific research into Arabic. Arabization will not succeed without accurate translations of Western research into pure Arabic.
3. Authorities should ensure that enough faculty members are available to teach scientific topics in Arabic for all levels of education. This then implies that they must provide appropriate teacher training programmes. Specialists in the mother tongue in this lexical committee should be consulted. The use of the mother tongue and mathematical language should be prioritized. Textbooks writers, publishers, and curriculum planners should collaborate with mathematics experts around the world to produce standard texts in mathematics in the mother tongue. As well, society in general should become educated on the need to support mother tongue initiatives related to mathematics instruction while relying on the opinions of teachers, students, and parents on any number of issues.

Recommendations to Professional Educators and Teachers

Language ideologies are integral to teacher education programmes and language policy discussions around creating equitable multilingual education. Teacher education programmes should engage teachers in collaborative ethnographies of language socialization and translingual practices as well as ideological analyses of language practices related to multilingual education.

Recommendations for Further Research

An important goal of linguists is to advocate for stronger forms of bilingual education to fulfill the responsibility of a language learning policy as a resource. Key questions emerging from the language as resource orientation include discovering how to facilitate language maintenance among linguistic minority communities. More branching of frames as resource orientations are needed to clarify how linguistic diversity relates to national unity and what differences exist between how the dominant national language and minority languages are viewed as resources. What ideological and implementation spaces are present in policies that allow for developing educational programmes that expand students' bi-/multilingual repertoires? In addition, how do educational programmes and curricula facilitate the development of intercultural understanding and lifelong bi-/multilingualism?

New ways of understanding the dynamics of bilingualism and multilingualism, particularly within the classroom context, can provide alternative opportunities for language learning and teaching. For instance, translanguaging is increasingly used to sustain the dynamic languaging of students. Given that French is read from left to right and Arabic from right to left, one question for future research is to examine how translanguaging affects students' cognition in learning mathematics when dealing with two languages that must be read in opposite directions.

In considering language conflicts between Moroccan ethnic groups, further research can focus on whether the re-adoption of the French colonial language in Morocco will eliminate ethnic conflicts and restore the educational Moroccan system. Also, since the Tamazight language has now been recognized as an official language in Morocco although its future is still unknown, researchers can determine if teaching mathematics in the Tamazight language will suffer similar consequences at the tertiary level as Arabization did.

This chapter may help practitioners understand how multilingualism and cultural identity affect mathematics education, which in turn can open avenues of investigation for mathematics education researchers and prompt meaningful school reforms reflecting concerns about rigor, relevance, reasoning and sense-making, particularly in relation to high school level mathematics education.

References

Boukous, A. (2009). Globalization and sociolinguistic stratification in North Africa: The case of Morocco. In C. B. Vigouroux & S. S. Mufwene (eds), *Globalization and language vitality: Perspectives from Africa* (pp. 127–141). London: Continuum.

Calvet, L. (1998). *Language wars and linguistic politics*. Trans. M. Petheram. Oxford: Oxford University Press.

Chakrani, B. (2013). The impact of the ideology of modernity on language attitudes in Morocco. Available online: http://www.tandfonline.com/doi/abs/10.1080/13629387.2013.791613?src=recsys&journalCode=fnas20 (accessed 22 March 2020).

Duckworth, A. L., & Quinn, P. D. (2009). Development and validation of the Short Grit Scale (GRIT–S). *Journal of Personality Assessment, 91*(2), 166–174.

Ennaji, M. (2002). Language contact, Arabization policy and education in Morocco. In A. Rouchdy (ed.), *Language contact and language conflict in Arabic* (pp. 1–27). London: Routledge / Curzon.

Ennaji, M. (2005). *Multilingualism, cultural identity, and education in Morocco*. New York: Springer.

Ennaji, M. (2009). Multiculturalism, citizenship, and education in Morocco. *Mediterranean Journal of Educational Studies, 14*(1), 5–26.

Fairclough, N. (1992). *Critical language awareness*. London: Longman.

Faour, B. (2010). Mapping early childhood services and programmes in Arab countries. The Regional Consultative Workshop on Advancing the ECCD Agenda in the Arab Region, ECCD = Early Childhood Care and Development, United Nations Educational, Scientific, and Cultural Organization (UNESCO). Available online: https://www.academia.edu/3196088/Paper_presented_at_the_Regional_ Consultative_Workshop_on_Advancing_the_ECCD_Agenda_in_the_Arab_Region (accessed 25 March 2010).

Fitouri, C. (1983). *Biculturalisme, bilinguisme et education* (Biculturalism, bilingualism and education). Neuchâtel and Paris: Delachaut et Nestlé.

Fox, S. E., Levitt, P., & Nelson III, C. A. (2010). How the timing and quality of early experience influences the development of the brain's architecture. *Child Development, 81*(1), 28–40.

Hakani, A., & Ghazaili, M. (2012) لرياضيات التحليل تمارين وحلول السنة الأولى من سلكا البكالوريا (Mathematics analysis, problems and solutions, first year of baccalaureate). Casablanca: Dar Attakafa.

Hakani, A., Fahmi, M., Ghazaili, M., Jayid, M., & Bouzite, N. (2012). المفيد في الرياضيات كتاب التلميذ (ة) السنة الثالثة من التعليم الثانوي الاعدادي (What's interesting in mathematics, the book of the student, third year secondary preparatory). Casablanca: Dar Attakafa.

Heckman, J. (2011). The economics of inequality: The value of early childhood education. *American Educator, 35*(1), 31–47.

Lakhdar-Ghazal, A. (1976). *Méthodologie générale de l'Arabisation du niveau* (General methodology of level Arabisation). Rabat: L'Institut d'Études et de Recherches pour l'Arabisation (IERA), Université Mohammed V de Rabat.

Melhuish, E. C. (2004). A literature review of the impact of early years provision on young children, with emphasis given to children from disadvantaged backgrounds. National Audit Office. Available online: https://ro.uow.edu.au/cgi/viewcontent.cgi?article=2678&context=sspapers (accessed June 2020).

Moustaoui, A. (2007). Minorizacion, desigualdad, y política lingüística en Marruecos (Minoritization, inequality, and language policy in Morocco). *Universidad Autónoma de Barcelona. AM, 14*, 129.

Peterson, C., & Seligman, M. E. P. (2004). *Character strengths and virtues*. Oxford University Press.

Sadiqi, F. (2003). *Women, gender and language in Morocco*. Leiden: Koninklijke Brill.

Sylva, K., Melhuish, E., Sammons, P., Siraj-Blatchford, I., & Taggart, B. (2010). *Early childhood matters: Evidence from the Effective Pre-School and Primary Education Project*. London and New York: Routledge.

Totsika, V., & Sylva, K. (2004). The home observation for measurement of the environment revisited. *Child and Adolescent Mental Health, 9*, 25–35.

Tsui, A. B. M., & Tollefson, J. W. (2007). Language policy and the construction of national cultural identity. In A. B. M. Tsui & J. W. Tollefson (eds), *Language policy, culture and identity in Asian contexts* (pp. 1–21). Mahwah, NJ: Lawrence Erlbaum.

Wagner, D. A., & Spratt, J. E. (1988). Intergenerational literacy: Effects of parental literacy and attitudes on children's reading achievement in Morocco. *Human Development, 31*, 35–69.

Young, M. E. (2009). *Early childhood development: Critical path to economic growth: An overview of ECD in the MENA region.* Washington, DC: World Bank.

Zellman, G. L., Martini, J., & Perlman, M. (2011). *Identifying Arabic-language materials for children that promote tolerance and critical thinking.* TR-856-OSD. Santa Monica, CA: RAND Corporation.

Zellman, G. L., Perlman, M., & Karam, R. (2014). How Moroccan mothers and fathers view child development and their role in their children's education. *International Journal of Early Years Education, 22*(2), 197–209.

Zellman, G. L., Ryan, G. W., Karam, R., Constant, L., Salem, H., Gonzalez, G. C., Goldman C. A., Al-Thani, H., & Al-Obaidli, K. (2009). *Implementation of the K-12 education reform in Qatar's schools.* MG-880-RAND Corporation. Santa Monica, CA: RAND Corporation.

Zouhir, A. (2013). Language situation and conflict in Morocco. In O. O. Orie & K. W. Sanders (eds), *Selected Proceedings of the 43rd Annual Conference on African Linguistics* (pp. 271–277). Somerville, MA: Cascadilla Proceedings Project. www.lingref.com, document #2975 (accessed 20 June 2019).

Part Three

Support and Development of Mathematical Practices in the Teaching and Learning of Mathematics in a Specific Linguistic Setting in Africa

6

Supporting the Development of Content-Specific Language-Responsive Mathematical Teaching Practices in Multilingual Classrooms in Africa

Jill Adler and Anthony A. Essien

Introduction: Why Content Specific Focus

Consider the relatively simple tasks (a) and (b) in Figure 6.1, each of which requires the calculation of the value of *x*:

(a) Solve for *x*: (i) $2x - 7 = 5 - x$ (ii) $2x - 7 > 5 - x$
(b) Find the value of x in each triangle in Figure 6.1.

Think for a moment about the language you would use to describe the solution process in each: the vocabulary you might use, how you would write out your solution, and the mathematical knowledge and thinking needed in each case. What is the same and different about the language-in-use given that the first are a linear equation and an inequality, written in symbolic algebra; and the second are geometric figures, each an isosceles triangle? What do the above questions mean for teaching and learning in multilingual contexts?

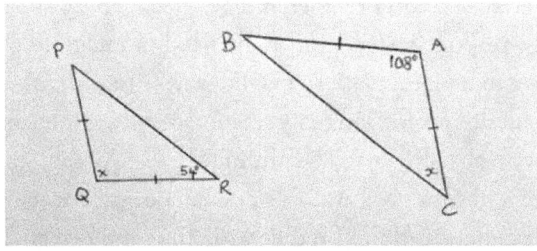

Figure 6.1 Geometric task.

You would no doubt recognize some of the different mathematical and language demands of algebraic in contrast to geometric tasks – for example, what the unknown or variable represents, or the equal sign and concept of equality in each. As Pimm (1987) revealed many years ago - as he introduced the field to the sociolinguistics of Michael Halliday (1978) and the notion of the mathematics register – the representations that we use to communicate mathematics are infused with language. In the above task, if we focus on the symbol x, in (a) (i) the word we use to denote its meaning is 'unknown' – there is a specific value that satisfies this equation. In contrast, in (a) (ii), x is a variable – with infinite values satisfying the inequality and depending on whether x is a natural or real number. In both the geometric tasks, x is an unknown number, and part of a measure in degrees of a particular angle. In (b) the language demands include interpretation of notation, the markings of equal sides of the triangle. The meaning of x and the words we use to talk about it, and so the language demands of the task at hand changes across these tasks, depending on their mathematical content. These tasks thus present learners with different language demands, notwithstanding that their forms are largely figural and symbolic. When teaching and learning mathematics is in a language that is not the mother tongue or spoken language, the visible and hidden language demands of the tasks increase, thus giving some meaning to the focus of this chapter: content-specific language-responsive teaching in multilingual classrooms. Of course, and of interest to us in this chapter, the question then arises of what then is needed in mathematics teacher education to prepare and support teachers in this work in multilingual contexts.

Our focus on content-specific language-responsive mathematics instruction has its roots in the seminal work in the South African context on teaching and learning mathematics in multilingual classrooms (Adler, 2001; Setati, 2005; Essien 2010, 2020, 2021; Robertson & Graven, 2019). We draw on more recent content-specific focused work that has been carried out in the global North, particularly Prediger and Zindel (2017); Erath et al. (2021); Prediger (2019); Post and Prediger 2022); and Prediger and Neugebauer (2021). Key for content-specific language-responsive teaching is the need to integrate 'mathematics and language learning in a mathematics-specific way' (Prediger, 2019, p. 368). While this work on content-specific language-responsive teaching practices is recent, in reality, research has shown and continues to show that closing language-induced achievement gaps is of utmost importance in the teaching and learning of concepts with understanding (Prediger, 2022). In multilingual contexts where students come to class with varying proficiencies in their home languages as well as in the language of learning and teaching (LoLT), language-induced achievement gaps are even more prominent necessitating a more urgent need to attend to language practices that can enhance mathematical learning and thus contribute towards closing such gaps. Our goal in this chapter is to argue for the significance of content-specific language-responsive mathematics teaching for research and practice across African countries, and to elaborate what is entailed in its enactment, inferring from the recent research emerging from the global North. In doing this, we intend to fill a significant gap in literature regarding language-responsive teaching. While seminal relevant work has been done in the South, there has been less emphasis on the integration of content entailments. The fact that work on language-responsive teaching has been done mainly in the global north and not in multilingual contexts in post-colonial countries where language features in mathematics classrooms are very different motivates our work in this paper.

As illuminated earlier in the introduction to this book, there are substantive differences in multilingual features of mathematics classrooms across the continent. We thus begin with a critical reflection on emergence of research on content-specific language-responsive mathematics teaching, its location, detailing the complexities entailed.

Content-Specific Language-Responsive Mathematical Teaching Practices

In their work on language-responsive mathematics teaching, Prediger and Zindel (2017) explicitly articulated a research agenda on specifying language demands in topic-specific ways, and called for research with this integrated focus. Interesting studies have ensued. For example, in a study of the teaching of algebraic concepts in Barcelona, where Catalan is the language of learning and teaching (LoLT), and learners, particularly immigrant learners are Spanish speaking, or perhaps speakers of other languages, Planas (2021b) illustrates why it is important for teachers and so teaching to communicate explicitly, meanings associated with algebraic concepts, and particularly the concept of equivalence in equation solving. This is content-specific language, produced not only by specific words, but how these are constructed in meaning-related sentences. From her observation of teaching and reflection on this with teachers, she showed that teachers did not spontaneously work in a deliberate way with the multiple meaning potentials possible in their and their students' description of how they are solving an equation and why. Specifically, the notion of equivalence that is critical to meaningful equation solving was not in focus in the classroom teaching, nor visible in the teachers' initial reflections. At the general level, Planas shows that important ways of using words and expressions critical to mathematical meaning making are consequently left implicit, reducing opportunities for their learning by students. She thus argues that teaching talk is important and needs to be the object of professional development and its research.

What is, can or needs to be included in a focus on content specific language practices requires reflection. Rezat and Rezat (2017), and in line with the above, do not argue for specific concepts like equivalence (Planas, 2021b) or place value (Poo & Venkat, 2021) or variable (Adler, 2021). From a study of teaching and learning geometric construction, they argue that teachers' awareness of 'genres' (and what others might include in discourse practices) is an important aspect of their knowledge for teaching. In the context of geometry from which we drew the examples in our introduction, what constitutes a proof, for example, and how a proof is built through sequential geometric statements and reasons for these, in responding to a geometric task, cuts across geometric topics and specific contents. This 'genre', and others like what it means to define in mathematics, are less in view in the research reviewed above.

Of course, awareness does not equate with enactment (see, for example, Essien, Chitera & Planas, 2016), where the interplay between teaching talk and learning talk is critical. As has been argued, enacting and researching appropriate teaching talk is tension-filled (Planas, Adler & Mwadzaangati, 2022). The foregrounding of teaching talk appears, or is experienced as in conflict with or diminishing of learning talk in class, or focusing on learning talk in research. And thus, we turn our attention now to what is entailed in LRMT.

What is Language Responsive Mathematics Teaching?

In an expansive longitudinal research project focused on Mathematics Learning under Conditions of Language Diversity (MuM) at the Technical University of Dortmund in Germany, Prediger and colleagues have explored a wider range of research problems related to what they have called language-responsive mathematics teaching (Prediger, 2022). They define language-responsive mathematics teaching (we abbreviate this to LRMT) 'as instructional approaches to enhance the language needed for mathematics learning' characterizing these as 'approaches offering rich content- and language-integrated learning opportunities' (Prediger et al., 2022, p. 255).

Their main goal is that opportunities for mathematical learning need to promote conceptual understanding, and they elaborate the design principle of connecting multiple representations and language registers in mathematics education to link students' experiences with these to enhance conceptual learning (Prediger et al., 2022). The design principle combines the classical mathematics education principle of using multiple representations (Lesh et al., 1987) with what is entailed in working across different language registers necessary for access to mathematics. Added to this is learning in more than one language in a multilingual context (e.g. in Prediger & Uribe, 2021). This central design principle for LRMT indicates some of the complexity of this work as relating languages, language registers and representations. In doing this and also in other design principles, emphasis is placed on the integration of content and language in the opportunities that are opened up for learning (Prediger et al., 2022). In other words, the key point being made here is that the goals for students' learning in the mathematics classroom need to include explicit language learning goals together with content learning goals.

Research on teaching and learning mathematics in multilingual classrooms, over the past two decades, has helped us learn that these dual goals are important but not easily or simply put together (Essien, 2021; Moschkovich & Zahner, 2018; Wessel, 2019; Poo & Venkat, 2021; Adler, 2001). For example, referring back to our opening thought experiment and task (a) above, linking the linear equation and the inequality with their graphical representation as two intersecting lines provides a situation where content-specific talk can be extended beyond deriving procedures for solving equations and inequalities (and these themselves are important) to include talk about: the intersection point, what it represents, how this relates to the solution of the equation, and where the y-values of the one line are greater or smaller than the other, and how this relates to the solution of the inequality. Inviting learners to explain in their own words, and in their languages, what they 'see' and how they interpret the graphs requires the teacher to navigate across languages, the everyday and more mathematical registers produced, while linking symbolic and graphical forms and all with deep understanding of the linear function. Where attention has been drawn to the importance of drawing on all learners' languages as resources for learning, research has shown how such use by learners enables meaning-making (Barwell, 2020; Planas, 2021b). As Prediger and her group have shown and argued, learners' everyday language use is not always sufficient for meaning-making, and leveraging this is the work of the teacher. Hence, the title of our paper as content-specific language-responsive mathematics teaching/teaching practices.

It is interesting to note here, and we will return to this point later in the chapter, the resonance between LRMT and the research and development that has evolved over many years, in the USA in particular, on culturally responsive mathematics teaching (CRMT) or culturally relevant pedagogy. The linkages are not surprising since CRMT was geared towards mathematics classrooms constituted by cultural and linguistic diversity. The linking approach, however, is not in the integration of language and content learning goals, but at a more focused level of recognizing and including in the learning process, the funds of knowledge (e.g. Civil, 2016) and so too language resources students brought to their learning (Planas, 2018). But in addition, it can be argued that funds of knowledge in the culturally responsive approaches sometimes assume that students already bring in all they need for meaning-making, whereas LRMT starts form the idea that learners linguistic capital may need to be leveraged (through an intermediate language) before they really serve this purpose.

Another related concept to LRMT is the CLiL (content and language integrated learning) which entails acquiring disciplinary knowledge while still learning or acquiring competence in a (foreign) language (Dalton-Puffer & Smit, 2013). With differing approaches all arguing for integration of content and language, or content and culture, the question that follows is what this means at the level of practice.

What Does Language-Responsive Mathematics Teaching Mean in Practice

We know from extensive research in the field that 'language-responsiveness' is not only about fostering more communication and discussion in class and so the communicative function of language (Moschkovich 2013; Planas and Schütte 2018). Language also has a critical epistemic function - as a tool for thinking and knowledge acquisition (Pimm, 1987; Prediger & Zindel, 2017). When drawing on students' language repertoires, this will include their everyday-language, and these need to be linked with and extended to relevant academic mathematical language. This is more than just vocabulary – it is also about critiquing, arguing and explaining. As Prediger (2019) argues:

> Among all discourse practices, describing general patterns and explaining meanings have turned out to be most relevant for language learners: language

learners can develop procedural knowledge without rich discourse practices, but little conceptual knowledge is developed unless they succeed in participating in the discourse practice of explaining meanings (Adler, 1995; Moschkovich, 2013).

Prediger, 2019, p. 372

Prediger (2019) builds upon a large body of research on language-responsive mathematics instruction as summarized by Erath et al. (2021) and unpacks what exactly that means for the work of mathematics teachers, across different mathematics content areas. She identifies five 'jobs' that teachers need to be acquainted with in order to enact language-responsive mathematics teaching. LRMT in the first instance needs to include the teacher 'identifying mathematically relevant language demands' and we would add here that these have content specificity, and then providing 'cognitively and discursively rich' learning situations or tasks 'demanding' learners' language-use, where this would including having learners discuss and write out their thinking and explanations. A next job is 'noticing' in learner productions (be these verbal utterances or in written text) what language resources learners use and what else or additional they might need to be able to use. The next jobs are 'supporting' and successively 'developing' learners' further use of relevant language resources, and these would include, for example, connecting learners' 'everyday language to school academic language and technical language and constantly working towards further development' (Prediger, 2019, p. 372).

Each of the five 'jobs' outlined above - identifying, demanding, noticing, supporting and developing – as we show below, are not trivial in and of themselves. How teacher education can enable mathematics teachers' learning what is involved and how to do this work in their multilingual classrooms, adds a further layer of complexity, and one we hope to take steps towards illuminating in this paper.

Where Has the Focus on LRMT Come From? Why is It Being Promoted?

In Germany, like elsewhere in the world where language diversity is constitutive of mathematics classrooms, and as noted earlier, there are attainment gaps in mathematics. While these are usually attributed to socio-economic conditions, as cities and so schools have changed through migration movements globally, these gaps are now also seen as language-induced particularly in immigrant communities in the global North. If language is a divider, then it is incumbent on the field to (a) figure out what, how and why language is a factor and for whom, and then (b) how to intervene to disrupt inequality and so strive for social justice. Language has been identified as a critical factor in performance of South African learners in the international comparative assessments like TIMSS and PIRLS (Reddy et al., 2016), hence the significance of improving learners' languages and languaging, and thus LRMT practices also for our context.

In earlier studies on teaching and learning mathematics in multilingual classrooms, there was recognition that inviting learners to participate more in class, through discussion of tasks or problems with their peers, or sharing their thinking and solutions with others and communicating their mathematical thinking was important (Lampert & Cobb, 2003, for an overview). However, 'moving them on', i.e. enabling their language skills to be supported and developed (as in the 'jobs' identified above) was not straightforward, and not a spontaneous outcome of focused mathematical learning (e.g. Adler, 1999). At the same time, with a stronger focus on the multiple language resources learners bring to class and so enabling the use of their everyday languages or mother tongues was important, but linking this to what it meant to move the content on was not straightforward either (Setati, 2005).

By way of example, a study on explaining as a language practice common in German classrooms (Prediger, 2022) (learners are frequently asked to explain their thinking, or report their solution pathways to a problem) showed that this is a common practice, and valued as a means for learning. Explaining thinking is, thus, viewed as important for learning – or what they captured as explaining to learn was valued. However, results showed that capabilities for this practice varied across learners within and across classrooms, indicating inequitable distribution of opportunities to learn through this practice. Prediger (2019) pointed out, however, that it was not evident what it would mean for teachers and teaching to enable learners' learning to explain. These are highly discursive classrooms, where dialogue and interaction between learners and learners and the teacher is common. This is not the case in many postcolonial contexts. Our experience in doing Lesson Study in both South Africa and Malawi, for example, shows that while students are often invited to the board to explain (or show) how they responded to a task, they typically write procedural steps without discursive elaboration of how these are derived (Adler & Ronda, 2017). Prediger (2022) makes a similar point, thus raising the question across contexts, of what it would mean for research and development to both develop the discourse practice in teaching of explaining to learn (and so more opportunities for learners to do this in class) and then to supporting learners in these classrooms to develop their explanations, and so their learning to explain.

In all the above, there is the assumption that language as a resource needs to be harnessed, and in language-responsive ways. There is debate in the field on the construct language as resource (Planas, 2018), with arguments from a dialogic perspective (Barwell, 2016, 2018) that a more adequate conceptualization is languages as sources of meaning, and that what students actually use is situated, and so not static. Referring to repertoires in use, Uribe & Prediger (2021) contrasted their emergence in three different 'multilingual constellations'. They show that different constellations (determined by language of schooling policies, the language of instruction, the languages of the learners, and of the teacher(s)) with different groups of students were associated with different repertoires in use, as well as how they connected languages, registers and representations. This diversity in the way students use their resources is not surprising, with implications then for teaching and teacher education related to LRMT not being reduced to one size fits all.

There have also been attempts to disaggregate different aspects of LRMT, with particular focus on the value of and relationship between lexical and discursive practices for conceptual learning (Prediger et al., 2022). The argument made, following earlier research (Moschkovich, 2015) is that attention to vocabulary is insufficient – mathematical discourse practices like reporting, explaining, arguing are indeed more important. While there is recognition that lexicalization is critical to appropriate discourse practices, it tends to be subordinated and considered less important. The analytic distinctions between these is important for teasing out different language practices, and their content entailments. Lexicalization has particular relevance with content foci, and discourse practices are more applicable across contents. Emphasizing the importance of discourse practices so as to ensure that there is attention beyond vocabulary is needed. However, the subordinating of vocabulary, and particularly in contexts where students are learning the LoLT while learning mathematics, might lead unintentionally to it being ignored (Planas et al., 2022). Indeed, studies with cases that show rich discourse practices linked to conceptual understanding, point out that in enactment, teachers do pay attention to lexicalization or should do it more consequently (Prediger & Zindel, 2017; Prediger, 2019).

There are key issues embedded in the above definition and characterization of LRMT. The first key issue is that it emerges in the context of a project focused on mathematics learning 'under conditions of language diversity'. There are two aspects buried in the notion of language diversity. One is what has elsewhere been referred to as a multilingual classroom context – a classroom where learners (and in some cases the teacher, too) bring a range of main languages or languages they speak outside school that are different from the language of instruction. This is the situation in many post-colonial contexts, and so in many African countries, where the language of instruction has remained the colonial language albeit for diverse and complex reasons. In this 'condition', students/learners have more or less fluency in the language used in class to teach mathematics. The other is that even in more language homogeneous or monolingual classrooms, where the teacher and all learners speak the language of instruction outside school as well, there can be differences in what has been called their academic language proficiency (Schleppegrell, 2007; Moschkovich, 2015), that is, differences in their experiences and familiarity with the way a more elaborate, explicit and abstract language is used in school. What is different in post-colonial contexts, is firstly that the language of instruction is not the majority language nor the spoken language of the teacher. As Adler (2001) argued many years ago, the language infrastructure supporting teaching and learning in schools is thus very different from contexts where the language of instruction is the dominant and majority language (such as in Germany).

Language Responsive Mathematics Teaching Research in South Africa

While limited, there are studies opening up research linked with LRMT in post-colonial countries, particularly in South Africa. At an early learning level, and so in the first grades in school, Poo and Venkat (2021) compared two contrasting ways in which learners' home languages were drawn into classroom processes. In one classroom, the learners' language Sepedi, was largely drawn on to restate something that had not been understood, and so a practice of code-switching or substitution. In the other classroom, the learners' language (also Sepedi) was drawn on, but integrated with other discursive means for enabling meaning making, specifically different representations. This multi-discursive or multimodal approach of the teacher, they argue, opens up more opportunities for learning, through possibilities for deeper conceptual meaning-making. This linking of languages, registers and representations reflects Prediger's model of language-responsive mathematics teaching registers. Of interest to us is that Poo and Venkat describe this multi-modal approach as translanguaging, a slightly different, perhaps mathematically specific and useful description, from other descriptions or definitions of translanguaging (e.g. Makalela, 2015) where deliberate planning for fluid use of multiple languages is emphasized. While working across languages, registers and representations in ways that support both content and language learning in fluid and flexible ways certainly gels with interpretations of translanguaging, what is out of view here is whether and how these were deliberately planned, and so with translanguaging as explicit means. Poo and Venkat are clear that theirs is an exploratory paper, offering short excerpts from two teachers and so with caution as to the claims made about the greater potential of translanguaging and for our purposes here by inference LRMT. They call for more research in different classroom language configurations, at different levels and with different mathematical content. We concur, and hence the focus of this chapter.

At the secondary level, and in a setting where learners and the teachers' main languages were out of view, Adler (2021) describes word use and justifying as two language practices critical for mathematical learning, linking these with the theoretical constructs of lexicalization and discourse practice. Her focus is not on the elaboration of what these are in classroom practice, but rather on what it means to mediate such practices in mathematics teacher professional development. The rationale for the research and development work reported is that if language-responsive mathematics teaching is important, then the teaching practices associated with this need to be elaborated and then offered in teacher education. The elaboration here is that, and particularly in multilingual contexts, word use, meanings at the level of words and sentences (lexicalization) is important – but of course not outside of wider mathematical discourse practices like explaining, and so justifying ideas, processes and procedures. While lifting up discussion on LRMT to the level of teacher professional development, a great deal more research is needed on whether and how these are taken up by teachers and then with what impact on learning.

A third study, also in South Africa, and in the science classroom is similarly important. Conducted too with an interest in translanguaging practices, Probyn (2019) provides us with illustrative examples of a teacher, who unlike the others in her study, broke the mould of 'postcolonial monolingual ideologies' by integrating not only learners' main languages but also their funds of knowledge – their knowledge of practices related to the science content they were discussing in their home and cultural life; while simultaneously developing their Academic Language in Science (clarifying the meanings of filtration and sedimentation, in English and isiXhosa), and integrating the use of these words in the science discursive practice of moving from observation to explanation, and through dialogic interactions. This illustration of translanguaging, of working with learners' resources in their language and culture, and linking these through dialogic interaction to scientific explanations of an observed phenomenon in science, can also be described as language responsive science teaching – where goals for both language and content learning are integrated in the enactment of the lesson.

In all of the above, LRMT is seen at play in primary and secondary school levels. To bring our goal of elaborating what this means in practice, in and for teacher education conditions in Africa, we provide illustrations of tasks for teachers from our own research and practices in South Africa, one in professional development, the other in pre-service teacher education. We analyse the tasks for the 'jobs' of LRMT that they make (or do not make) available for teachers to learn, and how they meet the key design principle of linking representations, language registers and languages. From this, we make recommendations on what work at the level of both research and practice lies ahead.

Case 1: LRMT in Mathematics Professional Development

A Task Used with Teachers and Its Potential for Learning LRMT

The task in Figure 6.2 below is from a course for mathematics teachers[1] working in multilingual Grades 8 and 9 classes. The goals of the task were to offer in-service teachers opportunities to develop knowledge of and practice firstly for what is entailed in explaining mathematics; and then for their teaching so that learners can develop their mathematical explanations. It is important to note that neither here (nor in the example below) were the 'jobs' referred to in the literature above on LRMT in view. There was, nevertheless, a focus on how words are used and justifications built. As research has shown, learners are not equally proficient at explaining or justifying their mathematical thinking, and this is a conceptual issue, made more complicated if they are not proficient in the language of instruction. Teachers thus need to be able to support their students' learning to explain, and this was a goal of the task. The choice of the content in the task – operations on integers – was deliberate. We were aware from research, from our observations in schools, and from communication with teachers, of how learners struggle to make meaning of negative numbers when they first start using these new mathematical objects.

When we used this task with teachers, there were very interesting and fruitful discussions on the different learner responses, and which was 'best' from the teachers' perspectives. Discussion, with our mediation as teacher educators, included the learners' word use of 'minus' and 'cancel' as prevalent in the school mathematics register, and the more technical use of 'negative' to denote the sign

> **Teaching and learning 'explaining' – word use and justifications**
>
> > A grade 8 learner task
> > Calculate -7 + 4 = ... and explain why you think your answer is correct
>
> **The task for teachers**
>
> The task above was given to learners in a Grade 8 class. Most students wrote the answer -3 but their explanations were different. There were five different kinds of explanations (L1 – L5 on the right)
>
> 1. Which of these explanations do you think Grade 8 learners in your school will be likely to offer?
> 2. Which of these explanations do you consider to be the best? Justify your response.
>
> L1: Minus 3, because when you work with numbers with different signs you take the smaller number from the bigger and then put the sign of the bigger. So 7 take away 4 is 3, and because its minus 7 you get minus 3.
>
> L2: Minus 3 because I have minus 7 and plus 4. So four minuses cancel with four plusses and I am left with minus three.
>
> L3: Minus 3: I owe Sipho R7 and pay him back R4, so now I only owe him R3.
>
> L4: Minus 3: You have to start at minus 7 on the number line and jump four places to the right so you land on minus 3.
>
> L5: Negative 3: I am adding positive 4 to negative 7; positive 4 added to negative 4 is zero, leaving me with negative 3.

Figure 6.2 Task adapted from Wits Maths Connect Project course materials (see https://www.witsmathsconnectsecondary.co.za/projects).

of the number, and 'zero' as the sum of positive and negative four. There was also discussion on the use of everyday language like bigger/smaller; owing and paying and linking these with positive and negative numbers.

There were particularly interesting arguments about the first learner response, L1. As a procedure it 'works'. You arrive at the correct 'answer'. However, from the perspective of mathematics, there is confusing use of words to describe integers. Negative seven (-7) is not the 'bigger' number. More critically, encouraging procedures that bypass working with '-7' as a number, does not provide learners with opportunity to learn how to work with and come to understand this new object in mathematics. The details of these discussions, interesting as they were, is not the main point here. Rather, we analyse this task in relation to the opportunities it opens up for *teachers to learn some of the LRMT 'jobs' of identifying, demanding, noticing, supporting and developing* described above.

Identifying Mathematically Relevant Language Demands

Identifying language demands entails having deep knowledge of the content in play, and for teachers this includes what challenges learners might encounter when meeting this content. It is well known from research, and teachers' experiences, that as negative numbers are abstract objects, many learners find them and the operations on them, difficult to understand. A key language issue is learning a new meaning for the symbol '-'. In elementary school, '-' signifies the operation subtract, and is typically associated with the words 'take-away' and 'minus'. When learners meet integers, '-' now has two different meanings: it is both operation (subtract), and sign (negative). If the school mathematical word 'minus' is used to signify both the operation (subtract) and the sign (negative), then, and more so in multilingual classrooms where learners are learning English while learning mathematics, difficulties can emerge. The words 'sign', 'operation', 'minus', 'subtract', 'negative' need attention not in isolated ways, but in how they are used to make meaning of -7 as a mathematical object and what it means to operate on it. In addition, given their abstract nature, context relevant situations for operations with negative numbers, and representations for these (like the number line, or owing and paying) are not always easily interpreted.

These language and representation 'demands' – words used, registers and situations for operations on negative numbers – were intentionally built into the task through the way the five learner responses were constructed. As we anticipated, when teachers considered and evaluated the different learner responses, their attention was drawn to these context-specific language issues. What this means, is that in teacher education, opportunities for teachers to identify and discuss content-specific 'language demands' (the discourse practices and the word use) such as those discussed here are important; and, a task such as this affords such opportunities.

Providing Cognitively and Discursively Rich Learning Situations or Tasks that Demand Learners' Language Use

This job is implicit in Figure 6.2, as it is located in what is given as the 'learner task'. We note here that in our use of this, we did not explicitly discuss the learner task with teachers, and we return to this later. However, what is important in the construction of the learner task, is that it 'demanded' that learners 'explain' their thinking. While the calculation could be considered a straightforward task, the cognitive and discursive demand of this writing task was high, as it required providing a conceptual explanation of operations with negative numbers which is challenging at this level. It is through the demand to explain their thinking that the different responses from learners can be provoked.

The task for teachers modelled what a discursively rich learning situation could be for their learners (i.e. asking learners to explain their thinking/ reasoning), and then provided the opportunity for teachers to engage with a range of student reasoning, how the students expressed what procedure they used and why it worked.

Noticing, Supporting and Developing Learners' Language

These three jobs were those most in focus in the use of this task with teachers. The intention was for them to work on what makes a 'good' explanation. And this is a function of how words are used and ways of reasoning about the task. The five learner responses, while all reaching the same 'answer' of '-3', reflect different register use and different conceptual clarity. In Prediger's terms, noticing would include attention not only to whether and how valid were the procedures learners used, but also to the different discourse practices produced (reporting a procedure or explaining meanings) and those aspects of word use related to negative numbers discussed above. Prediger suggests that supporting and then developing learners' language entails 'connecting everyday language to school academic language and technical language and constantly working towards further development' (2019, p. 372). The different learner responses provide examples of what it could be mean to move from the everyday and school registers (or money on the one hand, and 'minus' and 'cancel' on the other) towards adding positive and negative numbers. They also exemplify reporting as well as explaining that goes beyond procedural steps, to rationales for these.

In the above, we have described and analysed the task and how it was used, pointing to possibilities or opportunities for teachers to learn about LRMT. Much of the discussion was on word use. This was a function of how the learner task was set up and thus possible learner responses for teachers to engage with. Moreover, from the perspective of LRMT in different multilingual classrooms across Africa, there is no attention in the task to the use of different languages. In addition, while some of the learner responses wrote about representations (like the number line), different ways that the operation can be represented diagrammatically, in addition to in words, were not in focus. For enhanced LRMT, and the translanguaging for multilingual settings like those in Africa, the task could thus be extended to open further learning opportunities. In the next section we discuss these extensions, relating them to the literature and why they could be beneficial.

Extending the Task

If teachers are to not only identify and notice (two jobs above) language demands and so use of different registers, but also different representations, then the learner task needs to include this, as suggested in the box below.

Grade 8 learner task:

(a) Calculate -7 + 4 = ...
(b) Report on how you calculated it and explain why you can do it this way. You may use words from any of your languages to provide this explanation.
(c) If you think this is possible, provide a diagram or illustration that will help make your explanation clearer.

The teacher task could be extended as follows:

Five learners all wrote the answer -3 but their explanations and illustrations were different:

1. Which of these explanations and/or illustrations do you think Grade 8 learners in your districts will be likely to offer?
2. Which would you want to include in your teaching so that you can ensure diverse learners understand how to add integers? You could choose all or one, or some. Justify your choices.
3. What mathematics register related to this task would you want to explore further in your learners' home language(s)?

L1:

(a) -3
(b) Minus 3, because when you work with numbers with different signs you take the smaller number from the bigger and then put the sign of the bigger. So, 7 take away 4 is 3, and because its minus 7 you get minus 3.
(c) I don't know how to draw this.

L2:

(a) -3
(b) Minus 3 because I have minus 7 and plus 4. So four minuses cancel with four plusses and I am left with minus three.
(c) [illustration: four minus signs boxed with four plus signs, and three minus signs remaining outside]

L3:

(a) -3
(b) Minus 3 because if I owe Sipho R7 (this is like the minus 7) and pay him back R4 (this is like the +4) then I will only owe him R3.
(c) [illustration: seven dots in a row; below, four dots crossed out and three dots labelled "owe 3"]

L4:

(a) -3

(b) Negative 3. You have to start at negative 7 on the number line and jump four places to the right because you are adding four and so you land on negative 3.

(c)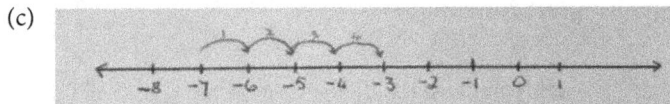

L5:

(a) -3

(b) Negative 3: I am adding positive 4 to negative 7; positive 4 added to negative 4 is zero, leaving me with negative 3.

(c)

These extensions to include attention to translanguaging and connecting representations open up opportunities for teachers to discuss (1) how deliberate use of words and explanations in multiple languages adds possibilities for students' meaning-making; and (2) whether the different representations are appropriate, and then what each offers in terms of meaning-making of operations with integers.

Case 2: LRMT in Pre-Service Teacher Education

A Task Used with by a Teacher Educator and Its Potential for Learning LRMT

The task in Figure 6.3 was given to multilingual pre-service teachers in a statistics class with a specific focus on distribution in two variables. It was taught by a bilingual teacher educator who did not share the same home language as most of the pre-service teachers. The PSTs were expected to first discuss the most important variables (most important things to consider) for a transport company whose business is to move stuff (e.g. furniture) for people who are relocating. The second part of the activity required PSTs to narrow these variables down to the two most important ones.

What is quick to notice in the task is the fact that the mathematics topic is not immediately obvious. After reading the introductory part of the task, the teacher educator initiated a whole class discussion by calling on the pre-service teachers

> **Situation 6: Fuel consumption of trucks**
>
> Consider a transport company using just one type of truck. Before each transport job, the company has to specify the price for the job. In order to specify a price before a job, the company needs to estimate how much their costs will be for doing the job.
>
> **Task 1: Identifying variables and postulating the relationships between them**
>
> Discuss: Leaving the overhead costs aside (i.e. salaries, etc.), what are the main costs in this kind of business? How are they related? How can we measure them?

Figure 6.3 The transport company task.

to explain what the task was about. Then she asked the PSTs to determine the variables that are necessary for a transport company to consider in determining how much to charge clients who are relocating:

Excerpt 1

1	Teacher educator (TE):	...Good, we can start. Here is the problem to consider from which what we gonna learn is going to emerge. Let's read the problem since we are also trying to become teachers. I can also ask you to read it loud for the class.
		(*Student reads the question of Task 1*)
		Hey stop, stop, stop. Now I want you to turn the papers over, turn it over; what is it that we have to consider, before you get to the task, what is this about?
2	PST1:	I was thinking of something that has to do with trucks, transport or something.
3	TE:	Transport, did you get that? You are not looking again now, you've read and you expand on this. What do you remember about the trucks and the transport?
4	PST2:	The companies have to transport some... it has to do some job...

5	TE:	Anybody else on that? So there's some job to be done, there is something about one truck. Turn the back, turn back the page and you can see it. That's exactly one truck. Read again. What does it ask?
6	PSTs:	One truck.
7	TE:	One type of truck ok that is how last week we said we look at a type of car, remember?
8	PSTs:	Yes.
9	TE:	Ok so it doesn't just have one truck, it has one type of truck. Does it say how many trucks? It doesn't say, maybe it doesn't matter, right.
10	TE:	. . . Ok. What do you gather a transport company does? What do you think a transport company does?
11	PST1:	Depending on the transport company . . . supposed to travel from one place to another.

There is an important language learning activity that the teacher educator asked of the pre-service teachers: They must first read the task, understand what they have read, and then express their own understanding of the context. This leads the discussion to the question as to what a transport company does, and subsequently into the key variables that are necessary for such a company.

In terms of the LRMT 'jobs', and specifically in term of the job of providing cognitively and discursively rich learning situations or tasks that demand language use, the task provided by the teacher educator, like in Case 1 above, has a strong focus on explanation and how justifications are built, on conjecturing and critiquing conjectures, or more generally, on what we have referred to elsewhere (Essien & Adler, 2016; Essien, 2016) as authorizing practices – that is – practices that deal with judgments about what is mathematically legitimate or not. The continuation of the task as seen in Table 6.1 indicates that this task was not a completely open-ended task – that the teacher educator was aware of which variables she wanted to narrow down to in order to teach the pre-service teachers about the concept of the line of best fit.

It is useful to engage with instances in which these key variables were suggested by pre-service teachers and what language-related mediational practices came into play/focus.

Table 6.1 The transport company task (cont. from Figure 6.3)

One of the main costs is the cost of fuel, and the main factor influencing the amount of fuel used is the distance. But the load weight also plays a role: the greater the load weight, the higher the fuel consumption. The table below gives information that was recorded for previous transport jobs.			
Job number	Distance (km)	Load weight (kg)	Fuel used (litres)
1	1,304	5,445	879
2	1,320	2,954	639
3	1,151	4,705	698
4	1,371	4,378	787
5	325	3,673	176
6	1,630	5,995	1,113
7	1,023	5,357	600
8	620	4,988	382
9	73	1,992	35
10	1,071	5,529	680
11	370	4,140	218
12	1,423	4,062	843
13	394	4,068	221
14	1,536	1.678	682
15	1,633	3,736	887
16	435	3,644	241

Previous transport jobs: Distance, load weight and amount of fuel used.

Excerpt 2

1	TE:	Ok, what does this company have to do when they get a call like this?
2	PST2:	They have to transport the stuff so that they can…they have to know what they're transporting from which place and to which place so that they can …
3	TE:	Yes, do you say km readings are important, they have to go from here to there; km readings are important for you, why?
4	PST2:	Because it's like the km readings will determine how much they will charge.
5	TE:	Do you agree? That how much they charge depends on how far they have to drive? If you disagree, … anything else you want to say that it can depend on?

6	PST3:	Think that should be how much fuel they need to go to the place
7	TE:	And what will that depend on? And what will that depend on?
8	PSTs:	The load.
9	TE:	Why the load?
10	PST4:	It's like, ok the load takes up a lot of petrol if you are doing that right, it does like at the end of it the more petrol we use to carry something around and since there is, I was gonna say that they could use different transport but we are given that it's only one type of transport so am gonna stick with the petrol that ...
11	TE:	Is that an assumption you can agree with?
12	PST5:	No. I was thinking about it. It depends on the nature of the product I have to transfer, for example you can transport twenty tons of cotton.
13	TE:	Cotton? What do you mean by cotton?
14	PST5:	Yeah for example; they can also transport twenty tons of stones of which the volume of twenty tons of cotton will be much bigger compared to the volume of twenty tons of stone so that one will also determine the price, on how much the customer needs to pay them.
15	TE:	Ok, so we've got various variables now, that one is an interesting one that I haven't thought of so let's see what sense we can make of it.
		So am just gonna jot down what we've said so far. [writing on the board] we said this company transports things, stuff and they charge for it, there is a fee they charge for it, right. The first thing was km reading; in the km reading we say the distance matters; you also said fuel consumption matters and then you said something like the mass of the load matters and up to there we were also clear and then we were challenged that it's not just the mass that matters, what else can you say, can you give me a term for what matters? Not just the mass.
16	PST7:	The nature of the stuff that you transport and I made an example of ...
17	TE:	But I looked at your hand, you said (*extending arms wide*) cotton, what is it that you're indicating to be, you not

		indicating to be hard and soft, not the nature what were you indicating to be (*extends arms*).
18	PST7:	For example the volume of 20 tons of cotton will be entirely different from the volume of 20 tons of a stone.
19	TE:	So it was not the nature of the stuff that you depend on, right it was the volume, the howmuchness of it do you get? So all of these [showing on board] we saying matters.
20	PST8:	So if you were carrying something that is breakable and you were to drive very slowly.
21	TE:	Will time be a variable that you would take into account?
22	PSTs:	Yes.
23	TE:	So you are saying that this would be, you mention drive slowly *neh* for some reason; so with a specific kind of load that they're carrying it might take more time, ok. Can you explain to us a bit more in terms of the time? What impact would it have on the company's business? If they just transport things like that? […] Anybody else on this argument please?
24	PST8:	I think that the second … because the time that the truck will take to move the stuff from one point to the other affects the business and the production of the business, how effective the business is. So I was thinking that time will be an important factor
25	TE:	Anybody against that? Anybody that would argue for not time the second variable but mass? Cos we have distance, you want to argue for that?
26	PST9:	Ma'am I wouldn't separate them I would take time and mass load as one variable because depending on your mass will depend on how much time you will take.
27	TE:	You think so? When you think of … other situations, other possibilities her challenge is depending on the mass, you will take more or less time depending on the mass.
28	PST9:	But it's not only the mass cos sometimes there is traffic and other things and then time will also be slower, regardless of having more mass or less mass so I wouldn't say I would take them together because time, sometimes there is traffic and sometimes there is no traffic.

| 29 | PST10: | What if we just leave the traffic outside and then ... (*laughter*). |
| 30 | TE: | Statisticians do that, statisticians decide which variables they're not gonna deal with, they're going to let them vary randomly; let's hear, you say? |

In Turn 2 in the above excerpt, PSTs uses a colloquial language to explain that a transport company moves things from one place to the other. The teacher educator revoices this by indicating which variable the PST was referring to. The discussion starts with the fact that the company needs to know 'what they're transporting from place to place' (Turn 2), then goes to km reading (Turn 3), and then to the distance (how far they have to drive) in Turns 5 and 15. Fuel use is also indicated at an important variable and through the discussion about what fuel use will depend on, load as a variable is proposed. What is important to note in the class discussion is that for the teacher educator, it was not only the identification of variables that was important – but also which variables matter and why and how these are named.

Through this activity, from identifying different variables for a transport company and postulating the most important variables, the class moved on to engaging with more complex statistical concepts like interpolating from a given data set, determining the fuel consumption of a given weight, what errors in the trendline mean, finding the total errors on a trendline, and reflecting on/ discussing the formula for errors on a trendline. Even though there are no representations used in this introductory class to the trendline concept in the currently reported class, in subsequent classes, many representations were used to discuss the meaning of the trendline. A 'traditional' classroom on the same concepts in statistics would have been giving the PSTs bivariate data and asking them to draw the trendline or giving them the formula for trendline and asking PSTs to use it to determine the relationship between the two variables in the data set. Our take is that it is the nature of this task as presented to the PSTs that enabled to a larger extent, the fulfilment of the other 'jobs' in LRMT, as we elaborate below.

In terms of the job of identifying mathematically relevant language demands, the understanding of the meaning of a variable and what the term signifies is key to a broader understanding of the concept of distributions in two variables. What is interesting to note here is that the word 'variable' is not mentioned initially. The teacher educator rather starts from the everyday by asking the question 'what do you gather a transport company does'. The second question the teacher educator asks the PSTs was to consider what the cost of transporting goods will depend on. In doing this, she introduced the variables to consider without necessarily using this term[2]. The first use of the term variable comes in Turn 12 where the teacher educator says 'so we've got various variables now'. It can be argued that through this, the PSTs understood that the various factors that needs to be considered by the transport company to ascertain the cost of moving goods are called 'variables'. From then onwards, we see a more frequent use of the term (e.g. 'will time be a variable?' in Turn 21). By so doing, it can be argued that the teacher educator supported and then *successively developed* the PSTs language repertoire through connecting their everyday language to the school academic language (Prediger, 2019). For being able to leverage their language in this way, she needed to 1) have *identified* that the concept of variable is an essential language demand, 2) have elicited their everyday language by *demanding* first utterances, and 3) noticed the possible connecting points within the PSTs' contributions before being able to leverage them towards the concept of variable. In this way, the other LRMT jobs are crucial for developing students' language.

For learners in multilingual classroom such as this class, it was important to provide PSTs with the opportunity of not only developing that mathematics register, but that too of enculturating the PSTs into becoming proficient users of the language of teaching and learning for their own meaning-making, and for the purpose of teaching (Essien, 2021) at the end of their qualification. Asking for explanations and justifications as the teacher educator did, is one way of achieving this, and it could be extended by making these jobs explicit in a reflective look back. But beyond this, it is noteworthy that only English is used in this class during this lengthy and important discussion. This represents, in our opinion, a missed opportunity to harness the other languages present in the class. Our take is that this is possible even if the teacher educator does not share the same home languages as the pre-service teacher. We will return to this point in the subsequent section.

Discussions on the Two Tasks in Relation to Content-Specific LRMT

We have provided detailed illustrations – cases – of two contrasting tasks for teachers, one in in-service and the other preservice teacher education practice in South Africa. We did this with a bifocal LRMT lens. We attended to design principles of varying language registers and representations of mathematical ideas for opening up conceptual learning opportunities, and to discursive practices that support engagement with mathematical ideas. At the same time, we reflected on the learning opportunities opened up for prospective and practicing teachers being exposed to or learning the 'jobs' of content-specific LRMT (Prediger, 2019), and thus with an eye to what LMRT can mean in mathematics teacher education practice.

The selection of two contrasting cases of tasks for teacher learning was intentional. The tasks are contrasting in a number of ways. Firstly, they are differently structured enabling us to ask: what do we learn from both structured and unstructured tasks? At the surface level, it could appear that Case 1 was more deliberately designed. It has structured into it, learner responses to the addition of integers, and so both different use of registers by the learners, and in the revised task, extension to include different representations and the possible use of the different languages present in the class. This structuring creates possibilities for teachers to discuss (and so a discursive space for them) how learners might talk/write about integers, how they name them as objects and how they explain how they operate on them, and so the registers and representations they use, and then what it means to notice these, and what it could mean to move learners towards more mathematically robust word use and explanations not only in English but in other languages present in the class.

Case 2 introduces preservice teachers to the work with an open task – eliciting from the PSTs their own ideas of key variables for transporting goods. The developing discourse as the teacher educator interacts with the PSTs steers towards naming these, in ways that reveal what she draws on their pre-knowledge, and how this can be connected with what, from the task perspective, are key variables. All this happens verbally, and so attention to word use and justifications for what matters for such transport are carefully mediated. A clue as to the deliberate preparation by the teacher educator as to what is key for her, is the table (Table 1) that is only introduced after there has been extensive discussion. Here, too, however, the PSTs have opportunities to learn what are key variables and why, without these initially being presented to them.

While the tasks are differently structured, they both illustrate the relevance of the language demands of content-specific LMRT. In Case 1, we see specific words (e.g. minus, subtract, negative) and the importance of distinguishing the operation and sign when talking about integers and particularly operations with negative numbers. We also see different representations (diagrams, concrete discs, number line) and what they communicate to support (or not) conceptual learning. In Case 2 we see the importance of identifying and naming key variables in the context of statistical problem -solving, and by so doing, we see the importance of paying attention to developing the mathematics register. We also see an example of an extended dialogue around a task and how explanations and justifications are elicited by the teacher educator and used for meaning-making. Whereas in Case 1, the teachers themselves are to simulate typical teaching jobs, in Case 2, they experience when the teacher educator provides a model of how to enact them in a classroom discussion. Their learning opportunity on statistics- and language-integrated teaching might have been deepened by a reflective look back on what the teacher educators did with them.

What the above points to is that the LRMT jobs of identifying, noticing, supporting and developing learners' language requires preparation – knowing about research insights into student learning of the topic, the lexicon and multiple representations related to the concept, so that these can be either built into a structured task, or held in mind while provoking and then listening to and supporting PSTs discursive engagement.

Second, with one task being drawn from in-service and the other from pre-service, we have been able to illustrate possibilities for and the importance of attention to LRMT across these two teacher education sites. Both tasks are drawn from actual teacher education practice, and so offer illustrations of ways of constructing opportunities for teacher learning.

Third, while both have content specificity, and are directed at teacher learning, their primary objects of learning are different. Case 2 presents PSTs with a contextualized mathematical problem, and so inducting teachers into *mathematical practices* they might not have had opportunity to engage with in their school mathematics learning, while the modelled teaching practices of the teacher educator stay more implicit. Case 1 presents practicing teachers with a mathematics teaching problem, and opportunities to learn and reflect *mathematics teaching practices*. It is beyond the scope of the data here to indicate that learning of both, mathematics and mathematics teaching, is possible in both tasks. In Case 1, we do not have data on how teachers discussed their responses to the task, and so what and how they learned more about integer addition themselves while engaging with its teaching. In Case 2, where we do have this kind of data, from what we know from the progression from this task into graphical representations and so on in later lessons, mathematics teaching practices were discussed, distinguishing what statisticians might be concerned with, and what teachers would need to attend to and why. Graphical representations were used, as with any other lesson on this topic, to show the line of best fit. But more importantly, representations of the different dots in relation to the regression line were used to explain error (or residual) in the regression model – that is, the deviation of the observed data from the regression line, and how the sum of the residuals around the regression line adds up to zero.

A fourth difference between the tasks is what elsewhere has been described as the difference between modelling and mediating mathematics teaching practices (Adler & Pournara, 2020; Adler, 2021). Case 1 sets out to deliberately **mediate** the discursive teaching practices of enabling learners to express and explain their thinking in words and diagrams, and the related LRMT jobs. Case 2 sets out to induct PSTs into important mathematical practices where they themselves express and explain their thinking. In this instance, the mathematics teacher educator **models** LMRT jobs and what is entailed in dialogic teaching. In each of these cases the primary object of learning is different as discussed above.

Fifth, and this is not about the cases being contrasting but how they also at a deeper level reflect a 'job' of LRMT that reflects cultural practices. As you read and engaged with Case 1, you might have wondered about the first learner response … that offered a procedure that works for adding integers, but, from our experience is strange to teachers in other countries. Figuring out -7 + 4 by 'subtracting the larger from the smaller and taking the sign of the larger' is a commonly used and even taught procedure across South African schools, and so can be referred to as a deeply entrenched school mathematics practice and ways of talking and using negative numbers. If it is to be problematized with teachers, it needs deliberate inclusion and engagement in teacher education. Such an example of learner thinking might not be useful in other contexts. Moving onto Case 2, as we know, many words are polysemic, and in the context of the problem, the word 'load' and its discussion might have been interesting. In an everyday language, the terms load, weight and mass can be taken to mean the same thing, even though scientifically, they are different and the PST talking about cotton makes that point.

Concluding Thoughts

While there is much to be learned about LRMT from the two cases, you might be asking, where in all the discussion above, is attention to translanguaging, and the use of multiple languages so crucial in postcolonial multilingual contexts.

Indeed, you might have been wondering about this from the outset, as both tasks are presented in English, and all of the dialogue in Case 2 is in English. These two cases are telling as they reflect predominant teacher education practice across many postcolonial contexts where the colonial language remains the official language of schooling particularly beyond Grade 4. We have thought a great deal about this as we developed this paper, reflecting critically back on our own practice and research, becoming more alert to how coloniality remains at work, years after independence, and what this means for our practice, our teachers' learning and their school practices. This is a key challenge for LRMT research and practice going forward. Future research and practice that draws on the language repertoires of teacher educators, teachers and PSTs will have much to offer the development of LRMT. In the global north, while teaching and teacher education might attend to drawing on multiple languages brought into and used in the teaching-learning context, the target language is the official and dominant language and the majority language. This is not the case in most African countries where the target language is not the spoken and majority language. As discussed in Chapter 1 of this book, these are very different language contexts or constellations (Uribe & Prediger, 2021), where many if not most teacher educators and teachers are teaching towards an official language that is not their spoken language. At present, there is little research that brings to light what LRMT then means and we have attempted through our cases and this chapter to at least bring this issue to the fore, and advocate for further research that can enhance a broader conception of LRMT as illuminated by particular conditions in the global south.

Acknowledgements

This work is based on the research supported by South African Chairs Initiative of the Department of Science and Technology, and National Research Foundation of South Africa (Grant No. 71218), and the National Research Foundation South African Numeracy Chair at Wits (Grant Numbers: 74703). Any opinion, finding and conclusion or recommendation expressed in this material is that of the authors and the National Research Foundation does not accept any liability in this regard.

We thank Susanne Prediger for insightful, helpful and critical comments towards the paper.

Notes

1 See Adler (2021) for elaboration on the project in which this task was used and for what purposes. The task in Figure 6.2 was developed by the first author and used in the course.
2 It must be noted that the PSTs in this class were encountering statistics for the first time given that as a product of the old South African curriculum, statistics as a topic was not done in schools.

References

Adler, J. (1999). The dilemma of transparency: Seeing and seeing through talk in the mathematics classroom. *Journal for Research in Mathematics Education*, 30(1), 47–64. Available online: http://www.jstor.org/stable/749629 (accessed 10 June 2022).

Adler, J. (2001). *Teaching mathematics in multilingual classrooms*. Dordrecht: Kluwer Academic Publishers.

Adler, J. (2021). Content and context specificity matter in the 'how' of language responsive mathematics teacher professional development. In N. Planas, C. Morgan & M. Schütte (eds), *Classroom research on mathematics and language: Seeing learners and teachers differently* (pp. 77–100): London and New York: Routledge.

Adler, J., & Pournara, C. (2020). Exemplifying with variation and its development in mathematics teacher education. In D. Potari & O. Chapman (eds), *International handbook of mathematics teacher education, Volume 1: Knowledge, beliefs, and identity in mathematics teaching and teaching development* (pp. 329–353). Rotterdam: Sense Publishers.

Adler, J., & Ronda, E. (2017). A lesson to learn from: From research insights to teaching a lesson. In J. Adler & A. Sfard (eds), *Research for educational change: Transforming researchers' insights into improvement in mathematics teaching and learning* (pp. 133–143). Abingdon: Routledge.

Barwell, R. (2016). Mathematics education, language and superdiversity. In A. Anjum & P. Clarkson (eds), *Teaching and learning mathematics in multilingual classrooms: Issues for policy, practice and teacher education* (pp. 25–39). Rotterdam: Sense Publishers.

Barwell, R. (2018). From language as a resource to sources of meaning in multilingual mathematics classrooms. *Journal of Mathematical Behavior*, 50, 155–168.

Barwell, R. (2020). Learning mathematics in a second language: Language positive and language neutral classrooms. *Journal for Research in Mathematics Education*, 51(2), 150–178.

Calor, S. M., Dekker, R., van Drie, J. P., Zijlstra, B. J. H., & Volman, M. L. L. (2020). 'Let us discuss math': Effects of shift-problem lessons on mathematical discussions and level raising in early algebra. *Mathematics Education Research Journal, 32*(4), 743–763. Doi: 10.1007/s13394-019-00278-x.

Civil, M. (2016). STEM learning research through a funds of knowledge lens. *Cultural Studies of Science Education, 11*, 41–59.

Dalton-Puffer, C., & Smit, U. (2013). Content and language integrated learning: A research agenda. *Language Teaching, 46*(4), 545–559. Doi: 10.1017/S0261444813000256.

Erath, K., Ingram, J., Moschkovich, J., & Prediger, S. (2021). Designing and enacting instruction that enhances language for mathematics learning: A review of the state of development and research. *ZDM – Mathematics Education, 53*(2), 245–262.

Essien, A. A. (2010). Mathematics teacher educators' account of preparing pre-service teachers for teaching mathematics in multilingual classroom: The case of South Africa. *International Journal of Interdisciplinary Social Sciences, 5*(2), 33–44.

Essien, A. A. (2016). Examining the joint enterprise in pre-service teacher education mathematics classrooms. In K. Brodie & H. Borko (eds), *Professional learning communities in South Africa.* Pretoria: HSRC (Human Sciences Research Council).

Essien, A. A. (2020). Norms of practices and pre-service teacher education for multilingual mathematics classrooms in South Africa. In I. Liyanage (ed.), *Multilingual yearbook 2020: Teacher education and multilingual contexts* (pp. 169–191). Cham: Springer.

Essien, A. A. (2021). Understanding the choice and use of examples in mathematics teacher education multilingual classrooms. *ZDM – Mathematics Education, 53,* 475–488. Doi: 10.1007/s11858-021-01241-6.

Essien, A. A., & Adler, J. (2016). Operationalising Wenger's communities of practice theory for use in multilingual mathematics teacher education contexts. In A. Halai & P. Clarkson (eds), *Teaching & learning mathematics in multilingual classrooms: Issues for policy, practice and teacher education* (pp. 173–194). Rotterdam: Sense.

Essien, A. A., Chitera, N., & Planas, N. (2016). Language diversity in mathematics teacher education: Challenges across three countries. *Mathematics education and language diversity: The 21st ICMI study,* 103–119.

Halliday, M. A. K. (1978). *Language as social semiotic: The social interpretation of language and meaning.* London: Edward Arnold.

Lampert, M., & Cobb, P. (2003). Communication and language. In J. Kilpatrick & D. Shifter (eds), *A research companion to principles and standards for school mathematics* (pp. 237–249). Reston, VA: National Council of Teachers of Mathematics.

Lesh, R., Post, T., & Behr, M. (1987). Representations and translations among representations in mathematics learning and problem solving. *Problems of Representation in the Teaching and Learning of Mathematics, 21,* 33–40.

Makalela, L. (2015). Moving out of linguistic boxes: The effects of translanguaging strategies for multilingual classrooms. *Language and Education, 29*(3), 200–215. Doi: 10.1080/09500782.2014.994524.

Moschkovich, J. (2013). Principles and guidelines for equitable mathematics teaching practices and materials for English language learners. *Journal of Urban Mathematics Education*, 6(1), 45–57.

Moschkovich, J. (2015). Scaffolding student participation in mathematical practices. *ZDM – Mathematics Education*, 47, 1067–1078. Doi: 10.1007/s11858-015-0730-3.

Moschkovich, J., & Zahner, W. (2018). Using the academic literacy in mathematics framework to uncover multiple aspects of activity during peer mathematical discussions. *ZDM – Mathematics Education*, 50, 999–1011. Doi: 10.1007/s11858-018-0982-9.

Pimm, D. (1987). *Speaking mathematically: Communication in mathematics classrooms*. London: Routledge & Kegan Paul.

Planas, N. (2018). Language as resource: A key notion for understanding the complexity of mathematics learning. *Educatinai Studies in Mathematics*, 98, 215–229.

Planas, N. (2021a). Challenges and opportunities from translingual research on multilingual mathematics classrooms. In A. A. Essien & A. Msimanga (eds), *Multilingual education yearbook 2021: Policy and practice in STEM multilingual contexts*. Cham: Springer. Doi: 10.1007/978-3-030-72009-4_1.

Planas, N. (2021b). How specific can language as resource become for the teaching of algebraic concepts? *ZDM – Mathematics Education*, 53(2), 277–288.

Planas, N., Adler, J., & Mwadzaangati, L. (2022). What is mathematics teaching talk for? A response based on three sites of practice in mathematics education. *ZDM – Mathematics Education*, 55, 521–534. Doi: 10.1007/s11858-022-01452-5.

Planas, N., & Schütte, M. (2018). Research frameworks for the study of language in mathematics education. *ZDM – Mathematics Education*, 50(6), 965–974.

Poo, M., & Venkat, H. (2021). Approaches that leverage home Language in multilingual classrooms. In A. A. Essien & A. Msimanga (eds), *Multilingual education yearbook 2021: Policy and practice in STEM multilingual contexts* (pp. 39–55). Cham: Springer.

Post, M., & Prediger, S. (2022, online first). Teaching practices for unfolding information and connecting multiple representations: The case of conditional probability information. *Mathematics Education Research Journal*. Doi: 10.1007/s13394-022-00431-z.

Prediger, S. (2019). Investigating and promoting teachers' expertise for language-responsive mathematics teaching. *Mathematics Education Research Journal*, 31, 367–392. Doi: 10.1007/s13394-019-00258-1.

Prediger, S. (2022). Enhancing language for developing conceptual understanding: A research journey connecting different research approaches. In J. Hodgen, E. Geraniou, G. Bolondi, & F. Ferretti (eds), *Proceedings of Twelfth Congress of the European Society for Research in Mathematics Education (CERME12)* (27 pp.). University of Bolzano / ERME (European Society for Research in Mathematics Education). Doi: hal.archives-ouvertes.fr/hal-03756062/.

Prediger, S., Erath, K., Weinert, H., & Quabeck, K. (2022). Only for multilingual students at risk? Cluster-randomized trial on language-responsive instruction. *Journal for*

Research in Mathematics Education, 53(4), 255–276. Doi: 10.5951/jresematheduc-2020-0193.

Prediger, S., and Neugebauer, P. (2021). Can students with different language backgrounds profit equally from a language-responsive instructional approach for percentages? Differential effectiveness in a field trial. *Mathematical Thinking and Learning*, 25 (1), 1–21. Doi: 10.1080/10986065.2021.1919817.

Prediger, S., & Uribe, Á. (2021). Exploiting the epistemic role of multilingual resources in superdiverse mathematics classrooms: Design principles and insights into students' learning processes. In A. Fritz, E. Gürsoy & M. Herzog (eds), *Diversity dimensions in mathematics and language learning: Perspectives on culture, education and multilingualism* (pp. 80–97). Boston, MA: De Gruyter Mouton. Doi: 10.1515/9783110661941.

Prediger, S., & Zindel, C. (2017). School academic language demands for understanding functional relationships: A design research project on the role of language in reading and learning. *EURASIA Journal of Mathematics, Science and Technology Education*, 13(7b), 4157–4188. Doi: 10.12973/eurasia.2017.00804a.

Probyn, M. (2019). Pedagogical translanguaging and the construction of science knowledge in a multilingual South African classroom: Challenging monoglossic/post-colonial orthodoxies. *Classroom Discourse*, 10(3–4), 216–236. Doi: 10.1080/19463014.2019.1628792.

Reddy, V., Arends, F., Juan, A. & Prinsloo, C. (2016) South Africa. In *TIMSS 2015 Encyclopedia of South Africa: Education policy and curriculum in mathematics and science* (1–14). Boston, MA: TIMSS & PIRLS International Study Center.

Rezat, S., & Rezat, S. (2017). Subject-specific genres and genre awareness in integrated mathematics and language teaching. *EURASIA Journal of Mathematics, Science and Technology Education*, 13(7b), 4189–4210.

Robertson, S.A. & Graven, M. (2019). Exploratory mathematics talk in a second language: A sociolinguistic perspective. *Educational Studies in Mathematics*, 101, 1–18. Doi: 10.1007/s10649-018-9840-5.

Schleppegrell, M. J. (2007). The linguistic challenges of mathematics teaching and learning: A research review. *Reading & Writing Quarterly*, 23, 139–159. Doi: 10.1080/10573560601158461.

Setati, M. (2005). Teaching mathematics in a primary multilingual classroom. *Journal for Research in Mathematics Education*, 36(10), 447–466.

Uribe, Á., & Prediger, S. (2021). Students' multilingual repertoires-in-use for meaning-making: Contrasting case studies in three multilingual constellations. *Journal of Mathematical Behavior*, 62(100820), 1–23. Doi: 10.1016/j.jmathb.2020.100820.

Wessel, L. (2019). Vocabulary in learning processes towards conceptual understanding of equivalent fractions – Specifying students' language demands on the basis of lexical trace analyses. *Mathematics Education Research Journal*, 32, 653–681. Doi: 10.1007/s13394-019-00284-z.

African Language/English Bilingual Curriculum Materials: What Educative Supports Does the Bala Wande Package Offer Teachers?

Hamsa Venkat and Samantha Morrison

Introduction

In this chapter, our focus is on curriculum materials developed for early grade mathematics classrooms in a South African research and development project known as Bala Wande. Two key features of this project distinguish it from earlier larger scale intervention materials in South Africa. First, is its presentation of Home Language text in its Teacher Guide (TG) and accompanying Learner Activity Book (LAB) coupled with a full subtitling in English. This fully bilingual model has been developed for three South African languages (isiXhosa, Sepedi and Afrikaans). The model is responsive to the evidence in South Africa of the press for access to English among historically disadvantaged South African population groups as the language of access to socioeconomic mobility, even in the likelihood of this move occurring in the midst of less access to understanding of subject content in schools (Setati, 2008). Second, the extensive inclusion of attention to number structure marks a key difference between the Bala Wande materials and the Department of Basic Education's National Workbooks, in which attention to number structure is much more sporadic and diffuse (Morrison & Askew, 2022).

We explain the importance of these two distinctions in the South African context later in this chapter. For introductory purposes, we make the point that both of these distinctions imply elements of curriculum materials that are substantively 'new' in the terrain. What constitutes the substance of this newness and how the new elements are framed is important to understand in the conditions of the broader early grades' context, in order to interpret the affordances and constraints that are likely to ensue in teachers' work with the materials in classrooms where mathematics is taught in home language medium.

In this regard, our interest lies in exploring the extent to which the Bala Wande materials can be described as 'educative'. Schneider and Krajcik (2002) describe educative materials as materials that are aimed at enhancing teachers' pedagogical practices. The distinguishing feature of educative materials according to these authors is that they are: 'curriculum materials designed to address teacher learning as well as student learning' (p. 221). While based in work located in science education with goals of moving towards reform-oriented practices, the sense of need for improvements in teaching is widely pointed out in mathematics education also, although what constitute aspirations for teaching may vary across contexts, conditions and cultures.

Different aspects and extents of 'scripting' have been described by Remillard and Reinke (2012) as a key feature of educative curriculum materials. In a South African terrain that has seen a return to relatively high degrees of scripting in the last decade, and with this feature carried through into the Bala Wande curriculum materials, we focus on the following research questions in this chapter:

1. In what ways can the bilingual presentation of tasks and activities in Bala Wande materials be considered as educative for teachers?
2. How does this bilingual presentation of Bala Wande materials support the presentation of structural views of early number?

We address these questions in this chapter in the following sections, which we outline here as an advance organizer for the reader. We begin with a brief outlining of the background that leads to particular interest in the Bala Wande aspects of bilingual presentation and structural presentation of early number. We also detail the ways in which these two aspects are presented in the Bala Wande materials, with reference to the literature bases on these aspects. The writing on key features of educative materials and, in particular, aspects that have been considered as useful for looking at teacher learning are then presented, and used to lead into our analysis of an illustrative strand of tasks drawn from the 2021 Grade 1 Bala Wande Teacher Guide (Funda Wande, 2020a) and Learner Activity Books (Funda Wande, 2020b).[1] This analysis leads us, in turn, into a discussion of key aspects that are likely to need consideration to further strengthen the use of home languages as resources for the teaching and learning of early number in contexts of language diversity.

South African Background

Performance in mathematics at all levels of the education system in South Africa continues to be low, with evidence of learning lags beginning in the early grades and growing across grades (Spaull & Kotze, 2015). There is also evidence of gaps in teachers' mathematical content knowledge (Venkat & Spaull, 2015) and in their pedagogic content knowledge (Carnoy & Chisholm, 2008). Alongside this, there is also widespread evidence of largely traditional, teacher-led pedagogic forms in which collective chorused responses to closed teacher questions are common in the early grades (Hoadley, 2018).

Multilingual Mathematics Learning in South Africa

The national language policy in South Africa provides for home language medium instruction in the early grades (Grades 1–3), with the majority of children nationally in recent years learning in home language medium classrooms. However, the complexity of seeing language as a resource for learning in South Africa is marked sharply and clearly in outcomes that show lower performance for children learning in home language in comparison to those learning in English. Mohohlawane (2019) puts the situation in relation to reading outcomes succinctly in these terms:

> learners that are receiving their Foundation Phase education in indigenous South African languages are still performing far below their counterparts that are receiving this in English or Afrikaans.
>
> p. 127

Setati (2008) noted though, that work within mathematics education on multilingualism had tended to ignore the political role of language. In her paper, she points to the tensions between the epistemic access to mathematics provided by learning in a language that one is familiar with and the press from parents and some teachers for English in particular, which – in South Africa – is seen as the language of socioeconomic access. She concludes this paper by noting what is required:

> The challenge is bringing together the need for access to English and the need for access to mathematical knowledge.
>
> p. 114

While waves of curricular reform in the decade and a half that have passed since Setati's publication have included the dissemination of national learner workbooks in all eleven official South African languages, they present what Sapire and Essien (2021) describe as 'multiple monolingualism', with children expected to continue to work within the boundaries of a single language.

Attention to Number Structure in South Africa

Although the definition of 'structure' has been described as largely undefined (Kieran 2018), we use the term *number structure* to describe the skilful organization of numbers using number relations, number patterns, the part-part-whole construction of number and the properties of operations (Venkat et al., 2019; Wright et al., 2006). Empirical data shows South African learners' dependence on counting-based strategies (Schollar 2008) and working with examples in highly separate ways that negate attention to connections between established and derived results; for instance, 'I know eight plus eight is sixteen, so eight plus nine has to be one more, making the answer seventeen' (Venkat & Naidoo 2012). This lack of awareness regarding number relations, seen in teaching and learning, plays through into the repeated need to work with number problems using 'first principles' counting in ones approaches.

The Bala Wande materials – noting the imperatives on the ground for access to both mathematical meaning-making and access to English – published the first mathematics teaching and learning texts that were fully bilingual. A growing body of literature points to language as 'central to the processes of mathematical thinking, learning and teaching' (Radford & Barwell, 2016, p. 283). Thus, we consider the bilingual language presentation as a key cog in children's conceptualization of number structure.

Bala Wande Materials

In the Bala Wande Teacher Guide (Funda Wande 2020a), each page of detail on particular activities or concepts in one of the home languages has a facing page with the same details in English. This provides teachers with easy access to explanatory text on some concepts and activity outlines in the African language of the text and in English. This is important in the face of some evidence suggesting that early grades' teachers prefer teaching mathematics through the medium of English as they are more familiar with mathematical terms and vocabulary in English than in the African language (Essien et al., 2015). In the Learner Activity Books, task instructions and explanations in home languages are subtitled immediately below, in a smaller font, with the same instructions and explanations in English (see https://fundawande.org/learning-resources for the website that gives access to the Bala Wande materials – all of which are published in Open Access format).

Further, while earlier interventions have included English-Home-language bilingual dictionaries to support teachers with bridging between specialized mathematical terms that they may only previously have encountered in English (e.g. Botes & Mji, 2010), Bala Wande offers more immediate access to equivalent terms and phrases in English in these texts, although an English–Home-language bilingual dictionary (Funda Wande, 2020c) is also included in their materials package. This dictionary elaborates explicitly on the philosophy of fluid and responsive moves between languages and between mathematical registers based on the multilingual nature of learner needs in South African classrooms in these terms (English version below but isiXhosa version precedes this in the text):

> This bilingual dictionary includes the daily list of lesson vocabulary that is included in the lesson plans and the teacher's notes. In the dictionary you will find explanations and diagrams for the lesson vocabulary. [...]
>
> If you have learners in your class who are not yet comfortable in the LoLT (Language of Teaching and Learning), try and explain the word in a language they understand. You can also use gestures or pictures to help you explain a concept. Another strategy is to let learners who speak the same language discuss the concept in their home language, and explain to each other.
>
> Funda Wande 2020c, Introduction, English–isiXhosa bilingual dictionary

The Bala Wande Teacher Guide advice for teachers on work with language more broadly reflects the bilingual presentation of materials and similarly calls for teachers to freely use moves between languages as needed to support children's mathematical learning, referencing and equating 'code-switching' and 'translanguaging' within this advocacy:

> Ootitshala abaninizi bemathematika baseMzantsi Afrika bayazixuba iilwimi xa befundisa ngeenjongo zokunceda abafundi babo babe nokuqonda isigama semathemaetika. Oku kuthetha ukuba bayathsintshatshintsha phakathi kweelwimi ezimbini okanye ezingaphezulu xa becacisa imathematika. Uphando lubonisa ukuba ukwenza oku kuba luncedo kakhulu kubafundi. Ukuxuba iilwimi kunceda ootitshala nabafundi bakwazi ukusebenzisa izakhono zabo zolwimi ekufundeni endaweni yokunyinwa lulwimi olunye. Esi siqhelo sisetyenziswa nakumazwe ngamazwe kwaye sibizwa ngokuba yi-'translanguaging' ukuwela imida yeelwimi.
>
> Funda Wande, 2020a, p. 10

Many South African mathematics teachers already code-switch to help their learners understand mathematical concepts and terms. This means that they alternate between two or more languages when explaining mathematics. Research has shown that this is a very useful practice that does indeed help learners to understand. Code-switching allows teachers and learners to draw on all of their language skills to learn, rather than to be limited by one language only. This practice is used internationally and is also called 'translanguaging'.

Funda Wande, 2020a, p. 11

While nuances in how code-switching and translanguaging may differ are described in the multilingualism literature base (García & Wei, 2014), the Bala Wande messaging is clear about foregrounding the need for mathematics teaching and learning to occur through a fluid combination of verbal and textual multimodal resources. This contrasts with what Sapire and Essien (2021) have described as the monolingualism model that pervades the national workbooks. In this model, teachers and children in particular medium classrooms are confined to the singular language of the text, regardless of the widespread evidence of multilingual proficiency and dialect-oriented spoken language in South Africa. The guidance is also interesting given the evidence from Poo's (2022) study showing lower prevalence of moves between mathematical registers in the Sepedi medium instruction she observed in comparison to what was seen in English-medium instruction settings. Putting these two bodies of evidence together leads to our sense of the potential in the Bala Wande materials for a broadening of the narrow representational repertoire in language and mathematical terms that has tended to prevail in African home language classrooms.

Number Structure in Bala Wande Materials

Morrison and Askew's (2022) paper points to the ways in which Bala Wande's extensive use of 'structured representations' (representations that are designed to promote some or other aspect of number relations – for example, double decker dot arrangements for showing doubles or odd/even numbers, or ten frames for showing base ten relations) can be contrasted with their more limited presence in the 2021 Department of Basic Education's (DBE) national mathematics workbook for Grade 1 (DBE, 2021). Morrison and Askew note that the DBE materials therefore send a weak conceptual signal regarding the importance of number structure, with Bala Wande materials sending much stronger signals in this regard. They argue that the Bala Wande tasks offer better links to the literature base that tells us that a rich network of number relations provide a strong foundation for learners' flexible and efficient mental computation (Foxman & Beishuizen, 2002; Heirdsfield & Cooper, 2002). Conversely, learners who do not develop an understanding of number structure and relations are thus forced to solve calculations in higher number ranges using time-consuming and error-prone counting strategies.

There are several explicit references in the Bala Wande materials on the need to work with number structure from the outset. For example, the conceptual development aspects detailed as goals for the first week in Grade 1 include mention of:

> a structured way of counting ... by getting learners to put counters onto the items they want to count and then transfer the counters into a ten frame. ... learners start to see that it is easier to compare amounts of things using a structured representation. They should start using the structured representation to make comparisons.
>
> Funda Wande, 2020a, p. 41

An example of how attention to number structure in Bala Wande is signalled is in the daily 'Register' activity. This activity involves a laminated class poster consisting of multiple ten frames that children each fill in by making a dot in one block with an erasable-marker as they enter the room (see Figure 7.1).

Figure 7.1 Bala Wande register poster.

Once all learners have registered their presence on the register chart and are in their seats, the teacher looks – with the class – at the poster and asks 'How many children are in class today?' In the Teacher Guide and in the accompanying video excerpt, there are instructions for teachers on how to work this activity and how they should encourage children to state the total number.

Usuku ngalunye	**Each day**
Sebenzisa irejista ukuze ubale abafundi abaseklasini.	Use the register to count the learners in the class.
Ebhokisini kukho ipowusta yerejista yeklasi eyodwa. Ngosuku ngalunye umfundi ngamnye uza kuziphawula ngokubeka ichokoza okanye abhale oonobumba bokuqala begama lakhe kwirejista.	In the box there is a special class register poster. Each day each learner will mark themselves by putting a dot or their initials on the register.
Qinisekisa ukuba abafundi bazalisa izakhelo zamashumi kwirejista ngokulandelelana.	Ensure that the learners fill the ten frames on the register in order.
Ekuqaleni kwesifundo semathematika bala inani labafundi abakhoyo, umz., balishumi, ngamashumi amabini, ngamashumi amathathu, amashumi amane [*sic*, text includes 'anesine' here]. Ngamashumi amane [*sic*, anesine] abafundi abakhoyo namhlanje.	At the start of the maths class, use the register to count the number of learners present. For example, ten, twenty, thirty, forty, four. Forty-four learners are present today.
Lo msebenzi uphindaphindwa yonke imihla ubethelela imbono yokuba ukuhlela nokubala ngamashumi. kuyasebenza kwaye kwenza abafundi bayeke ukubala ngoononye. (Funda Wande, 2020a, p. 14)	This repeated daily activity reinforces the idea that grouping and counting in tens is efficient and steers learners away from counting in ones. (Funda Wande, 2020a, p. 15)

The Teacher Guide offers the following isiXhosa instructions with parallel English translation on the next page:

A learner who comes in late is asked to add his 'dot' into the register chart stuck on the front wall. The child fills in the 43rd circle (3rd circle in the fifth row) and sits down.

T: Sizakubala ukuba bangaphi abantu abazileyo esilolweni. Ok, siyayazi ngubani lo wonke ephelele?	*T*: We are going to count the number of people that are present. Do we know what is this full number?
Class: NguTen.	*Class*: Ten.
T: NguTen ne? Masiye Ke	*T*: Ten right? Let's count.
Class: Ten, twenty, thirty, forty, fifty.	*Class*: Ten, twenty, thirty, forty, fifty.
T: Hayi! Forty ngaphi?	*T*: No! Forty-what?
Class: Forty-three.	*Class*: Forty-three.
T: Forty-three. Good. So sibayi forty three apha ngoku, phi?	*T*: Forty-three. Good. So we're forty-three where?
Class: Esikolweni.	*Class*: In school.
T: Esikolweni. Eklasini. Good.	*T*: In school. In class. Good.

The video excerpt, involving an expert teacher working with an isiXhosa medium class, presents exemplar teaching of the register task with English subtitles listed alongside as follows:

In the Teacher Guide excerpt, there is specific guidance on when and how the register activity should be used in lessons, with counting in tens flagged as an 'efficient' approach that 'steers learners away from counting in ones'. But there is, additionally, explicit direction in the Teacher Guide text and in the video clip on the exact sequence of number words to use for counting in tens, with home language number words used in the text and English number words used in the exemplar video. In the latter, for example, the teacher begins to model the way of counting she expects using the register poster thus:

T: Sizakubala ukuba bangaphi abantu abazileyo esilolweni. Ok, siyayazi ngubani lo wonke ephelele? (*Gesturing a circle around the first block of ten.*)

Class: NguTen.

Here, there is acceptance of 'ten' as the total value of the composite unit with no recourse to counting in ones. This working with ten as a composite unit continues in the further count, with the teacher attentive to some children continuing to recite the multiples of ten number sequence and losing the focus on enumerating the total number of children in class in this process, seen in her interjection: 'Hayi!

Forty ngaphi?' At this juncture, the class offer 'forty-three' in response. This too is accepted without any return to counting in ones, and the teacher further clarifies through questioning that the referent for the 'forty-three' is the number in class.

There is explicitness on the exact sequence of number words to be used to leverage work with base ten number relationships (e.g. *balishumi, ngamashumi amabini, ngamashumi amathathu, ...* – in the isiXhosa Teacher Guide). Thus, the numerical language for attending to base ten number structure in the structured resource context is modelled explicitly. This approach, with text and videos exemplifying fluid moves between linguistic and between mathematical registers to support attention to number relations is a common feature of the Bala Wande teacher support materials, and works in conjunction with the structured resources within the Bala Wande package to encourage attention to number structure. This explicit modelling of language use, to foreground number structure, contrasts with the approach seen in earlier policies like the Foundations for Learning programme, which introduced structured resources like abaci into schools without direction on how teachers' language use with number needed to change to support attention to base ten thinking.

What this contextual framing alerts us to is the aspects of Bala Wande that are likely to be encountered as shifts in the landscape – namely, the ways in which language is expected to be worked with in order to support progression in early number beyond counting in ones. Our focus in this paper is in looking more deeply at the nature of the supports offered to teachers in the Bala Wande materials for working with these two 'new' features. We do this through an exploration of some of the ways in which the materials offer educative supports for multi-modal language working for attention to early number structure.

Educative Curriculum Materials – Analytical Concepts and Categories

A number of studies have considered features of what are now referred to as educative curriculum materials or ECM, drawing on the early work of Bruner (1977) and Ball and Cohen (1996). Remillard's extensive attention across a number of studies to the ways in which teachers might be supported to work with curriculum materials was particularly useful to us in thinking about the Bala Wande materials. An early distinction made by Remillard (2000) was to contrast the idea of curriculum designers devising materials aimed at 'speaking through teachers' with those aimed at 'speaking to teachers'. The former approach tends to prescribe teachers' instructional actions, while the latter – offering suggestions and perhaps even some prescriptions on instructional actions – would also attend to enhancing teachers' awareness of the rationales underlying the mathematical and pedagogical choices presented in curricular texts.

Davis and Krajcik (2005) extended the focus on educative materials highlighted in the earlier Schneider and Krajcik (2002) work, offering a range of aspects through which the nature of educative attention in texts could be studied:

1. help teachers attend to student thinking
2. provide subject specific content support
3. help teachers connect ideas within a given discipline
4. communicate curriculum designers' rationale for pedagogical choices
5. foster teachers' ability to effectively mobilize curricular materials within a specific classroom context.

This list of aspects offered us some lenses for thinking about the nature of the educative elements present within the Bala Wande materials. Our attention was directed towards the bilingual presentation and number structure aspects that we have highlighted as 'new' in the texts and therefore in particular need of more educative slants.

We were mindful too of the critiques levelled at more prescriptive materials. Firstly, we noted their standardization that works against the possibilities for engendering differentiated instruction tailored responsively to individual needs. Secondly, there is acknowledgement in national and international literature that educative materials tend not to engender changes in teaching on their own. Rather, it is the case that teachers require one-on-one support (coupled with educative materials) to take on new practices (Cobb & Jackson 2015). Bala Wande's research model included different mechanisms for the delivery of this support in different provinces – each province with a different language of learning and teaching (LoLT). In the Eastern Cape province, where isiXhosa is a prominent language and also the LoLT, coaches were hired and trained to support teachers in the implementation of the Bala Wande project. In the Western Cape province, with Afrikaans-medium schools, education department-employed Subject Advisors were asked to support the Bala Wande rollout as part of their broader teacher support role. School-leaver teaching assistants in Limpopo Province Sepedi-medium schools were selected for the Bala Wande project, and were trained to support teachers in class with lesson implementation. Whilst one-on-one support was delivered differently to Bala Wande teachers in different provinces, a similarity was that all teachers involved in the project received three days' training on how to work with the Bala Wande materials. This training was intended to offer additional routes for communicating the aims and rationales for the choices of tasks and approaches used in the Bala Wande package, in a South African terrain where a lack of a reading culture among teachers has been documented (Porteus, 2022).

Methodology

Our focus in this chapter is on a qualitative text-based analysis of the ways in which the fully bilingual home-language–English presentation in the Bala Wande materials should be deployed alongside structured resources to direct teaching attention to number structure. We use this analysis to consider the extent to which the Bala Wande materials can be considered educative. The Bala Wande materials package that we drew from for our analysis consisted of the following:

1. Bala Wande Teacher Guide (Funda Wande, 2020a) linked to the Learner Activity Book for each of the four terms in Grade 1 (Funda Wande, 2020b). The Teacher Guide includes captioned illustrated sequences detailing key parts of the sequence of task interactions.
2. Video clips illustrating and discussing how tasks and activities should be worked with.
3. Resources box, including teacher demonstration and learner manipulatives and equipment.
4. English/ Home Language Bilingual Dictionaries (Funda Wande, 2020c).

The Bala Wande lesson structure details the following:

- Mental maths
- Concept development (whole class)
- Pair/individual work on worksheet/Learner Activity Book and game-based tasks

With Morrison and Askew's (2022) analysis already pointing to the high prevalence of structured representations in the Bala Wande materials, our focus in this chapter is on how teachers are asked to intertwine language and representational moves as a key route to engendering awareness of number structure in the texts. In order to do this, we analyse selected tasks drawn from the Grade 1 Term 1 texts, when the attention to translanguaging and number structure was first introduced to Grade 1 teachers. We chose tasks that involved use of ten frames, a representation that was introduced in the first week of Term 1. The tasks that we have chosen are reflective of the broader use of structured representations in the Bala Wande materials, but focusing on the ways in which attention to language and number structure are encouraged in a small number of tasks allows for a more in-depth analysis of the nature of support they offer for educative use.

The tasks we work with are drawn from the lessons in Term 1 Week 6. The focus of Term 1 Week 6 tasks is labelled as 'Match, sort, count and compare numbers 6 to 10.' In the Term 1 Teacher Guide, weekly overviews of the focus of tasks in the LAB are provided, rather than detailed instructions for every task. Five video extracts are provided for Term 1 tasks with one linked to the focal week, leaving several tasks more open to interpretation on how to engage with them in classrooms. Davis and Krajcik's (2005) list of aspects for studying the educative features of materials, introduced above, is drawn into our analysis.

Analysis

The Teacher Guide excerpt following Figure 7.1 above details the Register activity with a high degree of specification on instructional sequence and, therefore, would fall within Remillard's 'speaking through teachers' category. The scripting of the counting in tens number sequence to use in enumerating the number of learners in class as seen in the ten-based register chart can also be viewed as supporting the mobilization of the register resource – one of Davis and Krajcik's educative aspects – in ways that draw attention to the efficiencies offered by the base ten number system. Given prior South African evidence of teachers ignoring base ten structure in their instructional work with structured resources (Venkat & Askew, 2012), the interpretation of this scripting of the sequence of number words to use as educative would seem to be justified. Flexibility in the language to be used for saying number words is seen in the video clip, where instructional talk in home language is coupled with acceptance of learners' fluent use of the tens sequence number words in English. This kind of flexibility is core to translanguaging approaches to learning, with Makalela (2015) noting its usefulness for both epistemic access and for developing linguistic repertoires.

Further, the inclusion of the curriculum writers' rationale for advocating counting in tens rather than in ones on the grounds of this being more 'efficient' tends to fall on the 'speaking to teachers' side. The curriculum designers' rationale (another of Davis and Krajcik's educative aspects) is explicitly communicated here. Additionally, this reference to the press for efficient working can also be read as an attempt at communicating 'brevity' as an aspect that is valued in mathematics (and therefore falling within the subject-specific support educative aspect) – in a context where such attunements to valued mathematical practices are frequently absent

In this section, we focus on the tasks and activities for the focal Term 1 Week 6, providing a task outline and detail on the supports offered in the Teacher Guide and video clip, before analysing the supports for language use and number structure in relation to the educative descriptors introduced above. The tasks are detailed as follows (English version below, the same details are available in isiXhosa on the previous page of the Teacher Guide). The first two lesson tasks are linked with a farm scene poster showing different numbers of farm animals. In these 'farm animals' tasks learners need to count, sort and compare the number of animals using counters and ten frames. Ten frames continue to be specified for use across the counting and comparison tasks in the third and fourth lessons during the week.

The skills and understandings to be developed during the week include: 'accurately count objects (up to 10 objects)' and 'instantly recognize the numbers 6, 7, 8, 9, 10 shown in ten frames' alongside being able to recognize and write the numbers 6 to 10 in symbols and words (p. 139).

This set of tasks is of interest to us in its ongoing foregrounding – not just of counting as an end in itself, but of seeing numbers in the 1–10 range in the ten frame resource. Teachers are encouraged to use this resource – which is in use from Week 1 onwards, to support children to see numbers in the 6-10 range in relation to 5 and 10 as 'benchmarks' (Van de Walle & Lovin 2007) that allow for

Table 7.1 Bala Wande Teacher Guide (Funda Wande, 2020a, p. 139)

Day	Lesson activity
1	Use matching and sorting to count 6–10 objects
2	Use matching and sorting to count 6–10 objects. Write the number symbols
3	Use matching and sorting to count shapes (number range 6–10)
4	Compare numbers (6–10)
5	Consolidation and assessment for learning

> - Ngokusebenzisa isakhelo samanani sifuna ukukhuthaza abafundi bakwazi ukubona amanani ngoko nangoko, umz. bakwazi ukunakana ⬚⬚ njengo-7 bengakhange babale izibalisi nganye-nganye.
> - Are learners instantly able to recognise numbers, for example, to recognise ⬚⬚ as 7 without having to count each individual counter.

Figure 7.2 Teacher Guide notes on what to look out for.

conceptual subitizing of the total quantity, rather than counting in ones – a skill that has been noted as helpful for later progress and attainment in mathematics (Clements et al., 2019). The notes on what teachers should look out for during the week are explicit about this aspect in both languages – see Figure 7.2 (Funda Wande, 2020a, pp. 140, 141).

In the exemplar video (an isiXhosa lesson with English subtitles) that accompanies the farm animals tasks the teacher asks a learner up to place a counter on each of the six rabbits. She then checks that the class know that there are ten spaces in the ten frame, and moves each counter into a ten frame alongside the poster on the board with children counting the six counters as she moves each one into the ten frame. Pointing to the ten frame with the counters, she asks: 'U-five no-one ngubani? ('What number do five and one make?') The class chorus 'Six' and the teacher then writes the numeral '6' alongside the ten frame on the board. The 'Conceptual Development' notes accompanying the video in the Teacher Guide echo this sequence of actions, noting that 'a continued use of a structured way of counting' is a key goal for the week (as in preceding weeks) that can be achieved by:

> getting learners to put counters onto the items they want to count and then transfer the counters into a ten frame (as they did in the range 0 to 5).
>
> Funda Wande, 2020a, p. 141

This activity is repeated in the context of counting the numbers of different shapes in the task presented in Week 6 Lesson 3. This illustration of counting on from 5 rather than starting from 1 in the Teacher Guide and the video reflects, as before, an attempt to support teachers with translating curriculum intentions into the mobilization of resources in instruction. As before, the mixed use of home language with English number words is also exemplified here, reflecting a philosophy of language use in the service of effective mathematical learning.

In Lesson 4, attention shifts to comparing quantities by putting counters into the ten frame in order to more easily identify and compare the quantities.

The notes to teachers for this activity provide illustrations of what to do in a captioned photo sequence:

> Photo 1: Two children at front, one with a pile of yellow counters in her hands and the other with a pile of red counters in his hands, and a caption from teacher's mouth asking: 'Ngubani onezininzi?' ['Who has more?']
>
> Photo 2: Image shows the two children having put their counters into ten frames on the board – 8 yellow counters and 6 red counters, respectively.
>
> Photo 3: Shows teacher pointing to the ten frames with the sentence: 'U-8 ungaphezulu kuna 6' ['8 is more than 6'] written above on the board.
> (Funda Wande, 2020a, p. 160)

Below these images, the notes offer an outline for how the activity should proceed and why the ten frames are being used as follows:

> Sebenzisa amanani ahlukeneyo ezibalisi ukuze abafundi bafumane ithuba lokuthelekisa amanani. Sebenzisa isigama esithi 'ingaphezulu kuna-' okanye 'ingaphantsi kuna-'. Imiboniso yezakhelo zeshumi inceda abafundi babone ukuba zeziphi ezininzi kwaye zeziphi ezimbalwa
>
> Use different numbers of counters to allow many learners opportunities to compare numbers. Use the language of **more than** and **less than**. The ten frame displays help learners to see which is more and which is less.'
>
> Funda Wande, 2020a, p. 160

Several aspects of these support materials are of interest. First, across all four lessons (Lesson 5 is always a consolidation/assessment lesson), there is clear specification of the tasks to be used (in Lessons 1 and 2 here) and how the teacher should work with them – aligned with the 'speaking through teachers' perspective. However, in Lesson 4, for example, while one whole class activity example is illustrated, the teacher is asked to work with other similar examples chosen by the teacher, thereby leaving room for teachers' selections of appropriate follow-up examples. Thus, the Bala Wande materials are not at the extreme end of scripted orientations on speaking through teachers. On the language side, in Lessons 1 and 2, we see once again the teacher using English words for the numbers alongside isiXhosa. This is important and responsive in relation to Essien et al.'s (2015) findings noting that Foundation Phase teachers found 'pure' home language forms difficult to use in classrooms as number words in the African languages are often longer to both say and to write in words than their English parallels. As in the register video excerpt, this video excerpt thus also carries through the messaging on translanguaging, with integration of multiple languages and multimodal registers incorporated in this brief excerpt.

On the mathematical side, the emphasis on seeing six as composed of 'five and one' without counting in ones is carried in the orchestrated connection between placing counters in one-to-one correspondence with the rabbits, then 'sorting' the counters into the ten frame and drawing attention to the base-5 structure in the teacher talk. It is this kind of assembly of mediational means for focusing on number structure that was noted as sometimes lacking in the analyses of Askew et al. (2019). The follow up activity draws attention to more than and less than number relations within the ten frame setting. In completing the instructional section, the conceptually subitized quantity is linked with its symbolic representation. Once again, the prescription of how to combine talk relating to subitized, rather than counted, versions of number with structured resources suggests a 'talking through teachers' orientation.

Discussion

We return to these tasks in relation to the list of aspects offered by Davis and Krajcik (2005) as avenues for making materials educative by speaking to teachers. In relation to guidance about attending to student thinking, there are markers in the Teacher Guide about distinctions to look out for that are noted as important in early number learning – for example, able to/not able to instantly recognize quantities in the ten frame, ability to recognize and write number symbols and accurately counting up to 10. While remaining at rather dichotomized levels of description rather than detailing progressions for these aspects, these descriptions are directed at teachers, and thus represent illustrations of 'speaking to teachers' with a focus on what to look for in student thinking.

Subject specific content support tends, more often, to be dealt with implicitly via the detailing on what tasks to use and how to use them. Remillard and Reinke (2012) acknowledge that even whilst this approach tends to speak through, rather than to teachers, this kind of scripted detail can be useful for inexperienced teachers and teachers trying to work with unfamiliar approaches:

> explicit scripts have the capacity to offer new pedagogical repertoire and routines, allowing teachers to consider and try out new questions to ask, words to use, and instructional moves to make.... Through use of these scripts, teachers might begin to develop new instructional repertoires and styles of interacting with students.'
>
> p. 13

We noted above the explicit message to steer away from counting in ones. Thus, efficiency is flagged as a mathematically valued aspect of progression in early number learning. This functions as the rather succinct global rationale offered in the Bala Wande Teacher Guide for a range of underlying prescriptions – counting in tens rather than ones, counting on from fives, etc. In this rather limited explication of the rationale for pedagogic choices, we see more limited attention to this aspect of educative materials, suggesting a prioritizing of take up and trying out of a new pedagogical repertoire in advance of more detailed attention to the rationales underlying language, resource and representational choices. The global reference to moving on from counting in ones also tends to mean that the burden of connection falls upon the resources and the language that are carried through across tasks, rather than expecting the teacher to explicate connections in her talk. As noted already, ten frames are used recurrently across the tasks in Term 1 and into subsequent terms, with language patterns in counting also carried across these tasks. In later Grade 1 tasks, ten frames are connected with part-part-whole images and used to connect addition and subtraction, but as before, these connections tend not to be flagged explicitly at the mathematical content knowledge level. Rather, the educative focus is on helping teachers to connect ideas within early number through the recurring use of particular language patterns in counting linked with structured resources that support these counting patterns. When coupled with the global rationale for efficient counting, there is a danger that many of the subtleties of task presentation can be missed. For example, in the counting of the various farm animals task above, one-to-one correspondence actions are linked with arranging the count into the structured ten frame arrangement, and thereon into a count using number words and a final symbolic representation of the quantity.

There is no explicit drawing attention here to the fact that multiple representations of numbers are involved, nor to this being important within early number learning. Similarly, there is subtlety in how the steps of working in the farm activity are presented that is not explicitly discussed. For example, the counters are not counted out as they are placed onto the rabbits in the farm image; they are counted in ones only as the teacher transfers them into the ten frame. For the task goals at hand this is useful, as the first laying out of counters deals with the one-to-one correspondence needed for counting, followed by the counting itself in a format that then allows for focus on composition in relation to 5. However, if a teacher interprets the task as only about identifying the number of rabbits, there are dangers that the task can play out with attention to counting only. If children count as they are laying counters out onto the rabbits, the move to the ten frame would have to be carefully mediated to avoid a sense of simply counting again. To do this well, the teacher would have to draw attention to understanding 6 in terms of its 5-wise relations.

In our broader looking across the resources, we noted too that a relatively small number of key structured representations are carried through across the tasks in the Grade 1 Teacher Guide and Learner Activity Books – ten frames, part-part-whole bar diagrams and number lines amongst these. Part-part-whole diagrams, for example, are introduced in Term 1 in the context of breaking a column of multilink cubes into two pieces and representing the lengths of the whole and two parts. They are then used across the remaining terms to work with number combinations involving a missing whole, to connect addition and subtraction sentences linked to particular part-part-whole sentences and to solve missing addend problems. Whilst this kind of careful selection of key representations does find support in the literature (Askew & Brown 2003), there is limited explicit attention to discussing the rationales for the importance of these connections in the Bala Wande texts. Given the gaps in content and pedagogic content knowledge bases that we noted earlier, our sense is that the texts do not attend to the connections aspect as educatively as is likely to be needed in the South African context.

We have already noted that the Teacher Guide contents and videos are geared extensively towards supporting teachers to mobilize the curriculum resources and use the language patterns modelled in the Teacher Guide and the video clips that are provided in the Bala Wande package. The prescription on how to work with the materials – at the level of content, sequencing, pacing and resources, tends to mean that responsively attending to learner thinking – as an aspect in Davis and Krajcik's list – is less in focus, even though there are some examples of responsive working in the video clips. The emphasis on teacher mobilization of resources in instruction rather than on responsive attention to learner offers has been noted in the broader South African terrain and linked to the widespread evidence of gaps in primary teachers' mathematical content knowledge (Venkat & Sapire, 2022).

Taken together, and given the South African contextual features that we outlined earlier and the evidence of Bala Wande suggesting a substantively 'new' focus on how language can be used to support working with number structure, we would argue that the Bala Wande resources are more educative in relation to some of the aspects identified by Davis and Krajcik (2005) than others. Supporting the mobilization of curriculum materials with the structured counting in tens and ones patterns in teacher talk appear as key educative priorities, with content knowledge support and mathematical connections featuring more implicitly. Pedagogical rationales tend to be presented at more global, rather than at the more granular level of tasks. The need to move on from counting in ones to using base ten structure for more efficient counting and calculating is flagged early and consistently across the Grade 1 Bala Wande resources. On this aspect, there is therefore communication of the writers' rationales for their pedagogical choices. However, as noted above, this feature is not carried through consistently across other ideas that are also important – for example, connecting between representations, and what progression in terms of representations and in terms of the detail of stages of moves from counting to calculating strategies can consist of.

Attention to learner thinking in instruction tends to be largely absent, getting mention largely as something to be dealt with in the weekly assessment tasks rather than woven into instruction. We note very limited attention to supporting teachers to tailor instruction towards particular student responses, or to highlighting common errors and misconceptions and how these might be handled responsively. This emphasis on a rather singular instructional model is mirrored in the National Workbooks and other large-scale instructional materials in South Africa, and may be reflective of a current context of weak teacher content knowledge in which the need for common understanding of key ideas and language and resource use for coherent instruction takes priority over the need for more differentiated instruction.

Concluding Thoughts

Taken together, we see that the case for considering the combination of tasks, resources and illustrative videos offered here as educative on the multilingual and mathematical fronts is stronger in some categories than in others. There is a new emphasis on guidance on the language patterns associated with counting in tens and with using base ten structure for teachers, alongside structured resources. We would suggest that the emphasis of the materials is geared towards being educative in relation to providing supports for flexible and fluid use of moves between languages and between multimodal representations in coherent ways during instruction in the context of structured resources. This takes into account the need that has been flagged extensively in South African research for progression beyond rudimentary counting in ones approaches.

From a policy perspective, what our analysis suggests may be required up ahead – in the Bala Wande and broader CAPS contexts – is the need for a tailored sequence of training for teachers as they start to become familiar with the language patterns needed to draw attention to number structure in the context of working with structured resources such as ten frames. What we mean by this is that while initial attention in training may simply be to encourage teachers to practice and try out tasks with their associated resource and language repertoires, over time this could expand to reflecting on this use in training sessions. Expansions can involve increased attention to 'speaking to teachers' rather than 'through teachers' with increased attention to rationales for task choices and their presentation and sequencing gradually configured into the training that is offered. Longitudinal research of this process could then track the fluency and flexibility of teachers' linguistic repertoires in the context of working with early number structure. Without this, there is a danger, not just that mathematical subtleties of language use in home language settings will be missed, but also that the broader coherence of mathematics will continue to be disrupted.

Notes

1   The isiXhosa version of Bala Wande, *Funda Wande* (2020a, 2020b, 2020c) are used for analysis purposes.

References

Askew, M., & Brown, M. (2003). *How do we teach children to be numerate?* Southwell: British Educational Research Association.

Askew, M., Venkat, H., Abdulhamid, L., Mathews, C., Morrison, S., Ramdhany, V., & Tshesane, H. (2019). Teaching for structure and generality: Assessing changes in teachers mediating primary mathematics. In M. Graven, H. Venkat, A. A. Essien & P. Vale (eds), *Proceedings of the 43rd Conference of the International Group for the Psychology of Mathematics Education*. Vol. 2 (pp. 41–48). Pretoria: PME (Psychology of Mathematics Education).

Ball, D. L., & Cohen, D. K. (1996). Reform by the book: What is – or might be – the role of curriculum materials in teacher learning and instructional reform? *Educational Researcher, 25*(9), 6–14.

Botes, H., & Mji, A. (2010). Language diversity in the mathematics classroom: Does a learner companion make a difference? *South African Journal of Education, 30*(1), 123–138.

Bruner, J. S. (1977). *The process of education.* Cambridge, MA: Harvard University Press.

Cobb, P., & Jackson, K. (2015). Supporting teachers' use of research-based instructional sequences. *ZDM Mathematics Education, 47*(6), 1027–1038.

Carnoy, M., & Chisholm, L. (2008). *Towards understanding student academic performance in South Africa: A pilot study of Grade 6 mathematics lessons in Gauteng Province.* Pretoria: HSRC (Human Sciences Research Council).

Clements, D. H., Sarama, J., & MacDonald, B. L. (2019). Subitizing: The neglected quantifier. In A. Norton & M. Alibali (eds), *Constructing number: Research in mathematics education.* Cham: Springer. Doi: 10.1007/978-3-030-00491-0_2.

Davis, E. A., & Krajcik, J. S. (2005). Designing educative curriculum materials to promote teacher learning. *Educational Researcher, 34*(3), 3–14.

Department of Basic Education (DBE) (2021). *Workbooks.* Available online: https://www.education.gov.za/Curriculum/LearningandTeachingSupportMaterials(LTSM)/Workbooks.aspx (accessed 25 January 2022).

Essien, A. A., Venkat, H., Takane, T., & Tshesane, H. (2015). *An evaluation of the use and efficacy of the GPLMS multilingual mathematics materials: Issues and prospects – Final report.* Johannesburg: Tshikululu.

Foxman, D., & Beishuizen, M. (2002). Mental calculation methods used by 11-year-olds in different attainment bands: A reanalysis of data from the 1987 APU survey in the UK. *Educational Studies in Mathematics, 51*(1), 41–69.

Funda Wande (2020a). *Bala Wande Grade 1 Term 1 Teacher Guide: isiXhosa.* CC BY 4.0. Available online: https://fundawande.org/img/cms/resources/BW%20Gr1%20Xhosa%20TG%20T1_V2.1_WEB_2.pdf (accessed 26 June 2023).

Funda Wande (2020b). *Bala Wande Grade 1 Term 1 Learner activity book: IsiXhosa.* CC BY 4.0. Avvailable online: https://fundawande.org/img/cms/resources/BW%20Gr1%20Xhosa%20LAB%20T1_V2.1_WEB_1.pdf (accessed 26 June 2023).

Funda Wande (2020c). *Bala Wande IsiXhosa–English Grades R-3 Dictionary.* CC BY 4.0. Available online: https://fundawande.org/img/cms/resources/BW%20GrR-3%20Xhosa%20Dictionary_V1.pdf (accessed 26 June 2023).

García, O., & Wei, L. (2014). Language, bilingualism and education. In O. García & L. Wei (eds), *Translanguaging: Language, bilingualism and education* (46–62). London: Palgrave Pivot.

Heirdsfield, A. M., & Cooper, T. J. (2002). Flexibility and inflexibility in accurate mental addition and subtraction: Two case studies. *Journal of Mathematical Behavior, 21*(1), 57–74.

Hoadley, U. (2018). *Pedagogy in poverty: Lessons from twenty years of curriculum reform in South Africa.* London: Routledge.

Kieran, C. (2018). Seeking, using, and expressing structure in numbers and numerical operations: A fundamental path to developing early algebraic thinking. In C. Kieran (ed.), *Teaching and learning algebraic thinking with 5- to 12-year-olds: The global evolution of an emerging field of research and practice* (pp. 79–105). Dordrecht: Springer.

Makalela, L. (2015). Translanguaging as a vehicle for epistemic access: Cases for reading comprehension and multilingual interactions. *Per Linguam*, *31*(1):15–29.

Mohohlwane, N. L. (2019). How language policy and practice sustains inequality in education. In N. Spaull & J. Jansen (eds), *South African schooling: The enigma of inequality, policy implications of research in education* (127–146). Cham: Springer Nature.

Morrison, S. & Askew, M. (2022). Number structure in learner workbooks. In C. Fernández, S. Llinares, A. Gutiérrez, & N. Planas (eds), *Proceedings of the 45th Conference of the International Group for the Psychology of Mathematics Education*. Vol. 3 (pp. 203–210). Alicante: PME (Psychology of Mathematics Education).

Poo, M. (2022). Patterned differences in Grade 3 mathematics teachers' working with representations across two language contexts: Implications for learning opportunities. *African Journal of Research in Mathematics, Science and Technology Education*, *25*(3), 225–35. Doi: 10.1080/18117295.2021.2004361.

Porteus, K. (2022). Improving rural early grade mathematics: Design principles and patterns of improvement. In H. Venkat & N. Roberts (eds), *Early grade mathematics in South Africa*. (pp. 97–118). Cape Town: Oxford University Press.

Radford, L., & Barwell, R. (2016). Language in mathematics education research. In A. Gutiérrez, G. C. Leder & P. Boero (eds), *The second handbook of research on the psychology of mathematics education: The journey continues* (pp. 275–313). Rotterdam: Sense Publishers.

Remillard, J. T. (2000). Can curriculum materials support teachers' learning? Two fourth-grade teachers' use of a new mathematics text. *Elementary School Journal*, *100*(4), 331–350.

Remillard, J. T., & Reinke, L. (2012, April). Complicating scripted curriculum: Can scripts be educative for teachers. In Annual Meeting of the American Educational Research Association, 13–17 April, Vancouver, BC.

Sapire, I., & Essien, A. A. (2021). Multiple monolingualism versus multilingualism? Early grade mathematics teachers' and students' language use in multilingual classes in South Africa. In A. A. Essien & A. Msimanga (eds), *Multilingual education yearbook 2021: Policy and Practice in STEM multilingual contexts* (pp. 75–95). Cham: Springer.

Schneider, R. M., & Krajcik, J. (2002). Supporting science teacher learning: The role of educative curriculum materials. *Journal of Science Teacher Education*, *13*(3), 221–245.

Schollar, E. (2008, February). *Final report of the primary mathematics research project*. Johannesburg: Eric Schollar & Associates.

Setati, M. (2008). Access to mathematics versus access to the language of power: The struggle in multilingual mathematics classrooms. *South African Journal of Education*, *28*(1), 103–116.

Spaull, N., & Kotze, J. (2015). Starting behind and staying behind in South Africa: The case of insurmountable learning deficits in mathematics. *International Journal of Educational Development, 41*, 13–24.

Van de Walle, J. A., & Lovin, L. A. H. (2007). *Teaching student-centered mathematics: Grades K-3*. London: Pearson.

Venkat, H., & Askew, M. (2012). Mediating early number learning: Specialising across teacher talk and tools? *Journal of Education, 56*, 67–90.

Venkat, H., & Naidoo, D. (2012). Analyzing coherence for conceptual learning in a Grade 2 numeracy lesson. *Education as Change, 16*(1), 21–33.

Venkat, H. & Sapire, I. (2022). Early grade mathematics in South Africa between 2000 and 2010: What did we know in 2010, and how did this set the stage for the 2010–2020 decade? In H. Venkat & N. Roberts (eds), *Early grade mathematics in South Africa* (1–14). Cape Town: Oxford University Press.

Venkat, H., & Spaull, N. (2015). What do we know about primary teachers' mathematical content knowledge in South Africa? An analysis of SACMEQ 2007. *International Journal of Educational Development, 41*, 121–130.

Venkat, H., Askew, M., Watson, A., & Mason, J. (2019). Architecture of mathematical structure. *For the Learning of Mathematics, 39*(1), 13–17.

Wright, R. J., Martland, J., & Stafford, A. K. (2006). *Early numeracy: Assessment for teaching and intervention*. London: Sage.

8

A Case of English Medium Instruction in Rwanda: Issues for Mathematics Teaching and Learning Research

Rachel Bowden, Innocente Uwineza, Jean Claude Dushiminana and Alphonse Uworwabayeho

Introduction

Mathematics competence is central to the Rwandan national development vision of becoming a regional science and technology hub (MINECOFIN, 2000; MINEDUC, 2013). However, mathematics examination results and the numbers of students opting for business, science and technology streams at upper-secondary are disappointing (Uworwabayeho, 2009; Dushimimana and Uworwabayeho, 2021). English Medium Instruction (EMI), which is mandatory in Rwanda from the beginning of primary school through tertiary education, is likely to be part of the problem. The use of former colonial/international languages in African education systems is highly problematic, and the sudden switch from French to English medium instruction in Rwanda has exacerbated negative impacts (Milligan et al., 2020). EMI inhibits mathematics teaching and learning (Setati, 2005, 2008), and more generally, access and participation in secondary education (Schroeder et al., 2021). Indeed, EMI is shown to undermine educational access, quality and equity for millions of children in low-and-middle-income-countries (LMICs) (World Bank, 2021; Milligan et al., 2020). EMI may in part explain why enrolment in secondary education in Rwanda remains under 40 per cent,[1] despite being part of basic education. Nevertheless, EMI in Rwanda is unlikely to be reversed, in the short term at least, because of the complex drivers behind the policy (Milligan and Tikly, 2016). As such, an urgent and important task for research is to identify how to enable EMI teaching and learning in Rwanda, and comparable contexts (ibid.). In this chapter, we discuss issues for researching EMI mathematics teaching and learning in relation to our case study of mathematics lessons in a government secondary school in rural Rwanda. We begin by defining EMI, and outlining the context of EMI in Rwanda, before considering EMI mathematics teaching and learning and research through a review of the literature. We then present our research design and, using a lesson extract and teacher and student perspectives, key findings from our study. Finally, we discuss our findings and study design in relation to previous work and outline issues for future research.

English Medium Instruction in Rwanda

A broad definition of EMI is provided by Macaro, as 'the use of the English language to teach academic subjects (other than English itself) in countries or jurisdictions where the first language of the majority of the population is not English' (Macaro, 2018, p. 35). Here, our focus is EMI in basic education in post-colonial low- and middle-income contexts where, as Milligan, Desai and Benson (2020) note, several factors combine to make EMI highly problematic. These include:

1. The impact of EMI in basic education (as opposed to later introduction in higher education) on literacy and cognitive-linguistic development.
2. The linguistic distance between indigenous local languages and English. Patterns of sociolinguistic inequality rooted in colonial era, where elite groups have historically greater access to official (ex-colonial and/or international) languages and where access to these languages is limited in relation to intersecting characteristics such as poverty, rurality, gender, ethnicity and disability.
3. Systemic factors related to poverty including health and safety issues for staff and students, lack of basic facilities in schools (e.g. safe and hygienic toilets, electricity, water), content-heavy curricula, and stressful working conditions for teachers.

A further defining characteristic is the subtractive orientation to EMI, which dominates in Rwanda and other LMICs (Trudell, 2016; Sibomana, 2022). Subtractive multilingual education (MLE) officially removes and replaces learners' familiar language (e.g. Kinyarwanda), with an additional language (e.g. English) (Erling et al., 2021). In Rwanda, subtractive EMI is evident in textbooks and examinations, written as if for monolingual users of English (Milligan et al., 2016). In practice, classroom communication is multilingual (Pearson, 2014;

Williams, 2017; Sibomana, 2022), and this enables EMI mathematics teaching and learning (Carter and Rose, 2021). However, teachers inhibit and hide the use of Kinyarwanda (L1),[1] which they perceive as going against official policy and undermining learners' access to English (Sibomana and Uwambayinema, 2016).

An alternative to subtractive EMI are additive and flexible approaches, which provide for the ongoing use and development of L1 alongside the gradual introduction of an additional language (L2) for subject teaching and learning (Erling et al., 2021; Sibomana, 2022). Numerous classroom studies indicate the benefits of such approaches for teaching and learning (e.g. Banda, 2018; Charamba, 2020). There is no data on the impact of large scale and systemic approaches to additive MLE in basic education in Sub-Sahara Africa (SSA), because programmes at scale do not yet exist (Sibomana, 2022). However, there is a solid body of research over several decades from middle- and high-income countries, which confirm the benefits of additive compared to subtractive MLE for language and subject learning (e.g. May, 2017; Collier and Thomas, 2017; Genesee, 2013). Additive and flexible approaches find theoretical support in the notion of transglossia (Lin, 2019; García and Li, 2014). From this perspective language exists within a single complex psycho-linguistic system, where the whole system is engaged and adapts as new language is learned (Herdina and Jessner, 2002; Cummins, 2017). This viewpoint confirms that transitions in the language of learning and teaching (LOLT) are always additive, whether this is supported by the wider education system or not. Given robust evidence against subtractive EMI, a key task for research is to open up alternative understandings and approaches for policy makers and other education system stakeholders (Jaspers, 2018; Sibomana, 2018).

The context of EMI in Rwanda is distinct from other Low-middle Income Countries (LMICs) in two main ways. First, the vast majority of Rwandans cite the national and official language Kinyarwanda as their main language, while less than 7 per cent report being able to read and write in English (Sibomana, 2022). Second, French was the main official language of colonial administration and formal education. English was first introduced as an official language (alongside Kinyarwanda and French) following the genocide, in order to facilitate the return of diaspora from neighbouring Anglophone countries (Steflja, 2012). The sudden introduction of EMI and subsequent policy shifts are more typical of post-colonial language policy (Niyibizi et al., 2015). As indicated previously, the switch from French to English has exacerbated the negative impacts of using a former colonial/international language as the medium of instruction in basic education. One factor is that the majority of Rwandan teachers are required to teach in a language they were not themselves taught through. In 1996, the Rwandan Ministry of Education announced that English was to be used alongside French in schools as an official instructional medium. Then, in 2008, a 'sudden'" decree instated English as the sole medium of instruction from primary one onwards (Pearson, 2014, p. 44). In 2011, the policy was altered to allow for Kinyarwanda medium education from primary one to three (ibid.). The policy was recently reverted to EMI from primary one onwards (Milligan et al., 2020). EMI has failed to have the desired impact on school leavers' English language proficiency (Sibomana and Uwambayinema, 2016; Siboma, 2022). Nevertheless, EMI is broadly popular in Rwanda, where English is associated with internationalism and social mobility (Tabaro, 2015; Habyarimana et al., 2017). A number of drivers converge to make a move away from EMI in Rwanda unlikely, in the short to mid-term at least (Milligan and Tikly, 2016). It is therefore important to understand how to enable EMI mathematics teaching and learning (ibid.). An important focus for research is to identify the linguistic and pedagogical resources and constraints in mathematics classrooms, in order to inform policies that enable and do not undermine mathematics teaching and learning (Sibomana, 2018).

Mathematics Teaching and Learning in EMI Contexts

Next, we turn to mathematics teaching and learning practice and research in EMI contexts. It is well established that EMI mathematics teaching and learning is complex, as teachers negotiate between teaching English and teaching mathematics, between a focus on form and a focus on meaning, and between teaching languages of power and languages of identity (Adler, 1999; Setati 2005, 2008). Even in monolingual classrooms, language teaching and learning is central to mathematics education, as students learn to use multimodal mathematical language, including symbols and visuals and verbal language (O'Halloran, 2015), and to combine every day and academic forms in mathematical communication (Moschkovich, 2013).

Researching EMI mathematics teaching and learning is also complex, and distinct understandings of multilingualism are reflected in research designs and findings. Early studies of EMI mathematics teaching and learning in South Africa reported that teachers code-switch between local languages and English, and between English and mathematics and these switches were understood to present a series of dilemmas for teachers (Adler, 1999). The concept of code-switching was subsequently criticized for reinforcing the notion that multilingual communication is a problem (García and Li, 2014). The connection between language ideology and teaching and learning was highlighted in Setati's (2008) study of EMI mathematics at upper-primary level. Setati found that conceptual mathematics discourse, conducted primarily through L1, was seen as less valid than procedural discourse conducted in English, because English was perceived as a language of authority and legitimacy. A transglossic orientation can be seen in Setati et al. (2008, p. 16) who view 'facility across language' as a resource and not a problem in their study of upper-secondary mathematics lessons. The transglossic turn can also be seen in Moschkovich's work with multilingual mathematics learners in the USA. Moschkovich (2002) takes a complex, 'situated and sociocultural' view of language to account language use to construct and participate in here and now interactions, and to reproduce or challenge wider discourses. Moschkovich's model of academic literacy in mathematics is consistent with transglossic perspectives, as it 'widens what counts as competence in mathematical communication' to include 'social, linguistic, and material resources' (2013, p. 197). Moschkovich (2015) challenges the notion that learners need to know academic English *before* participating in mathematics lessons, and the related deficit view that multilingual learners lack language. She demonstrates that language is not necessarily a barrier to activity, as long as learners are enabled to use their full linguistic repertoires to communicate and participate mathematically. In order to support academic literacy in mathematics, teachers should:

> not address academic language as an isolated goal, but integrate mathematical proficiency, practices, and discourse whenever possible.
>
> Ibid., p. 57

Whilst taking an increasingly nuanced and situated view of multilingualism, research on EMI mathematics teaching and learning in sub-Saharan Africa can be critiqued for assuming learner-centred education as a pedagogical ideal (Bowden et al., 2022). For instance, Setati et al., (2002) evaluate the impact of a teacher education programme designed to develop learner centred methods along with multilingual communication. They found that groupwork was readily adopted, but note 'unintended consequences' (p. 138), as increased talk in English lessons was co-related with reduced writing and that students had few opportunities to use formal spoken or written English. The authors conclude that the policy message that 'groupwork is good' should be reviewed in relation to different subjects and contexts of teaching and learning (pp. 144–146). Van de Kuilen et al. (2020), also question the pedagogical validity of groupwork, even in relatively well-resourced Rwandan schools, given the limited numbers of textbooks and large class sizes. Likewise, Msimanga (2021) notes the limited take up of so-called learner centred approaches in sub-Saharan Africa, and demonstrates how multilingual communication as part of whole class interaction engages students with scientific content and English.

Carter and Rose (2021) apply a typology of pedagogical quality not associated with any single form of classroom organization, in their study of 97 mathematics teachers, working in different schools (89% in rural areas). The study confirms van de Kuilen et al. (2020) assertion of the pedagogical competence of Rwandan secondary school teachers. Rose and Carter find that mathematics teachers establish supporting learning environments, and set clear instructional objectives. Moreover, the vast majority of lesson time is used for mathematical activity and students remain largely on-task. Over half of teachers assign learners meaningful roles during lessons, such as solving equations in front of the class on the board. The authors report that 38 per cent of teachers used Kinyarwanda in their lessons and this was positively associated with learners' active analysis of mathematical content (p. 35). It is reasonable to infer that, when not being observed and video-recorded, more teachers would have used Kinyarwanda, given other reports of classroom communication in rural Rwandan schools (Pearson, 2014; Williams, 2017; Sibomana, 2022). This calls into question the conclusions which the authors draw about mathematics teaching and learning in Rwandan secondary schools. The use of observation rubric may have limited a situated understanding of language and pedagogy. Van de Kuilen et al. (2020), who also used an observation rubric based on generic standards of learner-centred education (from Schweisfurth, 2015), concluded that the standards do not do justice to 'the complexity of teaching and interplay of various factors' (2020, p. 10).

This brief review indicates some of the complexities of researching EMI mathematics teaching and learning, and signals the importance of situated understandings of language and pedagogy. Next, we present our study of mathematics lessons in a government secondary school in rural Rwanda as an illustration of how we responded to these challenges and the findings which resulted. We finish the chapter by discussing our research design and findings in relation to previous work, and recommending issues and approaches for further research.

Research Design and Sample

The aim of the study was to investigate how a teacher constructs and how students participate in EMI mathematics lessons, and the linguistic and pedagogical resources and constraints in their classroom context. Case study was selected as an appropriate approach for investigating complex social phenomena, the case here being a mathematics classroom (Duff, 2008). The study centred on a single mathematics class to enable detailed investigation of classroom interaction and influences on classroom interaction in one particular case, which is understood as related to other cases (Blommaert & Dong, 2010). We conceptualized language and pedagogy as intertwined, sociocultural and situated phenomenon (Moschkovich, 2002). A fully government owned and funded combined primary and secondary school was selected, to investigate EMI mathematics teaching and learning in relation to relatively under-privileged students (Williams, 2019). Language policy was conceptualized as a layered system of texts and discourses (Johnson, 2018), including official policy statements, and the interpretation of policy in curricula, textbooks, examinations, teacher education and school and classroom communication. We define linguistic ideology as ideas about language and users of language (Blommaert, 2010), which may be inaccurate and serve particular political interests, and pervade language, texts and discourses (Fairclough, 2013). Our focus on the teacher's construction of language policy in lessons, reflects the potential teachers have to interpret language policy (e.g. Cincotta-Segi, 2011). We recognize that teachers' agency is constrained by social and material conditions (Johnson & Johnson, 2015).

Data included 10, double-period (80-minute) mathematics lessons recorded over a five-month period in 2018; a week of participant observation in school; post-lesson interviews with the teacher and groups of students; an in-depth interview with the teacher; and two focus groups with students. Data were gathered by a cross-national, multilingual research team led by the first author (the European researcher), who designed the study as part of her PhD. Where possible, research participants were invited to choose language/s for communication. Most interviews were conducted in Kinyarwanda and translated to English, with some teacher interviews conducted in English. Student focus groups were conducted in English and Kinyarwanda. Recorded lesson observations were conducted by all researchers. The Rwandan researchers translated Kinyarwanda to English. First author transcribed English, paralinguistic features (pause, word stress and intonation), non-verbal language (gesture, gaze and facial expression), written language and drawings from the board. The study raises a number of ethical issues, given the power imbalances between adults and young people, European and Rwandan researchers, and Rwandan researchers and the teacher (Bond & Tikly, 2013; Hultgren et al., 2016). To mitigate these issues, information and consent forms were translated into Kinyarwanda, and presented orally and in writing to staff and students. All interviews and focus groups were conducted out of lesson time, and students had the choice to opt in for interviews and to sit off-camera during recorded lessons. The teacher reviewed and commented on tentative conclusions. Publications from the study are co-authored, by all researchers involved.

In total, 13 hours of lesson recordings were transcribed, including verbal (multilingual), paralinguistic, non-verbal and mathematical language (Heller et al., 2018). Classroom interaction was analysed ethnographically, through the identification of contextualization cues, speech acts and speech events (Gumperz & Hymes, 1986). The following hierarchical units of interaction were identified. 'Instructional units', roughly equivalent to a single lesson period, were defined as having an explicit pedagogical objective presented by the teacher at the start and end of the unit. Within instructional units, distinct 'activities', which repeated across instructional units, were identified. Activities are defined as bounded units of interaction, with distinct roles for teachers and students and communicative objectives, serving the purpose of the instructional unit (Lemke, 1990). In the data set overall, six activity types were categorised. These were:

1. Preparation
2. Presentation
3. Demonstration
4. Summary
5. Student questions
6. Individual and groupwork

Of these, the first four were present in all instructional units in the data set while the last two were less frequent, with instances of 6 (group and individual work) least frequent of all.

Critical analysis comprised tracing connections between classroom discourse and discourses and ideology at school and in the wider education system and society (Fairclough, 2013). Interview, focus group and participant observation data were coded and connections were traced between classroom practice, teacher and student comments and EMI texts, discourses and ideology from the school and wider education system (Heller et al., 2018). For example, the teacher's claim that 'language is not that important for mathematics' (05.09.18 fieldnotes), was associated with claims made by Ministry of Education officials and the introduction of EMI for mathematics and science before other subjects (Pearson, 2014); the teacher's focus on showing and doing mathematics and his omission of textbook student talk-based activities.

Findings

Lesson Extract

This extract is taken from an instructional unit on cuboids. In this extract, we see the teacher attempting to begin the activity of 'demonstration', which is present in all lessons in the data set and has the longest duration of all lesson activities, across lessons. Typically, in 'demonstration', student volunteers complete example tasks on the board in front of the class. Meanwhile, the teacher stands to the side and offers support to the student at the board or guides other students to provide support when he sees this is necessary, often in response to requests for help from the student at the board. As a result, the process of doing the example and the task supports are available to seated students. The rest of the class complete the exercise in their notebooks; some work faster than the volunteer, others in lock-step, and some only copy the exercise into their books once it has been completed. Students correct their work by comparing it to the example on the board. Individual teacher feedback on the work of seated students is rare.

Here, we see the teacher responding to cues from the students that they require additional task support before beginning demonstration. The extract exemplifies the range of linguistic resources which the teacher draws upon to help students access English and mathematics in these lessons, and which students use to participate. Transcript conventions are provided in Appendix 1: Transcript Conventions at the end of this chapter. The extract begins as the teacher writes the following word problem on the board:

Extract

Example: The net of a cuboid consists of a series of rectangles. How many rectangles are there? What is the surface area of the cuboid if it measure 6 cm by 3 cm by 2 cm?
Solution

The teacher completes the text by underlining the word 'solution' in a single stroke, then walks to a desk front left. He puts down the textbook and picks up the set square and holds it aloft:

> Who can come to correct this question? Anyone who can come to correct the answer ... Hari uwaza ngo agerageze? (*is there anyone who can come and try*) ... heh? ...

He points to the example on the board as he says 'this question', then gestures out at the class. He moves to the left of the room, and moves his gaze over the students seated there. This is a bid to begin demonstration, and an invitation for students to volunteer. Instead, the students continue writing, chatting quietly or looking across the room. Their non-response is a sign to the teacher that they need additional task support. The teacher responds by drawing and labelling a diagram of the cuboid for the task:

> Let me try to calculate to draw the figure
> 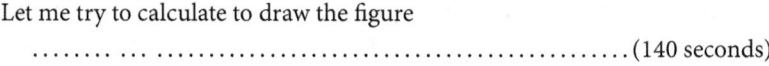 (140 seconds)

Then he makes another bid for a volunteer. He steps back to the left side of the classroom, talking as he moves away from the diagram. He looks at the diagram, then out at the class:

> Ntawaza ngo agerageze? (*Who can come and try*) ... who can come to find the surface area? ... can you try?

One student raises his hand and clicks his fingers. The teacher continues to look around the room. This particular student nearly always volunteers, and the teacher apparently interprets the non-response from most students to indicate the need for additional guidance. He points to the diagram of the cuboid in the middle of the board. He speaks loudly. Most students are facing the teacher at this point. 'How many rectangles are there?'

He leaves a pause of six seconds in which several students call out answers: Four. Four. Two. Four. Six. /Six/ 'He ends their turn by echoing the last response and extending it into a fuller answer: /Six/ rectangle. Sibyo? (*Isn't it?*)'

Teacher tag questions (such as Sibyo?) punctuate classroom interaction, where they function as a means to maintain and direct student attention, and provide opportunity for student participation.

A single student calls out: 'Four.' The teacher provides additional, visual guidance, turning to the second diagram of the cuboid on the board, and counting off the sides with his chalk as he talks. Iyi niyi, niyi niyi, niyi niyi yo hasi. Is six. Sibyo? (*This side and that, this side and that, and this side and the one* below. *Isn't it?*) The teacher looks up and pauses for three seconds. A single student calls out loudly: 'YES.' The teacher says: 'Sibyo? (*Isn't it?*)' The same student responds: 'Yes.' The teacher writes: S.A. (R.1), saying as he does so: 'Sibyo? Urabanza ushake surface area of rectangle one. Sibyo? SIBYO? (*Isn't it? You start by finding . . . Isn't it? Isn't it?*)' Then he writes: S.A (R.2), as he continues:

> Rectangle one and surface area of rectangle two. . . . Siko bimeze? Surface area of rectangle three. Noneho ugende ukuba kabiri ukuba kabiri (*Then you multiply by two*) Sibyo? . . . Siko bimeze? . . . (*Isn't it?*)

A single student answers: 'Yes.' The teacher finishes writing the formula, adding: S.A. (R.3). He turns away from the board and looks out towards the class, saying: 'Come . . .'

The teacher has provided additional task support, using English for mathematical language, along with mathematical symbols and the diagram on the board, and Kinyarwanda. He finishes by making another bid for a volunteer. When, again, no students volunteer, he proceeds to guide them through calculating the surface area of one of the rectangles:

> Rectangle ya mbere ngizi, zirimo ari face ebyiri. Sibyo?
>   (*The first rectangle is here. There are two faces. Isn't it?*)

The teacher points towards the length measurement label on the diagram as he says: 'This is length . . . Sibyo? (*Isn't it?*)'

Then he adds the labels '(l), (w), (h)' to the diagram as he says: 'Length, width, height Sibyo?' (*Isn't it?*). . .'

A single student answers: 'Yes.'

The teacher continues talking as he writes '2 (LxW)=', 'Wenda reka dukube kabiri. Sibyo? (*Let us multiply by two. Isn't it?*)

Length and width, Sibyo? (*Isn't it?*)'

Again, a single student answers: 'Yes.'

The teacher looks up at the class, and asks: 'Ni kangahe?' (*How much?*)

He leaves a six-second pause in which several students respond, although what they say is unclear. The teacher writes: '2 (6cm x 3cm),' then asks: 'Dukubye?' (*We multiply by?*)

He leaves a two-second pause in which several students call out; two are audible:

> 'Kabiri' (*Two times*)
>   'Ni cumi nagatanu, cumi na' (*It is fifteen*)

The teacher responds: 'Sibyo? . . . Turagira kangahe?' (*Isn't it? What do we get?*)

> A few students reply, their answer is unclear. The teacher writes '18' on the board, then continues:
>
> 'dukubye kabiri ni kangahe?... heh?' (*Eighteen multiply by two, we get*)
>
> A few students answer in the four second pause left by the teacher: ,'Itatu gatandatu' (*Thirty-six*).
> The teacher says: 'Centimetre square.'
> He writes: =36 cm²
> He moves to the left of the board, looks out towards the class and says:
>
> Hagire uza akore (*Who can come and try*)... for rectangle two... heeeh?
>
> The teacher looks around the room in the twelve-second pause that follows. This time, at least three students, seated on different rows, raise their hands and click their fingers.

This extract illustrates the teacher's purposeful pedagogical approach, which centres around the performance of example exercises. We see how the seated students direct the teacher to provide greater task support, non-verbally, through not volunteering to demonstrate the task, and how the teacher employs a range of multilingual and multimodal semiotic resources to do so. It is an example of how the teacher uses English for mathematical language, across lessons, as part of a flexible multilingual and multimodal semiotic repertoire which enables students to access English and mathematics.

Teacher and Student Perspectives

Next, we consider teacher and student perspectives on mathematics lessons and the use of English in lessons. Their comments in interviews and focus groups indicate a shared classroom language policy, which allows students to access mathematical meanings and practices, and the English they need to pass exams. The teacher states:

> When I teach, I prefer to use English only but students do not understand maths without explaining in Kinyarwanda (...) students like me to use both Kinyarwanda and English.
>
> 05.18, Teacher interview transcript

The students describe their preferences in almost the same terms. For example:

> I like studying mathematics in English but with some explanations in Kinyarwanda for understanding mathematics and English too.
>
> 19.09.18, Student group interview transcript

Across lessons, the teacher uses English for mathematical English terms and texts, which is the English students need to pass exams. Interestingly, the teacher seems to use the subtractive model of EMI to enable his main focus on mathematics, and English only in so far as it is part of mathematics. He describes himself as a mathematics teacher, and not an English teacher (Fieldnotes, 04.09.18), and states that teaching English is the responsibility of primary school English teachers (Fieldnotes, 04.09.18; 05.09.18).

When asked about their motivation for learning English, students do not refer to the international dimension of English as a 'global language', which is a discourse used by policymakers (Pearson, 2014; Sibomana, 2022) and other teachers at this school (Fieldnotes, 05.09.18). Instead, students state that they 'must' learn English to progress at school. This is illustrated by the comment of one student, who states:

> Learning English helps us to pass the exams of subjects taught in English.
>
> 05.18 Student focus group notes

Thus, like the teacher, the students are focused on the English they need to pass exams, which is arguably the English they are exposed to in these lessons.

Our data indicate some ways in which subtractive EMI and related discourses constrain classroom communication. For instance, students talk about their difficulties using English in lessons, positioning their 'lack' of English as the problem. As one student puts it:

> The issue is the lower level of English skills we have.
>
> 19.09.18 Student group interview transcript, S3

Students seem to compare their emergent and multilingual proficiency with the monoglossic 'ideal' of the coursebook, and perceive themselves to be lacking. This deficit perspective undermines students' confidence to communicate in lessons, as described by one student, below:

> The language issue that I had it was to ask questions but it was due the lack of confidence. I did not have enough confidence to ask in English.
>
> 19.09.18 Student group interview transcript, S1

Notably, the teacher also perceives students' limited English as indicative of the low ability of 'these students' (Fieldnotes, 04.09.18; 05.09.18). This seems to reinforce his negative perception of students who attend government twelve-year basic education schools, who as Williams (2019) reports are widely stigmatized in Rwanda.

Implications for Researching EMI Mathematics Teaching and Learning

In this section, we discuss the findings of our research in relation to other studies, and consider the implications for future research. Our study indicates that the teacher's purposeful pedagogical approach centres around engaging students with mathematical practices, as part of whole class interactions. As with Carter and Rose (2021), we find that almost all lesson time is used by the teacher and students to focus on mathematical tasks, with minimal time used for classroom management. Carter and Rose (ibid.) report that the teachers they observed provided little feedback to students. We suggest that feedback in these lessons is mainly non-verbal, as students compare their work with the example task on the board. This resonates with apprenticeship learning, as described by Lave and Wenger (1991), where learners self-correct by comparing their work with the 'professional' example they are part of constructing with guidance form an expert.

In general terms, we categorize this teacher's pedagogical approach as 'performance-mode', the dominant pedagogical form in sub-Saharan Africa, where lesson activities centre around the performance of subject-specific tasks (Barrett, 2007; Guthrie, 2018). Performance-mode pedagogy is a pragmatic response to contextual conditions associated with under-resourced education systems e.g. large classes, limited material resources, and long working hours for teachers (Barrett, 2007; Bernstein, 1996). Competence-mode pedagogy centres on the competence of individual learners in the class. The approach is more resource intensive, as teachers differentiate the use of time and space, tasks and evaluation strategies between students, which may be one reason why efforts to implement learner-centred education in low–middle-income countries s have stalled (Guthrie, 2018; Schweisfurth, 2015). There is not a good/bad dichotomy between the two: performance-mode pedagogy can include aspects of pedagogical quality, such as time on task, clear rules of behaviour, transparent feedback and the responsiveness of the teacher to students (ibid.). Indeed, we see similarities between this teacher's pedagogy and the simultaneous engagement with mathematical practice, language and meanings proposed by Moschkovich for multilingual mathematics learners (2015).

For EMI mathematics teaching and learning research, it is important to note that classroom talk has a distinct role in performance-mode and competence-mode classroom settings (Bernstein, 1996). In the former, established routines mean there is less need to verbally clarify activities and roles, or to provide feedback. Explanation comes as much from observation of and engagement with mathematical practice, as talking about practice. In the latter, verbal language has a greater role for classroom organization, and individualized task description and feedback (ibid.). For example, in the extract presented above students participate non-verbally to direct the teacher to provide task support. This insight would not have emerged from a study looking for student verbal participation alone. We do not question the central value of talk for mathematics teaching and learning, and as a key learning outcome. Our data confirm that EMI constrains student verbal participation in lessons and this undermines their active analytical engagement with mathematical content (Carter and Rose, 2021). However, we note that several influential EMI mathematics studies (e.g. Setati et al., 2002; Probyn, 2015), compare the practice they observe with competence-based pedagogical models of quality developed in middle and high-income contexts (e.g. Mercer, 1995). We argue that there is a need to research EMI mathematics teaching and learning as a situated phenomenon in order to recognize pedagogical resources and identify recommendations for development that are contextually feasible. For example, we suggest sustained collaboration between researchers and teachers, to inform researcher understanding of pedagogy and engage teachers agentively in pedagogical innovation (e.g. Barrett et al., 2021; William & Ndabakurane, 2017).

This study confirms that classroom communication in EMI settings is often multilingual (Heugh et al., 2017). The teacher uses a multilingual and multimodal semiotic repertoire to construct lessons, and enable students to access English and mathematics. He systematically uses English for mathematical verbal language, as part of a flexible multilingual and multimodal semiotic repertoire. This account contrasts with reports that teacher's use of L1 is ad hoc and haphazard (Probyn, 2015; Setati et al., 2008). His practice is also distinct from 'pedagogical translanguaging' (Makalela, 2019), because this teacher is not aiming to teach bi-literacy, but mathematical literacy. Again, this finding illustrates the need to allow teachers to lead on developing classroom language policies relevant to their pedagogical goals, rather than imposing fixed pedagogical models (Barrett et al., 2021). The teacher and students' description of their classroom language policy ('teach in English and explain in Kinyarwanda') echoes the teachers in William's (2019) report from Rwandan government schools, indicating that this systematic and flexible multilingual approach may be widespread. The integration of mathematical English with Kinyarwanda, and non-verbal and mathematical linguistic resources as part of classroom-mathematical practice to enable students to access English and mathematics resonates with the work of multilingual mathematics educators in the USA (Moschkovich, 2002, 2015). The principled and pragmatic pedagogical approach merits further research in EMI contexts.

In line with other studies, this teacher and other teachers at school, talk about EMI in relation to 'international English', whilst students reflect on the challenges of learning and assessment through English (Setati, 2005, 2008). This indicates differences in how EMI impacts teachers and students. As noted above, the teacher is able to interpret EMI in relation to his identity as a mathematics teacher, and legitimize his multilingual communication. Students, in contrast, are positioned as lacking language in comparison with the monolingual 'ideal' of the textbook. Like Probyn (2009), these students report that this undermines their confidence to talk in lessons. The teacher's description of 'these students' as lacking talent echoes Williams (2019), account of negative perceptions of students who attend government secondary schools. It is worrying, given the association between teacher's perception of students' ability to learn and the effort they make to help students learn (Brinkman, 2019). A negative result of the teacher's identity as a mathematics and not a language teacher is that while the teacher employs a range of language-supportive strategies (Barrett et al., 2021; Opanga et al., 2021; William & Ndabakurane, 2017), he does not describe them. This suggest that the teacher may have limited awareness and/or opportunity to develop the strategies which are central to student epistemic access and participation in these lessons.

Concluding Thoughts

In this chapter, we considered issues for researching mathematics teaching and learning in EMI contexts, drawing on our recent case study of mathematics lessons in a government secondary school in rural Rwanda. Our study was informed by our view of language and pedagogy as intertwined, situated and sociocultural phenomena (Moschkovich, 2002). This transglossic perspective enabled us to identify pedagogical resources and constraints, and draw recommendations for mitigating the negative impacts of EMI in Rwanda and comparable contexts. We conclude that the major problem with EMI is the subtractive and monolingual approach to EMI in official policy, that is reflected in textbooks, curriculum and teacher education. This ideology of EMI constrains classroom communication, and undermines the teacher and students' confidence in students' abilities. Thus, it is urgent and important for education researchers, policy makers, curriculum designers and teacher educators to move beyond subtractive and monolingual understandings of EMI. There is a need to learn from and with teachers, in order to develop language in education policy and educational resources which enable and do not constrain multilingual mathematics pedagogy.

Appendix 1: Transcript conventions

.....	Pause. Each dot is equivalent to one second
italics	Spoken quietly and not audible to the class
LOUD	Spoken loudly, 'shouting'
(italics)	Translation from Kinyarwanda to English
?	Rising intonation
!	Increased volume (between talking and shouting)

Conflict of Interests

The authors declare that they have no conflict of interest.

Notes

1   In 2018, 36 per cent (https://data.worldbank.org/indicator/SE.SEC. NENR?locations=RW, accessed 10 February 2022).

References

Adler, J. (1999). The dilemma of transparency: Seeing and seeing through talk in the mathematics classroom. *Journal for Research in Mathematics Education, 30*(1), 47–64.

Banda, F. (2018). Translanguaging and English-African language mother tongues as linguistic dispensation in teaching and learning in a black township school in Cape

Town. *Current Issues in Language Planning, 19*(2), 198–217. Doi: 10.1080/14664208.2017.1353333.

Barrett, A. M. (2007). Beyond the polarization of pedagogy: Models of classroom practice in Tanzanian primary schools. *Beyond the Comparative Education, 43*(2), 273–294. Doi: 10.1080/03050060701362623.

Barrett, A. M., Juma, Z. R., & William, F. (2021). Processes of pedagogic change: integrating subject and language learning through teacher education. In E. J. Erling, J. Clegg, C. M. Rubagumya & C. Reilly (eds), *Multilingual learning and language supportive pedagogies in sub-Saharan Africa*. Abingdon: Routledge.

Bernstein, B. (1996). *Pedagogy, symbolic control and identity. Theory, research, critique.* Rev. edn. Lanham, MD, New York and Oxford: Rowman and Littlefield Publishers.

Blommaert, J. (2010). *The sociolinguistics of globalisation*. Cambridge: Cambridge University Press.

Blommaert, J., & Dong, J. (2010). *Ethnographic fieldwork: A beginners' guide*. Bristol: Multilingual Matters.

Bond, T. N., & Tikly, L. (2013). Towards a post-colonial research ethics in comparative and international education. *Compare: A Journal of Comparative and International Education, 43*, 422–442.

Bowden, R., Uwineza, I., Dushimimana, J.C., and Uworwabayeho, A. (2022) Learner-centred education and English medium instruction: Policies in practice in a lower-secondary mathematics class in rural Rwanda. *Compare: A Journal of Comparative and International Education*. Doi: 10.1080/03057925.2022.2093163.

Brinkman, S. (2019). Teachers' beliefs and educational reform in India: From 'learner-centred' to 'learning-centred' education. *Comparative Education, 55*(1), 9–29. Doi: 10.1080/03050068.2018.1541661.

Carter, E., and Rose, P. (2021) *Teacher practices in Rwandan secondary mathematics classrooms: Findings from classroom observations*. Leaders in Teaching Research and Policy Series, March 2021. Laterite, Rwanda and REAL Centre, University of Cambridge.

Charamba, E. (2020). Translanguaging in a multilingual class: A study of the relation between students' languages and epistemological access in science. *International Journal of Science Education, 42*(11), 1779–1798. Doi: 10.1080/09500693.2020.1783019.

Cincotta-Segi, A. R. (2011). Signalling L2 centrality, maintaining L1 dominance: Teacher language choice in an ethnic minority primary classroom in the Lao PDR. *Language and Education, 25*(1), 19–31. Doi: 10.1080/09500782.2010.511232.

Collier, V. P., & Thomas, W. P. (2017). Validating the power of bilingual schooling: Thirty-two years of large-scale, longitudinal research. *Annual Review of Applied Linguistics, 37*, 203–217. Doi: 10.1017/S0267190517000034.

Cummins, J. (2017). Teaching for transfer in multilingual school contexts. In O. García, A. M. Y. Lin & S. May (eds), *Bilingual and Multilingual Education* (pp. 103–115). Cham: Springer. Doi: 10.1007/978-3-319-02258-1.

Duff, P. (2008). *Case study research in applied linguistics*. New York and London: Routledge.

Dushimimana, J. C., & Uworwabayeho, A. (2021) Teacher training college student performance in statistics and probability exams in Rwanda. *Rwandan Journal of Education*, 5(1), 68–81.

Erling, E. J., Clegg, J., Rubagumya, C. M., & Reilly, C. (2021). Introduction: Multilingual learning and language supportive pedagogies in sub-Saharan Africa. In E. J. Erling, J. Clegg, C. M. Rubagumya & C. Reilly (eds), *Multilingual learning and language supportive pedagogies in sub-Saharan Africa* (pp. 1–30). Abingdon: Routledge.

Fairclough, N. (2013). *Critical discourse analysis: The critical study of language*. 2nd edn. Abingdon: Routledge.

García, O., & Li, W. (2014). *Translanguaging. Language, bilingualism and education*. Houndmills, Basingstoke, and New York: Palgrave Macmillan.

Genesee, F. (2013). Insights into bilingual education from research on immersion programs in Canada. In C. Abello-Contesse, P. M. Chandler, D. Lopez-Jimenez, & R. Chacon-Beltran (eds), *Bilingual and multilingual education in the 21st century*. Bristol: Multilingual Matters.

Gumperz, J., & Hymes, D. (1986). *Directions in sociolinguistics: The ethnography of communication*. Oxford and New York: Wiley-Blackwell.

Guthrie, G. (2018). Classroom change in developing countries: From progressive cage to formalistic frame. In *Classroom change in developing countries: From progressive cage to formalistic frame*. London: Routledge. Doi: 10.4324/9781351130479.

Habyarimana, H., Ntakirutimana, E., & Barnes, L. (2017). A sociolinguistic analysis of code-switching in Rwanda. *Language Matters*, 48(3), 49–72. Doi: 10.1080/10228195.2017.1413127.

Heller, M. Pietikaeinen, S. & Pujolar, J. (2018). *Critical sociolinguistic research methods: Studying language issues that matter*. New York and London: Routledge.

Herdina, P., & Jessner, U. (2002). *A dynamic model of multilingualism: Perspectives of change in psycholinguistics*. Bristol: Multilingual Matters.

Heugh, K., Prinsloo, C., Makgamatha, M., Diedericks, G., & Winnaar, L. (2017). Multilingualism(s) and system-wide assessment: A southern perspective. *Language and Education*, 31(3), 197–216. Doi: 10.1080/09500782.2016.1261894.

Hultgren, A. K., Erling, E. J., & Chowdhury, Q. H. (2016). Ethics in language and identity research. In S. Preece (ed.), *Routledge handbook of language and identity*. London and New York: Routledge.

Jaspers, J. (2018). Language in education policy and sociolinguistics: Towards a new critical engagement. In J. W. Tollefson & M. Perez-Milans (eds), *The Oxford handbook of language policy and planning* (pp. 704–726). Oxford: Oxford University Press.

Johnson, D. C. (2018). Research methods in language policy and planning. In *The Oxford handbook of language policy and planning* (pp. 51–70). Oxford: Oxford University Press.

Johnson, D. C., & Johnson, E. J. (2015). Power and agency in language policy appropriation. *Language Policy*, *14*(3), 221–243. Doi: 10.1007/s10993-014-9333-z.

Lave, J., & Wenger, E. (1991). *Situated learning: Legitimate peripheral participation.* Cambridge: Cambridge University Press.

Lemke, J. (1990). *Talking science: Language, learning, and values.* Westport, CT: Praeger Publishers.

Lin, A. M. Y. (2019). Theories of trans/languaging and trans-semiotizing: implications for content-based education classrooms. *International Journal of Bilingual Education and Bilingualism*, *22*(1), 5–16. Doi: 10.1080/13670050.2018.1515175.

Macaro, E. (2018). *English medium instruction: Content and language in policy and practice.* Oxford: Oxford University Press.

Makalela, L. (2019). Uncovering the universals of ubuntu translanguaging in classroom discourses. *Classroom Discourse*, *10*(3–4), 237–251. Doi: 10.1080/19463014.2019.1631198.

May, S. (2017). Bilingual education what the research tells us. In O. García, A. M. Y. Lin & S. May (eds), *Bilingual and multilingual education.* Encyclopedia of Language and Education. 3rd edn (pp. 82–96). Cham: Springer International Publishing.

Mercer, N. (1995). *The guided construction of knowledge.* Bristol: Multilingual Matters.

Milligan, L. O., Desai, Z., & Benson, C. (2020). A critical exploration of how language-of-instruction choices affect educational equity. In A. Wulff (ed.), *Grading goal four: Tensions, threats, and opportunities in the sustainable development goal on quality education* (pp. 116–134). Leiden: Brill. Doi: 10.1163/9789004430365.

Milligan, L. O., & Tikly, L. (2016). English as a medium of instruction in postcolonial contexts: Moving the debate forward. *Comparative Education*, *52*(3), 277–280. Doi: 10.1080/03050068.2016.1185251.

MINECOFIN (Ministry of Finance and Economic Planning, Rwanda) (2000). *Republic of Rwanda Vision 2020.* July (pp. 1–31). Kigali: Government of Rwanda.

MINEDUC (Ministry of Education, Rwanda) (2013). *The Education Sector Strategic Plan 2013/4–2017/8.* Kigali: Government of Rwanda.

Moschkovich, J. (2002). A Situated and sociocultural perspective on bilingual mathematics learners. *Mathematical Thinking and Learning*, *4*(2–3), 189–212. Doi: 10.1207/s15327833mtl04023_5.

Moschkovich, J. (2013). Principles and guidelines for equitable mathematics teaching practices and materials for English language learners. *Journal of Urban Mathematics Education*, *6*(1), 45–57. Available online: http://ed-osprey.gsu.edu/ojs/index.php/JUME/article/viewArticle/204 (accessed 10 March 2019).

Moschkovich, J. N. (2015). Academic literacy in mathematics for English Learners. *Journal of Mathematical Behavior*, *40*, 43–62. Doi: 10.1016/j.jmathb.2015.01.005.

Msimanga, A. (2021). Creating dialogues in whole class teaching in multilingual classrooms: Language practices and policy imperatives. In A.A. Essien & A. Msimanga (eds.), *Multilingual education yearbook 2021: Policy and practice in STEM multilingual contexts* (pp. 57–74). Cham: Springer.

Niyibizi, E., Makalela, L., and Mwepu, D. (2015). Language-in-education policy shifts in an African country: Colonial confusion and prospects for the future. In L. Makalela (ed.), *New Directions in Language and Literacy Education for Multilingual Classroom in Africa* (97–122). Cape Town: CASAS (Centre for Advanced Studies of African Society, University of the Western Cape).

O'Halloran, K. L. (2015). The language of learning mathematics: A multimodal perspective. *Journal of Mathematical Behavior, 40*, 63–74. Doi: 10.1016/j.jmathb.2014.09.002.

Opanga, D., Uworwabayeho, A., Nsengimana, T., Minani, E., & Nsengimana, V. (2021). Practices in STEM teaching and the effectiveness of the language of instruction: Exploring policy implications on pedagogical strategies in Tanzanian secondary schools. In A. A. Essien & A. Msimanga (eds), *Multilingual education yearbook 2021: Policy and practice in STEM multilingual contexts* (pp. 97–115). Cham: Springer.

Pearson, P. (2014). Policy without a plan: English as a medium of instruction in Rwanda. *Current Issues in Language Planning, 15*(1), 39–56. Doi: 10.1080/14664208.2013.857286.

Probyn, M. (2009). 'Smuggling the vernacular into the classroom': Conflicts and tensions in classroom codeswitching in township/rural schools in South Africa. *International Journal of Bilingual Education and Bilingualism, 12*(2), 123–136. Doi: 10.1080/13670050802153137.

Probyn, M. (2015). Pedagogical translanguaging: Bridging discourses in South African science classrooms. *Language and Education, 29*(3), 218–234.

Samuelson, B. L. (2012). Rwanda switches to English: Conflict, identity and language in education policy. In J. W. Tollefson (ed.), *Language policies in education*. New York: Routledge.

Schroeder, L., Mercado, M. S., & Trudell, B. (2021). Research in multilingual learning in Africa: Assessing the effectiveness of multilingual education programming. In E. J. Erling, J. Clegg, C. Rubagumya, & C. Reilly (eds), *Multilingual learning and language supportive pedagogies in sub-Saharan Africa*. Abingdon: Routledge.

Schweisfurth, M. (2015). Learner-centred pedagogy: Towards a post-2015 agenda for teaching and learning. *International Journal of Educational Development, 40*, 259–266. Doi: 10.1016/j.ijedudev.2014.10.011.

Setati, M. (2005). Teaching mathematics in a primary multilingual classroom. *Journal for Research in Mathematics Education, 36*(5), 447–466.

Setati, M. (2008). Access to mathematics versus access to the language of power: The struggle in multilingual mathematics classrooms. *South African Journal of Education, 28*(1), 103–116. Doi: 10.4314/saje.v28i1.25148.

Setati, M., Adler, J., Reed, Y., & Bapoo, A. (2002). Incomplete journeys: Code-switching and other language practices in mathematics, science and English language classrooms in South Africa. *Language and Education, 16*(2), 128–149. Doi: 10.1080/09500780208666824.

Setati, M., Molefe, T., & Langa, M. (2008). Using language as a transparent resource in the teaching and learning of mathematics in a Grade 11 multilingual classroom. *Pythagoras, 67,* 14–25. Doi: 10.4102/pythagoras.v0i67.70.

Sibomana, E. (2018). Unpeeling the language policy and planning onion in Rwanda: Layer roles. *International Journal of Social Sciences and Humanities,* 2(2), 99–114. Doi: 10.29332/ijssh.v2n2.138.

Sibomana, E. (2022). Transitioning from a local language to English as a medium of instruction: Rwandan teachers' and classroom-based perspectives. *International Journal of Bilingual Education and Bilingualism,* 25(4), 1259-1274. Doi: 10.1080/13670050.2020.1749554.

Sibomana, E., & Uwambayinema, E. (2016). Kinyarwanda doesn't have a place in communication at our school: Linguistic, psychosocial and educational effects of banning one's mother tongue. *Rwanda Journal: Series B,* 3(1). http://www.ajol.info/index.php/rj/article/view/145353 (accessed 22 February 2022).

Steflja, I. (2012). The high costs and consequences of Rwanda's shift in language policy from French to English. In *Africa Portal.* Available online: https://www.africaportal.org/publications/the-high-costs-and-consequences-of-rwandas-shift-in-language-policy-reform-from-french-to-english/ (accessed April 2017).

Tabaro, C. (2015). Rwandans' motivation to learn and use English as a medium of instruction. *International Journal of Humanities and Social Science,* 5(2), 78–85.

Trudell, B. (2016). Language choice and education quality in Eastern and Southern Africa: A review. *Comparative Education,* 52(3), 281–293. Doi: 10.1080/03050068.2016.1185252.

Uworwabayeho, A. (2009). Teachers' innovative change within countrywide reform: A case study in Rwanda. *Journal of Mathematics Teacher Education,* 12(5), 315–324. Doi: 10.1007/s10857-009-9124-1.

van de Kuilen, H., Altinyelken, H. K., Voogt, J. M., & Nzabalirwa, W. (2020). Recontextualization of learner-centred pedagogy in Rwanda: A comparative analysis of primary and secondary schools. Compare, 52(6), 966–983. Doi: 10.1080/03057925.2020.1847044.

Williams, T. (2017). The political economy of primary education: Lessons from Rwanda. *World Development,* 96, 550–561.

Williams, T. P. (2019). The things they learned: Aspiration, uncertainty, and schooling in Rwanda's developmental state. *Journal of Development Studies,* 55(4), 645–660. Doi: 10.1080/00220388.2018.1453602.

William, F., & Ndabakurane, J. (2017). Language supportive teaching and textbooks (LSTT) for bilingual classrooms mathematics teaching and learning in Tanzania. *African Journal of Teacher Education,* 6(1). Doi: 10.21083/ajote.v6i0.3946.

World Bank (2021). *LOUD AND CLEAR: Effective language of instructions policies for learning.* Available online: https://www.worldbank.org/en/topic/education/publication/loud-and-clear-effective-language-of-instruction-policies-for-learning (accessed 10 February 2022).

Part Four

Language Issues in Teaching with Mathematics Register in an Indigenous (African) Language and Directions for Future Research

Preparing Teachers to Teach Mathematics in Home Languages in Malawi: What We Know, What We Need to Know and Directions for Future Research

Justina Longwe, Fraser Gobede and Mercy Kazima

Introduction

Language is considered a pedagogical resource that supports mathematics teaching and learning (Planas & Setati-Phakeng, 2014). Proficiency in the language of instruction is crucial in mathematics achievement because learning of mathematics occurs when learners realize the potential meaning engrained in language (Planas, 2018; Prediger, 2019; Setati, 2008). For the teacher, language is a key resource used for mediating learning (Essien, 2018; Scarino & Liddicoat, 2009). In Malawi, for instance, Kazima (2006) found that learners' first language has an influence on the meanings they attach to mathematical terms, some of which are different from the conventional mathematical meanings. This implies that the way language is used may promote or impede the learning of mathematics. Thus, the underachievement of Malawian learners reported in several studies (e.g. Brombacher, 2011; MoEST, 2010; MoEST, 2014; National Statistical Office, 2021) could be an indication that, among other factors, the language used for mediating learning does not fully support the development of important mathematical concepts in learners (Brombacher, 2019; Saka, 2019). For instance, during the 2010 Early Grade Mathematics Assessment (EGMA), the failure of Standard 2 learners to perform basic addition made Brombacher (2011) wonder if the learners understood what they were doing even though the questions were posed in their home language. As such, teachers need to know the issues surrounding language during mathematics teaching, more especially teachers who teach in multilingual classrooms – as is the case in Malawi. In this chapter, we focus on Malawi and discuss the use of indigenous languages for teaching mathematics during the early years of primary school, and how teacher education prepares the teachers for this. We pay attention to how pre-service teacher educators help pre-service teachers to learn to teach mathematics using home languages. We report on what we know about preparing teachers to teach mathematics in home languages. We do this by trying to answer the question: What do teacher educators do to prepare teachers to teach in home languages? Using lessons on the addition of whole numbers using a place value box as an example, we analysed lessons from two pre-service teacher education classes, and to see how primary school teachers teach mathematics using the same place value box, we analysed a Standard (Grade) 2 mathematics lesson on the same topic of addition of whole numbers. Our focus was on how the mathematics teacher educators and the primary school teacher used language and explained concepts about addition of numbers using a place value box.

Using Home Language in Early Grade Mathematics Teaching and Learning

Language is conceptualized differently in different settings. In multilingual settings, language often covers 'named languages' (Bowden & Barret, 2022, p. ii). There are many issues surrounding the teaching of mathematics in multilingual classrooms, and these issues are complex and can sometimes be contentious (Davis et al., 2015). Approximately half of the postcolonial countries in sub-Sahara Africa use English as a language of teaching and learning from upper primary to secondary schools. Most of these are former colonies of Britain. Preference of English is partly attributed to the status the language is accorded in economic as well as political circles, viewing widespread proficiency in English as an indicator of economic development (Milligan & Tikly, 2016). This status drives parents and even teachers to perceive early introduction to English as a language of teaching and learning as important for learners' academic achievement. For instance, even though research has often linked positive outcomes in learner achievement with the use of home languages (Jourdain & Sharma, 2016; Milligan & Tikly, 2016; Setati, 2008), it could appear surprising that when learners, teachers, and parents are asked to indicate their preferred language of teaching and learning, they may point to a foreign language, such as English (Davis et al., 2015; Roberts & Alex, 2020; Setati, 2008). In a study by Davis et al. (2015), for example, Grade 4 learners in Ghana acknowledged that they did not understand English and then reasoned that they wanted to learn mathematics in English so that they learn the language in the process. In Malawi a survey by the Centre for Language Studies at the University of Malawi found that parents prefer that children in primary school learn in English for the same reason that they should learn the language in the process (Centre for Language Studies, 2009). As Setati (2008), Milligan and Tikly (2016) argue, the choice of English is because of the opportunities the language offers despite the difficulties learners face learning with English. Thus, researchers, teacher educators, and teachers must be familiar with the underlying issues associated with the adoption and use of a particular language of teaching and learning.

Research and education policies in most parts of the world support the use of home languages for teaching and learning (e.g. Adler, 2001; Hariastuti et al., 2020; Setati et al., 2002). The benefits that learners get from learning in their home languages cannot be overemphasized. Scholars contend that the use of home languages, especially in the early years, tends to improve learners' cognitive development. Learners who learn mathematics in their home language learn better because they do not have to grapple with the additional constraints of learning the language of teaching and learning as they are already familiar with the 'linguistic structures' that they come across in their mathematics lessons (Sapire & Essien, 2021, p. 89). Additionally, teaching learners using their home language boosts their confidence, self-esteem and their creativity is enhanced; as such, they are able to actively participate in the lessons (Chitera, 2010). In emphasizing the importance of home languages on learners' learning, UNESCO (2003), as cited in Hariastuti et al. (2020), reiterated that 'no language can take the place of mother tongue in education and that no educational system can afford to disregard it without serious detriment to the mental and social development of the child' (p. 64).

Given the importance of using home languages in the teaching and learning of mathematics, it is important to recognize that effective implementation of these language policies depends on the knowledge that the teacher has in teaching mathematics in home languages. How well the teacher explains mathematical concepts in the home languages greatly influences learners learning of mathematics. We contend that the ability of teachers to foster effective mathematics teaching experiences in the home languages might not come naturally. Thus, how teacher education prepares them for multilingual classrooms is crucial. It implies that it is important for pre-service teacher education to accommodate the realities of teaching mathematics in home languages. This would not only help teachers teaching in home languages in Standards 1-4, but would also help teachers of Standards 5–8 to be able to use the home languages as a resource (Adler, 2001) in their multilingual classrooms. However, researchers bemoan the lack of proper teacher training for teachers to teach in home languages (Chitera, 2012; Essien et al., 2016; Planas, 2021). Teaching mathematics in home languages has its own challenges such as issues to do with the translation of mathematical concepts from English to the language of teaching and learning, being that most home languages lack vocabulary in mathematics and in most cases, teaching and learning materials are in English (Chauma, 2012; Chitera, 2010; Kazima, 2008; Lartec et al., 2014). This makes it challenging for teachers to explain mathematical concepts to learners in a way that they can understand. Thus, these challenges necessitate the need for teacher education to pay particular attention to the use of, and to use home languages in mathematics teaching and learning.

The Malawi Context

Malawi Language Policy in Education

Malawi's language policy in education requires that learners be taught in their home languages in the first four years of primary school, and thereafter in English. This language policy was introduced in 1996, with the justification that early years learners learn better and faster when they are taught through their home languages (Mjaya et al., 2006). This policy succeeded the 1968 policy which required that early years learners should learn all subjects, except English, in Chichewa, which is Malawi's national language, regardless of whether the learners and the teachers had Chichewa as their home language (Chitera, 2012; Mjaya et al., 2006). The introduction of the 1996 policy meant that early years learners would be learning in their home languages or in languages that are predominant in their areas, while Chichewa and English would be learned as subjects. Thus, the policy allows for multilingualism in the early years of primary school. However, implementation of the policy began without teachers receiving any formal training on the use of home languages as a medium of teaching and learning (Mjaya et al., 2006). Furthermore, there were, and still there are no textbooks in any other home language except Chichewa. It is worthwhile to note that in 2014, the government of Malawi announced a directive that English should be the medium of instruction in all primary school classes (Kamwendo,

2016; MoEST, 2016). However, this was not followed through and the mother tongue policy is still in place.

Although the 1996 language in education policy has been in use for over two decades, very little has been done to support teachers to effectively teach in home languages. In teacher training colleges (TTCs), pre-service teacher training is done in English, and the training programme does not provide guidance on how teachers can teach in the home languages, yet, the teachers' work of teaching in the first four classes expects them to teach using home languages. This poses a challenge to teachers, especially in the teaching of mathematics in multilingual classes. The teaching of mathematics involves the use of specialized terms that come in a register of their own, and to make this information comprehensible to learners, interpreting the terms into learners' home languages becomes necessary (Kazima, 2008), but teachers may not be able to do this effectively if their teacher education does not support them on how to do this. The absence of this element in teacher education may imply that mathematics teacher educators (TEs) are left to decide by themselves how they can help pre-service teachers (PSTs) to learn to teach mathematics using home languages in a multilingual classroom.

Mathematics Teaching in Primary Pre-Service Teacher Education in Malawi

In Malawi, pre-service primary school teacher education is currently done in specialized TTCs through a two-year Initial Primary Teacher Education (IPTE) programme, divided into six terms. A school term lasts 12 to 14 weeks depending on the school calendar, which is determined by the Ministry of education. An academic year comprises three terms. The academic calendar for the IPTE programme is the same as that of primary and secondary schools. Pre-service teachers spend the first two terms at the TTC doing taught courses, the following two terms in schools doing teaching practice, and the last two terms at the TTC again for more taught courses and final assessment. The programme produces generalist teachers that are expected to teach all subjects in all primary school classes. The mathematics curriculum in pre-service teacher education appears to be aligned with the language policy in that there is a special focus on the teaching of mathematics in the early years. The content that is taught in the first term of year one focuses specifically on the teaching of mathematics in the early years (MoEST, 2017). However, the language of teaching and learning is English and all curriculum materials that are used are in English.

Mathematics Teaching in Primary School

Mathematics is taught using home languages in the first four years of primary school, and thereafter taught in English in the upper classes (Standards 5 to 8). The teaching and learning resources for teaching in the early years are developed in a way that the syllabus and teacher's guides are in English, and the learners' books are in one vernacular language, Chichewa. It implies that there are no teaching and learning materials developed for other home languages.

Implementation Gaps

Looking at the teaching of mathematics in primary school and how PSTs are prepared to teach during their pre-service teacher education, it is clear that there is a gap in the implementation of the language in education policy. While PSTs are expected to implement the home language policy in their work of teaching, their pre-service teacher education neither includes courses on teaching in home languages, nor does the curriculum provide guidance on how the PSTs should be prepared to teach in home languages. This implies that teachers teach mathematics in a language that they were not trained to teach, or there is an assumption that mathematics TEs know how to train PSTs in using home languages. In this study, we explore what mathematics TEs do to prepare PSTs to teach in home languages, in the absence of curriculum guidance on how to train teachers to teach in home languages. We draw from our observations on what two mathematics TEs and one primary school teacher do in their lessons on the addition of whole numbers using a place value box.

Theoretical Framework

This research was guided by the Mathematics Discourse in Instruction (MDI) framework which was developed by Adler and Ronda (2015). Over the years, the teaching version of this framework, which is the Mathematics Teaching Framework (MTF) (Adler, 2021) has also been developed and improved. The MDI framework was chosen for use in our study because it is a research framework (ibid.) which is helpful in describing and interpreting shifts in mathematics that is made available during teaching (Adler & Alshwaikh, 2019), and it specifically targets mathematics teaching practices that teachers meet regularly in their work of teaching (Adler, 2017), implying that it is informed by the demands of teaching and learning mathematics. Also, the framework was developed from data collected in a multilingual classroom in an African context. Thus, the framework takes into consideration the challenges of teaching mathematics in a multilingual classroom.

The MDI framework considers four elements that are key to the teaching of mathematics, the object of learning, exemplification, explanatory talk and learner participation (Adler & Ronda, 2015). The object of learning refers to what learners are expected to know and be able to do. In a mathematics lesson, bringing the object of learning into focus is crucial because it brings learners' attention to what they are expected to learn. This object of learning is brought into focus through three mediational means, which include exemplification, explanatory talk and learner participation. Exemplification is concerned with examples and tasks used in a lesson, and how these provide opportunities for learners to learn mathematics. Explanatory talk refers to talk that names and legitimates important aspects of the object of learning, while learner participation is about how learners are invited to participate and demonstrate their mathematical reasoning in a lesson (ibid.). All these mediational means work together to achieve the object of learning. In this study, we used the element of explanatory talk to understand what mathematics TEs do to prepare teachers to teach in home languages. Explanatory talk unfolds through how teachers refer to mathematical objects and processes (naming), and how they legitimate what counts as mathematics (legitimation) (Adler & Ronda, 2015). We used this element of explanatory talk to analyse how mathematical concepts about the teaching of addition using a place value box were explained in the two teaching contexts where the language of teaching and learning was different. In a mathematics lesson, what teachers say and how they say it is crucial, especially to early years learners who largely depend on their teachers to learn (Adler, 2017). Thus, in our study, we regard explanatory talk in terms of language use and explanations that take place in order to communicate mathematically in a mathematics lesson. In a multilingual context language use also includes the use of home languages to describe mathematical concepts. This implies that the analysis of word use also involves interrogating word use when naming mathematical terms in home language.

Methodology

This study employed a qualitative case study approach (Creswell, 2014). Two mathematics TEs from one public TTC, and one primary school teacher were purposively selected for participation in the study. All the three participants were part of a larger study on strengthening numeracy in early years of primary education. Data collection was done through lesson observation for all the three participants. All the lessons were video-recorded, and analysis begun by transcribing the lesson videos so that the data could be kept in a readable form. Later the transcribed lesson data was divided into episodes, each of which was recognized by a change in content focus. Coding for explanatory talk, which included how mathematical concepts were named, was done using codes developed from the MDI framework. <u>Underline</u> indicated mathematical word use and *italics* indicated non-mathematical word use. Word use was coded as non-mathematical when ambiguous pronouns were used or when TEs' or PSTs' naming appeared to be incorrect or confusing. We extended the analysis to include use of home language, and coding for this was done by indicating whether it was available in that particular episode or not. In the data from pre-service teacher education lessons, we focused on language use and mathematical explanations provided by the TEs as well as the PSTs during the lessons on the teaching of the addition of whole numbers using the place value box. The focus was also on what TEs were doing in the lessons to help PSTs learn to teach mathematics in home languages. Regarding the data from the primary school lesson, our aim was to understand how primary school teachers use language and explain mathematical concepts in the home language. We did this by analysing data from a Standard 2 mathematics lesson on the same topic of addition of whole numbers using a place value box. Table 9.1 shows an example of how we coded the data.

Findings and Discussion

We begin the section by presenting findings on the use of language as observed in the two teacher education classrooms, then we present findings on the use of language as observed in the primary school classroom.

Observations on Use of Language in Teacher Education Classrooms

Here, we begin by giving a brief overview of the lessons from the two mathematics TEs (herein referred to as TE1 and TE2). After presenting an overview of the lessons, we use excerpts that offered opportunities for seeing the TEs' mathematical word use related to home language. As explained before, the

Table 9.1 An example of coding

Episode and object of learning	Utterances	Comments for word use
1.2 Teaching addition without regrouping	130. *TE*: So, am moving to <u>addition of whole numbers without regrouping</u>. May be for the sake of those who don't know what regrouping means, can you please explain. 131. *PST*: Umm, regrouping means, uh, when someone *adds two-digit number, for example, umm, 9+1*, it will give us 10, which means a learner can put 0 and remain with 1. 132. *TE*: Umm, okay, umm, where regrouping is involved we are talking about <u>transferring of value</u> from one <u>place value position</u> to another, are we together? 133. *PSTs*: Yes. 134. *TE*: Yeah. . . . So, when you are teaching learners, we should also start teaching them using concrete objects, if we are going to teach <u>addition without regrouping</u> we should use resources, and one of the most used resource, and of course, the most appropriate for the meantime, is this resource (shows a place value box). You remember this resource? 135. *PSTs*: Yes. 136. *TE*: When you were dealing with. 137. *PSTs*: <u>Place value</u>. 138. *TE*: <u>Place value</u>. What name is given to this? 139. *PST*: Place value box *TE*: A place value box, we can use a place value box to teach <u>addition without regrouping</u> . . .	**Mathematical word use:** in 130 132, 134, 137, 138 & 139 **Nonmathematical word use:** in 131 **Use of home language:** None

lessons focused on the teaching of addition of whole numbers using a place value box. A place value box is one of the teaching and learning resources which teachers use to teach place value of numbers. Because most schools in Malawi are not provided with readymade teaching and learning materials, teachers are required to improvise them, and in pre-service teacher education, improvisation is emphasized. Figure 9.1 is a representation of a place value box used by a PST, made from cardboard paper. The letters H, T and O stand for Hundreds, Tens and Ones, respectively.

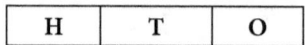

Figure 9.1 A place value box being used by a pre-service teacher.

TE1

The object of learning for TE1's lesson was: Modelling addition of numbers without regrouping, using place value box. The TE began this episode of the lesson by explaining to the PSTs that they were going to model addition of numbers, not involving regrouping, and that they were going to use place value box. He then asked PSTs to define 'regrouping,' and to explain what is meant by 'addition without regrouping.' Two PSTs provided their definitions, and the TE consolidated as follows:

134. *TE1*: It simply means adding numbers without affecting the other sections, so, as you will be adding in the ones column, the answer will not affect the tens column, likewise, up to the hundreds. So, the same applies to addition with regrouping. In regrouping it means the other columns will be?

135. *PSTs*: Affected.

The lesson continued with the TE giving tasks to individual groups. Some groups were asked to discuss and prepare a presentation on how to model the addition of two-digit numbers and others how to model the addition of three-digit numbers on a place value box. Then the PSTs went into their respective groups, planned and made their presentations before the whole class. The presentations were done in the form of mini-lessons, with the other PSTs playing the role of learners. The lesson ended by TE1 reminding the PSTs to teach addition by modelling using teaching and learning resources, and that modelling should always start from the ones column.

TE2

TE2 began the lesson by writing 'Addition of whole numbers without regrouping' on the chalkboard and explained to the pre-service teachers that they were going to look at how to teach addition of whole numbers without regrouping. He asked PSTs to define the term 'regrouping.' One PST defined it as:

131. PST: Umm, regrouping means, uh, when someone adds two-digit number, for example, umm, nine plus one it will give us ten, which means a learner can put zero and remain with one.

TE2 added to say:

132. TE2: Umm, okay, umm, where regrouping is involved we are talking about transferring of value from one place value to another, are we together?

TE2 continued to explain what the term 'without regrouping' means, and asked PSTs to always remember to teach such mathematical concepts using concrete objects like a place value box. Then, he asked the PSTs to give any addition problem that would not require regrouping. One PST gave 14 + 12. What followed was the PSTs practising how to model 14 + 12 using a place value box. The lesson ended by TE2 explaining to the PSTs that when they are teaching this to their learners, they should make sure that the learners, themselves do the modelling.

From our analysis of the lesson data, we observed that in all the lessons for both TEs, English was the language of teaching and learning all through. TEs and PSTs used English, and all mathematical concepts were named and explained in English. Even in instances where the PSTs were presenting their mini-lessons, practising how they would teach in schools, the activities were all done in English and not in home language which is the language of learning and teaching in early years of primary school. Mathematical terms such as regrouping, modelling, addition, were all named in English. For example, in an activity where TE2 asked PSTs to demonstrate how they would model the addition of 14 + 12 using a place value box, one PST asked if he could use home language. TE2's response is shown in the excerpt below:

142. TE2: (*writes 14+12 on the board*) . . . Can somebody come to the front and model the first addend fourteen in the place value box? Yes!

143. PST: Should I use local language?

144. TE2: Uh, this gentleman is asking whether he should use local language

145. PSTs: Yes.

146. TE: Where local language shall mean what?

147. PSTs: Chichewa.

148. TE2: Uh, Chichewa, no, use English.

The above dialogue shows the PST's awareness of the language in education policy in use in the early years of primary school. By asking if he could do the activity in the local language, the PST knew that he was expected to teach the same concepts in home language to his learners. So, he may have taken this as an opportunity to practise teaching in the language that he is going to use. But the TE emphasized on the use of English. While the PST's question provided an opportunity for himself and the others in the class to practise teaching in home languages, we feel that this was also an opportunity for the TE to assess the PST's readiness to teach in home languages by checking how they would name concepts such as regrouping, ones, tens in the home languages, and provide guidance where necessary. But this opportunity was not utilized. However, the TE's negative response may not be very surprising, considering that the language of teaching and learning in pre-service teacher education remains English and all the TTC curriculum materials are also in English, irrespective of the level where the concepts under focus would be taught. Also, the teacher education curriculum does not provide guidance on how TEs should help PSTs to learn to teach in home languages. Therefore, the TE could have just been following the prescribed language requirements for TTCs.

The finding that the two TEs in our study used English throughout the lessons concurs with Chitera's (2012) findings where she also found that all TEs who participated in her study used English in all the lessons that were observed despite the content under discussion being of early years classes. During her interviews with the TEs, Chitera asked them to explain what they do to help PSTs to learn to teach in home languages. They claimed that they allow their PSTs to use Chichewa when they are explaining concepts related to early years classes. However, the claim was not supported by the lesson observation data (Chitera, 2012). The observations made in our study and the findings reported by Chitera may imply that the decision to let PSTs practice teaching using home languages during the taught courses lies in the hands of the individual TEs, and that there is no common practice among mathematics TEs on how to prepare PSTs for the work of teaching mathematics in home languages. Reports that teachers are struggling to effectively implement the home languages policy (Chauma, 2012) may, therefore, not be surprising because competencies for effective implementation of the policy are expected to be obtained during teacher education.

Analysis of data from the two lessons by TE1 and TE2 also indicates that the lessons were similar in that they both focused more on equipping PSTs with knowledge of how to teach, and less on the mathematical content. Almost all the activities and explanations that were observed were directed towards how the PSTs can teach the addition of whole numbers using a place value box. This is not surprising because the PST education curriculum puts emphasis on teaching methodologies (MoEST, 2017). The content was mostly presented as examples of how to teach a particular topic, but not necessarily an in-depth interrogation of the underlying mathematical content. Although this was the case, findings from our analysis of the data reveals that there were some instances where mathematical explanatory talk was observed, implying that the TEs used mathematical language to explain concepts. For instance, the TEs provided a definition of the word 'regrouping,' as shown in utterrances 131 and 132 in the preceding excerpt. We feel this was important for PSTs to know the mathematical meaning, bearing in mind that this word is also used in ordinary English but with a different meaning. Research indicates that learners find it challenging to understand words that have different meanings when used in mathematics and in English as a language (Kazima, 2008). Thus, this explanatory talk provided opportunities for PSTs to link the word to mathematical language. However, considering that the PSTs will be required to teach this concept to learners in their home languages, it would have helped more if the explanatory talk had been extended to include how the PSTs can explain this using home languages.

Another observation that we made from our analysis of the data was that although there were instances where the explanatory talk was provided, there were some PST explanations that appeared to require modification (Adler & Ronda, 2016) and further explanation. An example of such instances is taken from TE1's lesson where a PST was demonstrating how to teach 33 + 12 using a place value box. See an excerpt below:

> **PST:** ...So, we model the addition of numbers without regrouping, so at this particular time we have the ones column and tens column, same as this place value box has got two compartments, ones and tens. So, if we are to add these two numbers, thirty-three and twelve, first we have to model, uh thirty-three, which means we have got **three under the ones and three under tens**, so first of all, we count, we are going to model three under the ones. We are going to have uh, three sticks; here is the place value box and we have got ones and tens. We have to count three loosened sticks and place them in the ones column. Here are the sticks, let's count together (*they count 1, 2, 3*). Here we have modelled **three in ones section**. Now, let's go to tens section. We are going to have how many? Three bundles of sticks, so let's count together, one, two, three, then we have modelled three loosened sticks under the ones and **three bundles of ten sticks under tens column**, therefore, we are going also to add, uh, two under what?
>
> **PSTs:** Ones.

In the above excerpt, the PST explained that to model thirty-three, it means there is 3 under the ones column and 3 under the tens column (see bolded areas). In his explanatory talk, the PST appeared to focus on the digits that were going to be placed on each place value position. While it is true that the digits that would appear under ones and tens are 3 and 3, respectively, further explanatory talk to stress on the value of each digit would have emphasized to the PST that the 3 under the tens column is not just three, but thirty or three tens. This aspect is important because research shows that most learners struggle with concepts to do with place value. This is mostly because when teaching place value, teachers tend to emphasize the place value positions rather than the values of the digits (Brendefur et al., 2018). Thus, the PST's explanatory talk would have been complete if the TE had extended the explanatory talk to emphasize the value that a digit holds in a particular place value position, as well as how this can be explained in home languages. This may be challenging for learners, especially in a multilingual classroom, to understand how the digit three, for example, would be written as 3, but carrying the value of thirty. However, the TE's explanation was not observed, and this would mean that the PSTs would not readily have the appropriate home language vocabulary when teaching their learners.

Observations on the Use of Language in a Primary School Classroom

We observed the same topic of addition of whole numbers using a place value box being taught in a primary school classroom, where home language is used. We did this to understand how primary school teachers implement the home languages policy, and we focused on the use of language and explanatory talk. The lesson was in Standard 2. As we did in the previous section, we begin by presenting a brief overview of the lesson.

The teacher began the lesson by revising counting from 1 up to 50 with the learners. Then, she introduced the object of learning for the lesson as '*kuphatikiza nambala mpaka 50*' (addition of numbers up to 50). This was followed by activities on writing numbers under place value headings like in the examples of 35 and 13 provided in Figure 9.2.

T	O
3	5

T	O
1	3

Figure 9.2 Writing numbers under place value headings.

All these activities were done by the learners. Then, the teacher involved learners in modelling the numbers on place value boxes, and later added the modelled numbers on one place value box and on the chalkboard as shown in Figure 9.3.

T	O
3	5
+1	3

Figure 9.3 Adding numbers on a place value box and on the chalkboard.

These activities continued using different examples, and later the teacher gave learners an exercise to do as individual work. Figure 9.4 shows the exercise that the learners were given.

		Ntchito		
T	O		T	O
	6		3	6
+2	2		+1	0

Figure 9.4 Individual work (the word *Ntchito* which was written on the board means Exercise/Work).

The teacher marked a few of the learners' exercise books, then concluded the lesson by revising the exercise.

Our findings from analysis of the data from this lesson indicate that throughout the lesson, the teacher used Chichewa as a medium of communication, but the place value headings were written the way they are written in English as T for tens and O for ones. The teacher pronounced these English terms to sound as Chichewa – what Kazima (2008) calls '"Chichewalised" English.' For example, ones was pronounced as '*ma wanzi*' and tens as '*ma tenzi*'. In the absence of a proper explanatory talk, this may be confusing to learners. In the teaching and learning of mathematics, learners need to know the what and the why of the mathematics they are learning. Thus, for learners to understand the meanings of the place value headings, the teacher needed to provide an explanatory talk that would help learners to know why they use T for '*ma tenzi*' and O for '*ma wanzi*'. For T, it might be easy for the learners to understand because there is a t in '*ma tenzi*' but for O in '*ma wanzi*', the learners may not connect it to O in ones as written in the English version. This appears difficult for the teachers to explain why there is use of O when it is pronounced as '*wanzi*'. Teachers can only develop such explanatory talk if they are exposed to proper language practices during their initial teacher education (Chitera, 2012).

We also observed that the teacher's explanatory talk was mostly brief questions that led the learners to get to name mathematical concepts or provide answers to mathematical examples. For example, in an activity to add 28 and 11, the teacher led as follows:

Teacher: Ndani amene angabwere kutsogolo kuno kudzatiphatikizira 28 kuphatikiza 11 pogwiritsira ntchito timabokosi tiri apati ndi mitengoyi? (Who can come forward and add 28 to 11 using these boxes here and these sticks?)

Throughout this activity, the teacher provided short questions, such as what number is this? How many bundles of sticks are we going to put under tens? Such questions led to learners modelling and finding the sum to 11 and 28. Such word use from the teacher provided opportunities for the learners to learn to name mathematical concepts and add numbers correctly. At the same time, it provided opportunity for the teacher to know if the learners were using mathematical language correctly and be able to make corrections where necessary.

Findings also indicate that the teacher provided some explanatory talk that reminded learners of important concepts on place value. For example, before getting to the addition of numbers, the teacher asked learners to write numbers under place value headings like ones and tens, and also model the numbers on place value boxes, and to state meanings of some concepts like how many items are contained in a bundle as indicated in the excerpt below:

Teacher: ... 13 [Brief silence] Ndiye paja tinanena kuti tikaika mma grupumu chonchi kamtolo zimakhala kuti zilipo zinthu zingati? (So, we said that when we group items in a bundle like this, how many items are there?) (*Holding some bundles of sticks in her hands.*)

This is the work that learners did when they were initially introduced to the different representations of place values of numbers. But considering that knowledge of these activities is useful in the learning of addition of whole numbers, the teacher provided opportunities for learners to go through it again. Thus, the teacher laid a foundation on which the learners would base their new knowledge. Being a multilingual classroom, such explanations and activities are important because although the learners are learning in a home language, the mathematical concepts may not be familiar to them. Thus, providing explanations that could remind them of what they had learnt before was important because this excerpt involved linking the idea of bundles in their home language to the concept of tens in English.

Findings from data analysis also revealed that there were some mathematical concepts that were not elaborated or emphasized by the teacher. For example, we observed that the value of digits in the addition problems was not emphasized, rather, the teacher put emphasis on the position of the digits. The excerpt below provides an example of such instances:

Teacher: Ati waphatikiza 28 kuphatikiza 11. Uku waikako timitolo titatu, uku waikako ma wani 9 (He says he has added 28 and 11. Here he has placed three bundles, here he has placed nine ones). (*Pointing to the sticks in the place-value box.*) *Ndiye nambalayo akuti 39* (And he says the number is 39). (*Pauses briefly and repeats 39.*) *Zikomo kwambiri ukakhale pansi* (Thank you very much. Go and sit down). (*Pauses briefly as the learner sits down.*) *Wakhoza ameneyi, eti?* (He is correct, right?)

Learners: Ee! (Yes!)

This utterance came after a learner had modelled the addition of 28 and 11 on a place value box. The teacher's explanatory talk emphasized where the bundles and loose sticks had been placed to make 28 and 11, and later added to make 39. However, the values of each digit in the numbers were not emphasized or explained to the learners. This oversight was also observed in the findings from TEs' lessons. The lack of such explanations is known to prevent learners from understanding place value concepts (Brendefur et al., 2018). The teacher's lack of explicit explanation to these concepts might be linked to the gap in the use of home language in pre-service teacher education. Because pre-service teacher education does not provide opportunities for PSTs to learn to explain the concepts of place value positions and values of digits in home languages, this teacher may have found it challenging to help the learners to learn to differentiate between place value position of a digit and the value of a digit in home language. Thus, it is important that mathematics TEs should place emphasis on such mathematical ideas so that PSTs can learn to enact them in learners' home language when teaching.

From our findings in this study we have observed that the primary school teacher found it challenging to provide equivalent home language terms related to the concepts of place value. We have attributed this challenge to gaps in teacher education concerning use of home language. Chitera (2012) observed that TEs seemed to value compliance to the official language of teaching and learning in teacher education colleges than addressing their PSTs' needs to be able to effectively handle teaching in home language as it is expected of them. We see this as a dilemma that the TEs are facing, necessitating some explicit guidance on how to handle the issue of home language in teacher education classrooms. We argue, therefore, that despite the TE curriculum being in English, it is important that the TEs take a language responsive approach (Prediger, 2019) to teaching PSTs by incorporating the use of integrated style to language use. They can do this by including mathematical terms as they are used in the early years of primary school.

Concluding Thoughts

In this study, we explored the question: What do teacher educators do to prepare teachers to teach in home languages? This question was explored in terms of what two TEs, and one primary school teacher do in their lessons on the teaching of addition of numbers using place value boxes. Using the element of explanatory talk from the MDI framework, we observed language use and the explanatory talk provided in these mathematics lessons. Based on the findings from this study and other research, we now know that there is a mismatch between pre-service teacher education and primary school classroom practice in terms of the implementation of the home language policy. We know that primary school teachers are teaching in languages that they were not trained to teach. As observed in this study, this makes in-service teachers to rely on their in-the-moment decisions on what language choices to make when faced with a situation demanding mediation of number sense in the classroom. We also know that the teacher education curriculum does not provide any guidance on how TEs can help PSTs to learn to teach mathematics in home languages. As such, TEs continue to teach in English and do not provide opportunities for PSTs to practise the teaching of mathematics in home languages. Furthermore, we now know that although primary school teachers are implementing this home language policy, they have challenges in explaining the mathematics concepts. We argue that these challenges stem from the lack of preparation during teacher education on how to enact the expected language practices.

This study found that there is no clear guidance of how TEs should implement the home language policy in teacher education institutions. Hence, the enactment of the language related issues in the pre-service teacher education classroom lies on the discretion of individual TEs. Knowing all this about the implementation of home language policy and the challenges teachers are facing teaching in the home languages, we contend that there is need for more research on evidence-based practices that have proven to be helpful in multilingual settings. For instance, should teacher education introduce separate courses on how to teach using home languages or should this be integrated in the existing courses? How can all major languages be addressed? Would modelling in Chichewa be transferable to other home languages? What can teacher educators do if they have different home languages from the pre-service teachers? How can effective home language mathematics teaching and learning be enabled and developed in teacher education? What are the barriers to the TEs using home language, and how can these be overcome? How do teachers and TEs currently understand multilingualism? What are key gaps in understanding, how can these be addressed through teacher education? There is great need for further research to address these and other unanswered questions.

Acknowledgements

This study was kindly funded by the Norwegian Programme for Capacity Building in Higher Education and Research for Development (NORHED) through the Strengthening Numeracy in Early Years of Primary Education Through Professional Development of Teachers Project (Ref: QZA-0498 MWI 16/0020).

References

Adler, J. (2001). *Teaching mathematics in multilingual classrooms*. Dordrecht: Kluwer Academic Publishers.

Adler, J. (2017). Mathematics discourse in instruction (MDI): A discursive resource as boundary object across practices. In G. Kaiser (ed.), *Proceedings of the 13th International Congress on Mathematical Education* (pp. 125–143). Cham: Springer.

Adler, J. (2021). Levering change: The contributory role of a mathematics teaching framework. *ZDM – Mathematics Education*, 53(6), 1207–1220. Doi: 10.1007/s11858-021-01273-y.

Adler, J., & Alshwaikh, J. (2019). Working with example sets: A productive focus in lesson study. In U. T. Jankvist, M. Van den Heuvel-Panhuizen, & M. Veldhuis (eds),

Eleventh Congress of the European Society for Research in Mathematics Education (pp. 3191–3198). Utrecht: Freudenthal Group & Freudenthal Institute.

Adler, J., & Ronda, E. (2015). A framework for describing mathematics discourse in instruction and interpreting differences in teaching. *African Journal of Research in Mathematics, Science and Technology Education, 19*(3), 237–254. Doi: 10.1080/10288457.2015.1089677.

Adler, J., & Ronda, E. (2016). A lesson to learn from: From research insights to teaching a lesson. In J. Adler & A. Sfard (eds), *Research for educational change transforming researchers' insights into improvement in mathematics teaching and learning* (pp. 133–143). London and New York: Routledge.

Bowden, R., & Barrett, A. M. (2022). Theory, practices and policies for 'late exit' transition in the language of learning and teaching: A literature review. *Bristol Working Papers in Education Series* #02/2022. Available online: http://www.bristol.ac.uk/media-library/sites/education/documents/bristol-working-papers-in-education/working-paper-bowden-barrett-2022.pdf (accessed 25 July 2022).

Brendefur, J. L., Strother, S., & Rich, K. (2018). Building place value understanding through modeling and structure. *Journal of Mathematics Education, 11*(1), 31–45. Available online: http://educationforatoz.com/images/Asempapa-JME_2018-1-1.pdf (accessed 12 August 2020).

Brombacher, A. (2011). *Malawi Early Grade mathematics assessment (EGMA): National Baseline Report.* Lilongwe: USAID.

Brombacher, A. (2019). *Research to investigate low learning achievement in early grade numeracy (Standards 1–4) in Malawi: The victory of form over substance.* No. EACDS131. Oxford: DFID (Department for International Development).

Centre for Language Studies (2009). *Sociololinguistic surveys of four Malawian languages with special reference to education.* Zomba: University of Malawi.

Chauma, A. (2012). Teaching primary mathematical concepts in Chitumbuka: A quest for teacher education. *South African Journal of Higher Education, 26*(6), 1280–1295. Doi: 10.10520/EJC132767.

Chitera, N. (2010). Language of learning and teaching in schools: An issue for research in mathematics teacher education? *Journal of Mathematics Teacher Education, 14*(3), 231–246. Doi: 10.1007/s10857-010-9167-3.

Chitera, N. (2012). Language-in-education policies in conflict: Lessons from Malawian mathematics teacher training classrooms. *African Journal of Research in Mathematics, Science and Technology Education, 16*(1), 58–68.

Creswell, J. W. (2014). *Research design: Qualitative, quantitative and mixed methods approaches.* 4th ed. Los Angeles, CA: Sage Publications.

Davis, E. K., Bishop, A. J., & Seah, W. T. (2015). 'We don't understand English that is why we prefer English': Primary school students' preference for the language of instruction in mathematics. *International Journal of Science and Mathematics Education, 13*(3), 583–604. Doi: 10.1007/s10763-013-9490-0.

Essien, A. A. (2018). The role of language in the teaching and learning of early grade mathematics: An 11-year account of research in Kenya, Malawi and South Africa. *African Journal of Research in Mathematics, Science and Technology Education, 22*(1), 48–59. Doi: 10.1080/18117295.2018.1434453.

Essien, A. A., Chitera, N., & Planas, N. (2016). Language diversity in mathematics teacher education: Challenges across three countries. In R. Barwell, P. Clarkson, A. Halai, M. Kazima, J. Moschkovich, N. Planas, M. Setati Phakeng, P. Valero, & M. Villavicencio Ubillús (eds), *Mathematics education and language diversity: The 21st ICMI study* (pp. 103–119). Cham: Springer. Doi: 10.1007/978-3-319-14511-2_6.

Ezeokoli, F. O., & Ugwu, E. O. (2019). Parents', teachers' and students' beliefs about the use and study of mother-tongue in the secondary schools in Akinyele Local Government Area, Oyo State, Nigeria. *International Journal of Education and Literacy Studies, 7*(2), 82–93. Available online: https://eric.ed.gov/?id=EJ1219573 (accessed 2 March 2022).

Hariastuti, R. M., Budiarto, M. T., & Manuharawati, M. (2020). Incorporating culture and mother tongue in mathematics learning: Counting operation in traditional houses using Banyuwangi. *Malikussaleh Journal of Mathematics Learning (MJML), 3*(2), 62–69. Doi: 10.29103/mjml.v3i2.2482.

Jourdain, L., & Sharma, S. (2016). Language challenges in Mathematics education: A literature review. *Waikato Journal of Education, 21*(2), 43–56. Available online: https://eric.ed.gov/?id=EJ1233433 (accessed 3 November 2021).

Kamwendo, G. (2016). The new language of instruction policy in Malawi: A house standing on a shaky foundation. *International Review of Education, 62*, 221–228. Doi: 10.1007/s11159-016-9557-6.

Kazima, M. (2006). Malawian students' meanings for probability vocabulary. *Educational Studies in Mathematics, 64*(2), 169–189. Doi: 10.1007/s10649-006-9032-6.

Kazima, M. (2008). Mother tongue policies and mathematical terminology in the teaching of mathematics. *Pythagoras, 67*, 53–63. Doi: 10.10520/EJC20895.

Lartec, J. K., Belisario, A. M., Bendanillo, J. P., Binas-o, H. K., Bucang, N. O., & Cammagay, J. L. W. (2014). Strategies and problems encountered by teachers in implementing mother tongue – Based instruction in a multilingual classroom. *IAFOR Journal of Language Learning, 1*(1). Available online: https://eric.ed.gov/?id=EJ1167236 (accessed 2 March 2022).

Milligan, L. O., & Tikly, L. (2016). English as a medium of instruction in postcolonial contexts: Moving the debate forward. *Comparative Education, 52*(3), 277–280. Doi: 10.1080/03050068.2016.1185251.

Ministry of Education, Science and Technology (MoEST) (2010). *Primary achievement sample survey: Report*. Domasi: MoEST.

Mjaya, A., Mkandawire, K., Kishindo, L., Kalikokha, C., & Lora-Kayambazinthu, E. (2006). The evaluation of Malawi's languange-in-education policy from 1968 to the present. *Journal of Humanities, 20*(1), 1–27.

MoEST. (2014). *Education sector implementation plan II for 2013/14–2017/18: Towards quality education, empowering the school*. Lilongwe: MoEST.

MoEST. (2016). *National Education Policy*. Lilongwe: MoEST.

MoEST. (2017). *Mathematics syllabus for initial primary teacher education*. Domasi: MIE (Malawi Institute of Education).

National Statistical Office (2021). *Malawi multiple indicator cluster survey: 2019–20, Survey findings report* (pp. 1–71). Zomba: National Statistica Office.

Planas, N. (2018). Language as resource: A key notion for understanding the complexity of mathematics learning. *Educational Studies in Mathematics*, 98(3), 215–229. Doi: 10.1007/s10649-018-9810-y.

Planas, N. (2021). Challenges and opportunities from translingual research on multilingual mathematics classrooms. In A. A. Essien & A. Msimanga (eds), *Multilingual education yearbook 2021: Policy and practice in STEM multilingual contexts* (pp. 1–18). Cham: Springer. Available online: https://link.springer.com/10.1007/978-3-030-72009-4 (accessed 2 March 2022).

Planas, Núria, & Setati-Phakeng, M. (2014). On the process of gaining language as a resource in mathematics education. *ZDM*, 46(6), 883–893. Doi: 10.1007/s11858-014-0610-2.

Prediger, S. (2019). Investigating and promoting teachers' expertise for language-responsive mathematics teaching. *Mathematics Education Research Journal*, 31(4), 367–392. Doi: 10.1007/s13394-019-00258-1.

Roberts, N., & Alex, J. (2020). Teacher preparation for primary mathematics in a bilingual, rural context in South Africa. In M. Inprasintha, N. Changsri, & N. Boonsena (eds), *Proceedings of the 44th Conference of the International Group for the Psychology of Mathematics Education* (pp. 484–490). Khon Kaen: PME (Psychology of Mathematics Education).

Saka, T. W. (2019). An exploration of mathematics classroom culture in selected early grade mathematics classrooms in Malawi. PhD diss., University of Johannesburg. Available online: http://hdl.handle.net/10210/296529 (accessed 14 March 2022).

Sapire, I., & Essien, A. A. (2021). Multiple monolingualism versus multilingualism? Early grade mathematics teachers' and students' language use in multilingual classes in South Africa. In A. A. Essien & A. Msimanga (eds), *Multilingual education yearbook 2021: Policy and practice in STEM multilingual contexts* (pp. 75–95). Cham: Springer International Publishing. Doi: 10.1007/978-3-030-72009-4.

Scarino, A., & Liddicoat, A. (2009). *Teaching and Learning Languages: A guide*. Carlton, Victoria: Curriculum Corporation.

Setati, M. (2008). Access to mathematics versus access to the language of power: The struggle in multilingual mathematics classrooms. *South African Journal of Education*, 28(1), 103–116.

Setati, M., Adler, J., Reed, Y., & Bapoo, A. (2002). Incomplete journeys: Code-switching and other language practices in mathematics, science and English language classrooms in South Africa. *Language and Education*, 16(2), 128–149. Doi: 10.1080/09500780208666824.

Epilogue

10

Whose Languages? Whose Mathematics?

Richard Barwell

I began my own thinking about language, language diversity and mathematics teaching in the 1990s, first as a teacher in linguistically diverse Pakistan and then in my postgraduate studies in the UK (the country of my birth). Thinking back to the research literature available at that time, two things strike me. First, there was much less written about language diversity and mathematics education and certainly few books. The present volume adds to the growing but still relatively slight collection of books on this topic. Second, Africa was one of the major geographic regions of cutting-edge research on this topic. Research produced in South Africa, in particular, has led the world in focusing on language diversity in mathematics classrooms and in mathematics education as a significant and important topic, and has been decisive in setting the research agenda and theorizing its different dimensions. This book continues that significant role and I write this epilogue with this point of view in mind. My organizing question is: 'What can researchers in the rest of the world learn from African research on language diversity and mathematics education?' In addressing this question, I highlight a series of critical tensions that the different contributions help to make visible.

My own research about language diversity is informed by contemporary sociolinguistics (Blackledge & Creese, 2010; Blommaert, 2010) and, in particular, Bakhtin's (1981) translinguistics. Three specific ideas are relevant for the purposes of this epilogue. First, it is more productive to think about speakers' *repertoires*, than to try to divide people into clearly defined boxes. The boundaries between languages are hard to define and largely artificial (a European export of dubious value: see Makoni & Meinhof, 2004) and all languages incorporate features of other languages. People rarely speak in clearly distinct and discrete languages; they use different bits of languages for different purposes. Even the idea of language proficiency, while intuitively simple, is difficult to define in practice. Speakers may be 'fluent' in one domain of activity and weak in another. The concept of repertoires focuses on what speakers actually do, rather than the extent to which they conform to some notional language norm or set of norms (see Barwell, 2016; Blommaert & Rampton, 2011).

Second, languages are fluid and changeable, and they intermingle. The extraordinary diversity of language is often called *heteroglossia*, which refers to the many ways in which language use varies. We can think of multiple languages, the multiple registers associated with different professional and social activities, multiple genres of different kinds of text, multiple accents, and so on. Bakhtin (1981) highlighted a profound tension at the heart of all language use. He noticed counteracting centrifugal and centripetal forces. Centrifugal forces drive the never-ending innovation of language use: every time we say or write something, we do it in a unique way, thus adding to this innovation. Centripetal forces drive the never-ending desire to standardize language; this desire is ideological in nature since it is related to received ideas about what 'good' or 'correct' language looks and sounds like. These two forces are always operating and are always in tension. This makes sense: the centrifugal force makes it possible to say new things in new ways, while the centripetal force is necessary to ensure that we can communicate with each other. The tension between them shapes many aspects of language use and language policy, including in mathematics classrooms.

Third, language in society is *stratified*, such that some forms of language align with dominant or powerful groups and others are considered inferior. Stratification is again based on ideology, since there is no objective 'better' in language, only variation. Stratification is relevant to mathematics classrooms in several ways, not least in the idea that there is a correct form of mathematical language and that to be successful, learners must appropriate this correct form. This idea is apparent in much writing that suggests how learners can be guided from everyday language to formal mathematical language, or from less preferred languages to the official language of instruction.

Fourth, language is *indexical*, in that forms of language are not simply conduits for passing messages; the form of the utterance serves to associate speakers and other participants with social groups, aspirations, diasporas, ingroups and outgroups and so on. Indexicality functions in classrooms, for example, for students to signal if they are serious or disinterested, to associate themselves with friendship groups, political alignments or social communities, gender identities and so on.

Every chapter in this book is a testament to the language diversity of the African continent. We see multiple languages in use in mathematics classrooms, in mathematics teacher education classrooms, in mathematics textbooks and in mathematics education policies and national language policies. I share some of what I learned from these chapters, organized around four critical points of tension.

Tension 1: Which Languages for Mathematics Teaching and Learning?

Most countries in Africa officially recognize multiple languages and most have policies that permit or encourage multiple languages to be used within the education system. This language diversity is an incredible source of riches, but it can make life complicated. In Rwanda, for example, English was 'suddenly' introduced as the language of schooling, despite few people in the country being able to read or write it, as recounted in the chapter by Bowden, Uwineza, Dushimimana and Uworwabayeho. In Morocco, as Aqil reports, different combinations of French and Arabic have been proposed or attempted. In each case (and others), the choice of the language of instruction involves a political dimension and has political impacts, with different groups being advantaged or disadvantaged depending on the policy. We also see tensions between different colonial languages and local languages. Regardless of the official policy, a similar tension is always present. On the one hand, a language in education policy exerts a centripetal force: it mandates some languages and not others and, sometimes implicitly, it mandates particular versions of the selected language or languages, such as a specific variety of Arabic, Chichewa, or English. On the other hand, learners and teachers come to mathematics class with complex repertoires composed of aspects of several languages. This diversity represents a centrifugal force which permits, in principle, a wide variety of combinations of languages or language varieties to be deployed. Strict application of a 'one language' policy requires learners and teachers to behave in an unfamiliar way, by only using and developing one part of their repertoires, while in most of their daily life, they make use of their full repertoire.

The parameters of this tension include the language strata in the local society. If, functionally, English or French is required to enter higher education, public service or join an international corporation, then a system that requires English or French to be used is likely to prepare a minority of students for these pathways. What happens to the students who will not take these pathways? In some contexts, English might also index diasporic connections – this seems to have been a factor in Rwanda's introduction of English. What does this mean for learning *mathematics*? The chapter by Shuukwanyama, Long and Maseko in Namibia adds further evidence to that of Setati (2008), that parents and learners often favour former colonial languages, precisely because they can open doors to valuable opportunities. These studies show that learners, in particular, are aware of the choice this entails between a socially valued language (a form of indexicality) and their understanding of mathematics. That is, the choice of language can have an impact on success in learning mathematics. Even where compromises are made, such as in the various forms of dual language instruction discussed in Essien, Sapire and Moleko's chapter, these tensions do not disappear. Working with two languages is more diverse than working with one, but less diverse than most societies. Moreover, in reality, as several chapters demonstrate, language policies are rarely followed to the letter. Learners will naturally draw on their broad language repertoire, while their teachers develop informal translanguaging practices to support them.

While these strategies are often developed in an ad hoc way, the chapters by Robertson and Graven, Bowden et al., and Adler and Essien, all show that more deliberative strategies can be implemented. Important work such as on language responsive mathematics instruction seeks to combine language learning goals with mathematics learning. This work has the promise of more structured guidance and support for mathematics teachers. As such, it seems to accept the centripetal requirements of language policies and looks for how to support learners to, for example, learn English. A question that comes to mind here is: what would a 'full repertoire' language policy look like, in which it is officially mandated that students use all the languages available to them? This question is relevant in most parts of the world.

Tension 2: Which Languages for Mathematics Teacher Education?

Several chapters reveal a previously under-reported tension arising in mathematics teacher education classrooms in contexts of language diversity. The centripetal force arises from a preference for a language that is 'further' from the learner than that used in mathematics classrooms. In Longwe, Gobede and Kazima's chapter from Malawi, we see that African languages are mandated in the language policy for the early grades and that English is then introduced. In practice, centrifugal forces mean that a mixture of languages including English is used in most mathematics classrooms. This heteroglossia presents a problem for teacher education, which, as it is part of higher education, is conducted, centripetally, in English. Similar situations arise in other African countries.

In their chapter, Adler and Essien set out their work on developing content-specific language responsive mathematics teaching. As an example, they describe working on mathematical explanations in professional development work with mathematics teachers. Mathematical explanations are content-specific discourse practices often overlooked in discussions of language and mathematics. They make the point that teachers need to learn how to support learners' use of mathematical terms at the discourse level as much as at the word level. This is important work that reflects the centripetal forces of the education system through its focus on English.

While the choice of English is to some extent ideological and related to the stratification of languages, there are also practical considerations in higher education that create a need for a single language. Higher education potentially brings together students from many regions of a country and employs instructors and researchers who participate in broader regional and international communities. English is one of the dominant languages of the international mathematics education community and many African researchers participate and hence must be proficient in English. In this context, English indexes participation in this international community. This is a clear example of how centrifugal and centripetal forces exist in tension. There is no clear resolution to this tension, although it is preferable to have a clear institutional strategy. In Malawi, according to Longwe et al.'s chapter, the preference is to insist on English, thus promoting cohesion in the mathematics teacher education classroom, but seeming to create a disconnect with respect to the contexts the students will eventually find themselves in as mathematics teachers. In Adler and Essien's chapter, a more deliberate approach is reported, in which carefully designed teaching strategies are explicitly developed and discussed with students. As with mathematics classrooms, mathematics teacher education students bring diverse language repertoires into the classroom and in most cases, multiple languages would be heard, even if only among the students. Who benefits most from the current language in mathematics teacher education policies? Would a 'full repertoire' approach to teacher education be possible? What would it look like?

Tension 3: Which Languages for Mathematics Textbooks?

Some chapters examine different questions relating to mathematics textbooks. Aqil's chapter from Morocco highlights the complex semiosis of combining French and standard Arabic along with algebraic expressions and diagrams, sometimes reading from right to left, other times from left to right. In relation to the complex layers of languages within society, the textbook represents a sort of heteroglossic compromise. This approach reflects both a centrifugal divergence from the standard idea of a single-language textbook, but also a centripetal reduction from the full diversity of Morocco's sociolinguistic context into standard forms of two languages. Interestingly, Aqil seems to see even this as problematic.

Rather like in mathematics teacher education, publishing processes mean that choices must generally be made. It is not practical to print large runs of textbooks in multiple different languages. The choice always has a political dimension and very often reflects the stratification of languages in society. As described in Azrou's chapter from Algeria, the dual history of French and Arabic mean that both have a privileged place.

In South Africa, Venkat and Morrison are attempting to push in the opposite direction by preparing texts that reflect languages other than English (isiXhosa, Sepedi and Afrikaans) and support teachers to use them in their teaching. Even in this scenario, however, standardized forms of African languages must be used. Indeed, the texts themselves index what might be considered a standard form. This standardization extends to the use and interpretation of the mathematical register of the three other languages. In a context of language flux, the texts do not simply reflect the mathematical register; they contribute to them. How can multiple languages be incorporated into published mathematics materials? As digital and mobile technologies become ubiquitous, it may be that, released from the burden and cost of printing books, a greater diversity of mathematics teaching texts in different languages will be possible.

Tension 4: Whose Mathematics are we talking about?

The general ideas about language mentioned at the start of this epilogue apply just as much to mathematics as they do to languages. I was struck in reading the book how familiar to me most of the mathematics is. Many of the printed mathematics questions and tasks could be found in much of the world. The familiarity of the mathematics throughout the book suggests a strong centripetal force that promotes a unified view of mathematics. Research has shown, however, that doing mathematics in different languages might mean doing different mathematics (Barton, 2004). Does the work in this book inadvertently index a particular abstract Eurocentric ideology of mathematics. Where might we find mathematical heteroglossia?

A recent paper by Mesquita et al. (in press) provides several instructive examples. In Mali, for example, counting numbers in Bamanankan are ordinal in nature and are related to the sequence of births of the children in a family. For larger numbers, multiplier words are derived from the sound made by kola nuts and the baskets in which they are carried. In Algeria, meanwhile, they report a difference in relation to money. In school mathematics, exercises for calculations with money use the official currency, the dinar. But in much language and commercial activity outside of school, prices are referred to in 'old francs' so the amounts referred to are different. These are examples of the diversity of mathematical practices and mathematical meanings derived from social practices that may be suppressed by the centripetal force of a standardized international mathematics based on European notions of abstraction in which mathematics is separated from social practices.

We see some hints of variation in mathematics in Essien et al.'s example of differences in interpreting the English word 'least' and Azrou's analysis of conditional forms in Arabic and French, although both seem to be in the service of learning the European mathematics. In Venkat and Morrison's chapter, the structure of number systems is incorporated into mathematics teaching in various languages, but I wonder if there are other meanings in those languages that are missing. The question here, then, is about whether in seeking ways to teach mathematics in the context of language diversity, mathematical diversity is being overlooked. This is an important issue for the wider international mathematics education community. As I argued 20 years ago, the bias towards English in our field risks overlooking many valuable ways of thinking and doing mathematics and may contribute to the extinction of some languages (Barwell, 2003).

Closing Thoughts

The chapters in this book offer many valuable insights to mathematics educators around the world. Language diversity in mathematics education remains an area of research in which African researchers are world leaders. The same cannot necessarily be said of the policies and systems adopted by African education systems, which often carry the traces of the practices of European colonial powers. Africa is, in demographic terms, a young continent. In each of the coming decades, there will be more than a billion children in Africa and the proportion of children in the world who are African will double from roughly 23 to 46 per cent, with the sharpest increase in sub-Saharan Africa. There will be challenges in these decades but also opportunities. The tensions I have described are inherent in language diversity; there is no way to eliminate them. In these tensions, however, are opportunities for creativity, to do things differently, as several of the chapters in this book show. When so many children in the world are in Africa, there is a chance for African educators to shape how mathematics is taught around the world. My hope is that they will show the world how to teach mathematics in ways that honour, preserve and enhance the language diversity that enriches all our lives.

References

Bakhtin, M. M. (1981). *The dialogic imagination: Four essays*. Ed. M. Holquist, trans. C. Emerson & M. Holquist. Austin, TX: University of Texas Press.

Barwell, R. (2003). Linguistic discrimination: An issue for research in mathematics education. *For the Learning of Mathematics, 23*(2), 37–43.

Barwell, R. (2016). Mathematics education, language and superdiversity. In A. Halai & P. Clarkson (eds), *Teaching and learning mathematics in multilingual classrooms: Issues for policy, practice and teacher education*, pp. 25–39. Rotterdam and Boston, MA: Sense Publishers.

Blackledge, A., & Creese, A. (2010). *Multilingualism: A critical perspective*. London and New York: Continuum.

Blommaert, J. (2010). *The sociolinguistics of globalization*. Cambridge: Cambridge University Press.

Blommaert, J., & Rampton, B. (2011). Language and superdiversity. *Diversities, 13*(2), 1–21.

Makoni, S. & Meinhof, U. (2004). Western perspectives in applied linguistics in Africa. *AILA Review, 17*, 77–104.

Mesquita, A., Conceição, M. C., Acher-Spitalier, S., Coulibaly-Togora, H., Fumo, P., Patronis, T., & Pavlopoulou, K. (in press). Comment comptons-nous dans nos langues ? Des particularités de la numération en certaines langues. *Actes du 8e colloque de l'Espace mathématique francophone*.

Setati, M. (2008). Access to mathematics versus access to the language of power: The struggle in multilingual mathematics classrooms. *South African Journal of Education, 28*, 103–116.

Index

academic
  development 32
  linguistic skills 32
  performance 96
  proficiency 29, 31, 37
additional language 4, 26, 27, 172, 173
additive
  approaches to bilingualism 29
  bilingualism 26
  MLE 173
Adler, Jill 115
African
  contexts xiv, 2, 6, 15
  research 147, 166, 219, 223, 225
algebraic expressions 224
Algerian culture 48, 55
apartheid
  government 25
  rule 24
  system 26
Aqil, Moulay Driss 95
Arabic
  Arabic–French 95
  language 48, 51–52, 54, 56, 97, 108
Arabization 50–51, 95, 97–100, 102, 105, 107–110
articulated language 10, 15
autonomous
  languages 3
  language systems 8
  linguistic systems 9
awareness of language use 12, 15
  PST awareness 206
  teachers' awareness 118, 157
  teachers' poor awareness 68
Azrou, Nadia 47, 51

Bantu Education Act 25
Barwell, Richard 219
Berber language 49

bilingual
  approach 29
  education 29, 30, 37, 95, 97, 107, 109
  mathematics classrooms 77, 87
  mother-tongue-based-bilingual-education 39
  presentation 148, 151, 157
  programme 10
  proficiency 37–38
  routes 35
  speakers 37
  teacher 131
  Welsh–English model 37
  vertical bilingual development 37
bilingualism 8, 26, 27, 29, 31, 33, 37, 97, 98
  subtractive 31
body language 40
Bowden, Rachel 171

centrifugal forces 220, 223
classroom management 184
code-switching 6, 34, 36, 49, 59, 62–63, 68, 77, 86–87, 90, 124, 151–152, 175
coexisting language 60
cognitive
  academic language proficiency 31
  academic skills 31
  development 9, 96, 197
  growth 31
  -linguistic development 172
colloquial language 49, 137
colonial
  history 2, 6
  language 2, 6, 14, 76, 110, 124, 142, 221–222
colonization 3
community-based educator 25
competence-mode
  classroom 185
  pedagogy 184
conventional mathematical meanings 195
cross-linguistic issue 2, 3

Index

cuboids 179
cultural diversity 95
Cummins BICS/CALP 37–38
Cummins' linguistic interdependence hypothesis 31, 32

decoding 31
descriptive appellation 4
dialects 2, 15, 49
   Algerian dialect 49, 52, 53
   dialect-oriented 152
diaspora 173
diasporic connections 222
'discursive drift' 36
dual language 107, 222
Dushiminana, Jean Claude 171

embedded language 10, 12
EMI mathematics teaching 171, 172, 173, 174, 175, 176, 177, 184, 185
English
   medium instruction 74, 171, 172, 173, 175, 177, 179, 181, 183, 185, 187, 189, 191
   policy 34
epistemic access 36, 149, 159, 186
Essien, Anthony A. 1, 6, 195, 197, 198
Eurocentric ideology 225
exploratory engagement 34

foreign words 49
Foundation Phase
   education 149
   mathematics 10
   mathematics project 12
   teachers 162
framework
   MDI 200, 201, 202, 212
Freudenthal 32, 37, 38
full linguistic repertoire 25, 37, 175

genocide 173
geometric task 115
Gobede, Fraser 195
Graven, Mellony 23

historic colonial politics 6
home language 2, 3, 4, 6, 7, 14, 15, 27, 33, 73, 74, 74, 79, 81, 83, 86, 89, 116, 131, 138, 147, 148, 149, 150, 151, 155, 156, 159, 161, 162, 167, 195, 196, 197, 198, 199, 200, 201, 202, 203, 205, 206, 207, 208, 209, 211, 212, 213
   African home language classrooms 152
   English-Home-language 151, 156
   home language medium of instruction 124
   home language medium classroom 149
   learners' home languages 79, 124, 199
   as second-language medium of instruction 29

indigenous
   African languages 2, 3, 39
   language textbooks 4
   local languages 172
in-service teachers 1, 126, 212
instructional
   approaches 79, 118
   unit 178, 179
intellectualization 39
international contexts 9

Kazima, Mercy 195
Kinyarwanda 15, 173, 174, 176, 177, 178, 181, 182, 183, 185, 186, 187
Krashen's theory 39

language-as-problem orientation 6
language-as-resource 1, 3, 5, 6, 7, 8, 9, 10, 11, 12, 13, 14, 15, 76, 78, 79, 83
   strategy 7
language-induced challenges 6
languaging 4, 37, 38, 110, 122
languages
   additional language 4, 26, 27, 172, 173
   awareness 11, 23, 25, 56–57, 65, 67, 68, 118, 150, 157, 158, 186, 206
   first language 1, 4, 24, 87, 172, 195
   language conflicts 110
   language differences 68
   language diversity 2, 19, 68, 76, 78, 118, 121, 123, 148, 219, 221, 222, 225, 226
   Language in Education Policy 26, 29, 187, 199, 200, 206, 221
   language ideology 10, 175

language of instruction 14, 47, 48, 50, 60, 61 63, 64, 65, 67, 77, 79, 85, 123, 124, 126, 195, 220, 221
language of learning and teaching 2, 4, 5, 6, 13, 14, 28, 74, 117, 157, 173, 205
language orientations framework 89
language policies 21, 25, 27, 33, 64, 73, 74, 75, 76, 78, 79, 80, 84, 89, 97, 98, 109, 149, 173, 177, 182, 185, 192, 197, 199, 200, 212, 213, 220, 221, 222
language repertoire 8, 12, 14, 33, 120, 138, 142, 167, 222, 223
language-responsive mathematics 116, 117, 118, 120, 121, 124, 225
learners' first language 29, 87, 195
learner-centred 175, 184
lexico-grammatical linguistic input 31
lingua franca 48
linguistic
    capital 3, 4, 120
    diversity 2, 25, 107, 109, 120
    dynamics 2
    dynamics of the African contexts 2
    ideology 177
    interdependence hypothesis 31, 32
    pluralism 5
    'purity' 24
literacy 27, 30, 96, 102, 172, 175, 185
    academic literacy 175
    development 30
logical negation 53
Long, Caroline 73

mathematical
    concepts 6, 32, 38, 75, 76, 77, 82, 83, 84, 85, 87, 88, 90, 151, 195, 197, 198, 201, 202, 205, 210, 211
    discourse in instruction 200
    discourses 57
    expressions 56
    heteroglossia 225
    language 39, 61, 88, 89, 105, 109, 120, 174, 178, 181, 182, 207, 210, 220
    practices 113, 141, 160, 184, 225
    proof texts 53
    reasoning 53, 201
    register 4, 5, 9, 61, 119, 151, 152, 156, 224
    symbols 53, 99, 104, 108, 181

mathematics textbooks 4, 56, 57, 64, 68, 88, 95, 99, 102, 221, 224
meaning-making 3, 7, 8, 14, 24, 25, 30, 32, 33, 34, 36, 40, 119, 120, 124, 131, 138, 140, 150
mediate learning 10
medium of instruction 6, 14, 29, 73, 74, 77, 79, 88, 99, 173, 174, 198
minoritized learners 36
mixed
    fluidly 12
    language 8, 10, 11, 12, 13, 36
monoglossic ideologies 10
monolingual 1, 2, 12, 172, 186
    approach to EMI in official policy 187
    understanding to EMI 187
mother-tongue 35, 39, 74
    -based-bilingual-education 39
    -based education 26,
    languages 77, 78, 87, 90,
    -medium education 30
monolingual
    bias 23, 24, 25, 27, 29
    classrooms 124, 174
    postcolonial monolingual ideologies 125
    routes 35
    students 64
multi-bilingual presentation 4
multilingual classrooms 6, 7, 14, 36, 63, 66, 73, 75, 76, 78, 79, 82, 87, 90, 115, 116, 119, 121, 122, 128, 129, 195, 196, 197, 198
    contexts 2, 4, 9, 10, 12, 13, 14, 67, 115, 116, 117, 125, 141
    countries 59, 64, 66
    learners in 63
    proficiency 152, 183
    students 1, 64
multilingualism
    in Africa 19
    in education 19
    in foundation phase mathematics 10, 12
    multiple monolingualism 149
multimodal
    approach 124
    communication 25, 40
    mathematics education 174,

mathematical language 174
nature 25
registers 163
repertoires 41
representations 166,
resource 152
semiotic resources 182
semiotic repertoire 182, 185
multimodality 40
multiple languages 6, 8, 15, 33, 124, 131, 141, 142, 163, 220, 221, 223, 224
multiplication action 35

natural language 4, 55
negate 55, 56, 150
negating 56, 57
negation 24, 53, 54, 55, 56, 57, 58, 75, 61
non-cognitive skills 96
non-fixed language 50
non-native users 24
non-verbal language 177
numeric flow diagram 34, 35

official language 2, 29, 31, 47, 48, 49, 60, 73, 78, 79, 97, 98, 110, 142, 173, 212, 220

pedagogical
   approach 182, 184, 186
   choices 157, 166
   models 185
   practice 148
   rationales 166
   repertoire 163, 164
   resources 9, 81, 87, 174, 177, 185, 186
   translanguaging 185, 166
pedagogy issues 93
   competence-mode pedagogy centres 184
   culturally relevant pedagogy 120
   language pedagogy 9
   mathematical pedagogy 23
   mathematics pedagogy 187
performance-mode pedagogy 184
power imbalances 178
probability 58

quadrilaterals 37, 38
qualitative research 96

rainfall task 1, 3
repertoire approach 23
right-to-left
   mathematical directionality 104
   writing 3
Robertson, Sally-Ann 23

second-language
   medium 29
   teaching 23, 24, 39
semiotic
   modes 25
   repertoires 14
   source 40
Shuukwanyama, Tulonga T. 73
specialized mathematical meanings 4
square 37, 38, 180, 182
stratification of languages 223, 224
students' learning 53, 56, 62, 99, 119, 126
subtractive multilingual education 172
surface area of rectangle 181,
systematic marginalization 24
systemizing translanguaging 10

teacher autonomy 15
transglossia 173
transgressing official policy 36
translanguaging
   approaches 159
   initiatives 36
translating 53, 63, 68, 84, 85, 108, 161
translation 2, 3, 4, 12, 13, 14, 15, 36, 53, 56, 58, 61, 64, 77, 81, 82, 83, 84, 85, 87, 89, 98, 107, 109, 110, 155, 187, 198, 208

utterance 203

vernacular language 49, 200,
vertical mathematization 32, 37

Welsh–English bilingual model 37
world language 2, 5, 6

www.ingramcontent.com/pod-product-compliance
Lightning Source LLC
Chambersburg PA
CBHW071825300426
44116CB00009B/1436